Palgrave Studies in Disability and International Development

Series Editors
Shaun Grech
Malta

Nora Groce
University College London
London, UK

Sophie Mitra
Lincoln Center Campus
Fordham University
New York, NY, USA

We are pleased to announce the new book series, the Palgrave Studies in Disability and International Development. With this series, we open space for innovative research, debate and critical writings aimed at pushing forward the frontiers of discourse, theory and practice. We are seeking strong new monographs reporting on empirical work, edited books, as well as shorter theoretical writings, and are especially interested in interdisciplinary offerings. We welcome unsolicited book proposals. We accept completed manuscripts, but would also be happy to hear about current research or about writing projects still in-process. The series is intended to span a range of areas and we would welcome proposals on any topic related to international development and disability, including, though not limited to: Inclusive education Employment and livelihoods Social protection Disability and poverty Human rights and disability rights Health and health care Discrimination and exclusion Religion and spirituality Disability definition and measurement (Data and Disability) Rehabilitation and community based rehabilitation Enabling and disabling environments International development programs and their impacts on disabled people Disability cultures and identities Histories of disability Postcolonial issues Indigenous concerns Inclusive research and decolonizing approaches.

More information about this series at
http://www.palgrave.com/gp/series/14633

Beth Harry

Childhood Disability, Advocacy, and Inclusion in the Caribbean

A Trinidad and Tobago Case Study

Beth Harry
University of Miami
South Miami, FL, USA

Palgrave Studies in Disability and International Development
ISBN 978-3-030-23857-5   ISBN 978-3-030-23858-2   (eBook)
https://doi.org/10.1007/978-3-030-23858-2

This Palgrave Macmillan imprint is published by the registered company Springer Nature Switzerland AG.
The registered company address is: Gewerbestrasse 11, 6330 Cham, Switzerland

I dedicate this book to the children and families of the Immortelle Children's Centre, past and present, and to the memory of my daughter, Melanie Teelucksingh, and her classmate Khayam Ali.

FOREWORD

Some 15.3% of the global population consists of persons with disabilities (World Report on Disability, 2011). Caribbean surveys of childhood disability however show higher prevalence than global estimates such as 18.9% (2006) in Guyana; 23.7% (2006) in Suriname; 24% (2007) in Jamaica; and 16.1% (1984) in the Republic of Trinidad and Tobago. Several Caribbean countries have attempted to streamline a disability and development agenda which resulted in legislative and policy changes, and adoption of the 2006 United Nations Convention on the Rights of Persons with Disabilities (CRPD).

Eleven Caribbean countries are CRPD signatories: Antigua and Barbuda, Bahamas, Barbados, Belize, Dominica, Grenada, Guyana, Jamaica, Saint Lucia, Suriname, and Trinidad and Tobago. Countries with CRPD accession include Saint Vincent and the Grenadines, and Haiti. Disability policies are also available in Guyana (1997), Jamaica (2000), Barbados (2002), Trinidad and Tobago (2006), and the Cayman Islands (2014–2033). Further, six countries have disability legislation: Guyana (2010), Haiti (2012), Bahamas (2014), Jamaica (2014), the Cayman Islands (2016), and Antigua and Barbuda (2017). Comparatively, Trinidad and Tobago's Equal Opportunities Act of 2008 addresses various types of discrimination (sex, race, and disability, among others).

Data paucity and evidence-based inter-sectoral programming to implement treaty, legislative and policy commitments, however, remain very weak. The marginalized sociocultural disability identity bolsters stigma, isolation, low expectations, and outcomes. This is evident in quantifiably poorer educational and labor market situation of persons with disabilities (PWDs) compared with persons without disabilities (non-PWDs). The United Nations Economic Commission for Latin America and the Caribbean (ECLAC, 2011) states that 18% of children with disabilities 5–14 years were not pursuing any education versus 4% of non-PWDs in eight Caribbean countries. Children with disabilities in Grenada and Trinidad and Tobago were 16 and seven times more likely to be without access to education compared with non-PWDs (ECLAC, 2011). For the working age (15–64 years) in particular, PWDs were five and ten times more likely to be without access to education compared with counterparts without disabilities in Jamaica and Trinidad and Tobago (Gayle-Geddes, 2016).

ECLAC (2011) also found that 34% of working-age PWDs were employed compared with 59% of non-PWDs in the eight Caribbean countries. Comparatively, 49% and 28% of working-age PWDs were employed in Jamaica and Trinidad and Tobago versus non-PWDs at 75% and 62% respectively (Gayle-Geddes, 2016). Relatedly, disability is identified as a main driver of poverty across the region (Caribbean Development Bank, 2016). Grounded research that document the macro, meso and micro history of the disability and development agenda is scarce in the Caribbean. This book squarely takes on this critical task through the lens of a small private school in Trinidad and Tobago called Immortelle.

Immortelle's story is an ethnographic study that lucidly captures the challenges and successes of developing and sustaining educational services for PWDs. The narrative of Immortelle's genesis and continuity over four decades reflects the agency and resilience of PWDs, parents, and non-governmental organizations, as well as the unique roles played by the private sector and government agencies. This narrative bears similarity with the advocacy thrust in other post-colonial Caribbean countries. Although educational and other public provisions have improved over time resulting from advocacy, disability services receive low public priority and remain largely piecemeal. Accordingly, the author argues, "the government provided increasing support for private schooling of children [with disabilities] whom the public schools are not equipped to serve, but there is still no mandate for educational provision for these citizens." Immortelle therefore "faces continual personnel and financial sustainability issues" despite the country's high human development rank and economic development profile (Human Development Indices and Indicators 2018 Statistical Update).

The book identifies the inherent conflict between the country's vision of *equality* and implicit doubt about the value of PWDs. The intervening role of political influence is intricately nuanced by the author as it inhibits, yet possesses, unparalleled ability to effect positive change amid sociocultural continuity. Themes of advocacy and competition for limited resources, inadequate public education system and related services such as diagnostic, therapeutic and school to work transition programs demand the development of "systems" that are responsive to the needs of PWDs. The necessity of enacting legislation, providing public funding, creating non-bureaucratic institutional arrangements to support implementation of policy commitments, and a holistic national agenda to strengthen the acceptance of PWDs, are skillfully articulated in the book.

Disability mainstreaming is therefore positioned as fundamental to all sustainable development processes. The heterogeneity and intersectionality of disability with other vulnerabilities associated with gender, race, age cohort (childhood, adulthood, and elderly), and urban/rural location, as well as considerations of disability severity and disability types, are underscored. Responsive policymaking and service provision are critical linchpins of the no one left behind mantra of the Sustainable Development Goals. The book offers critical developmental considerations to embed progress made, and a platform for guaranteeing a more *inclusive* rights-based human development agenda in Trinidad and Tobago, with important lessons for the wider Caribbean.

Caribbean Development Bank   Annicia Gayle-Geddes
February 7, 2019

REFERENCES

Caribbean Development Bank. (2016). *The changing nature of poverty and inequality in the Caribbean. New issues, new solutions.* Wildey: Caribbean Development Bank.

Gayle-Geddes, A. (2015). *Disability and inequality: Socioeconomic imperatives and public policy in Jamaica.* New York: Palgrave Macmillan.

Gayle-Geddes, A. (2016). A situational analysis of persons with disabilities in Jamaica and Trinidad & Tobago: Policy imperatives for the 21st century. In P. Block, D. Kasnitz, A. Nishida, & N. Pollard (Eds.), *Occupying disability: Critical approaches to community, justice, and decolonizing disability* (pp. 127–141). New York: Springer Ltd.

United Nations Development Programme. (2018). *Human development indices and indicators 2018 statistical update.* New York: United Nations Development Programme.

United Nations Economic Commission for Latin America and the Caribbean. (2011). *Availability, collection and use of data on disability in the Caribbean region.* Port of Spain: Subregional Headquarters for the Caribbean.

World Health Organization. (2011). *World report on disability.* Retrieved February 1, 2019, from http://whqlibdoc.who.int/publications/2011/9789240685215_eng.pdf

ACKNOWLEDGMENTS

Support for this book came from many quarters and in many forms—participants in Trinidad/Tobago, research support in Miami, and my family members.

I thank my sources at Immortelle: Jacqui Leotaud, the Principal of the Immortelle Children's Centre, for her enthusiastic and open-hearted response to my invitation to participate in the project, sharing her personal journey both as a parent and as the driving force behind the Immortelle. I thank her also for allowing me free access to the school for the purposes of this research and for opening doors to the numerous stakeholders who play a key role in the disability community in Trinidad/Tobago. Sincere thanks also to the teachers at Immortelle, who welcomed me into their classrooms and shared their personal views about their work through tape-recorded and informal conversations. And my heartfelt thanks go to the 24 families who participated by sharing the most deeply personal aspects of their journey as parents. Of these families, nine were particularly close to my heart as I recalled our loving relationships during the 1980s—the first decade of Immortelle's existence.

Second, I thank the 28 community members—advocates, professionals, service providers, and policymakers—whose interviews provided me with a broader view of the landscape of disability issues in the society. Their frank sharing of information and even of controversial perspectives demonstrated the courage and strength of purpose needed by all who would advocate for the most vulnerable among us.

With regard to resources for this research project, I thank Dr. Isaac Prilleltensky, my Dean at the University of Miami's School of Education and Human Development, for his support of my sabbatical year in 2015 and for providing funds to assist me in the costs of travel to and from Trinidad/Tobago as well as the heavy costs of transcription of some 80 lengthy interviews. Thanks to NTasha Barrett, for her outstanding professional services in transcribing those interviews. It was wonderful to have this done by someone with a local ear for the enchanting nuances of Trinibagonian language! I thank Dr. Patrice Fenton, who was at that time a doctoral student at the University of Miami, for her thoughtful and patient assistance in the technological aspects of the data analysis. Thanks to Alina Yurova of Palgrave, for supporting acceptance of this book, Mary Fata for her guidance throughout the submissions process, and Drs. Lani Florian and Maya Kalyanpur for their helpful feedback on early drafts of the manuscript. Finally, warm thanks to my friend, Christine Craig, for her invaluable assistance in the final editing of the manuscript, in particular the huge challenge of reducing the word count from an initial 130,000 words to 100,000!

Above all, my deep appreciation to my husband, Bernard Telson, for his daily support of my research and writing and for putting up with my extended absences over the three years of my work on this project. I thank my son, Mark Teelucksingh, for his continuing love and interest in the life of his sister Melanie and in the work that she inspired. Finally, I continue to be grateful to Clive Teelucksingh, Mark and Melanie's father (now deceased), for his support during the early years of my struggle to establish the Immortelle.

Praise for *Childhood Disability, Advocacy, and Inclusion in the Caribbean*

about ability, as well as the triumphs of transforming intolerance toward disabilities. In the end, we gain a cultural understanding of educational access and opportunity."
—Alfredo J. Artiles, Dean, *Graduate College, Ryan C. Harris Professor of Special Education, Arizona State University, USA*

"A must read for anyone interested in international developments in education, this book provides an inside account of the development of Immortelle, a Centre for educational provision for children with disabilities in Trinidad and Tobago. By bringing to life the voices of those who nurtured and sustained Immortelle as a centre of excellence, the book enhances the country's reputation in the Caribbean region as a place of tolerance, love and creativity."
—Lani Florian, *Bell Chair of Education, Moray House School of Education, The University of Edinburgh*

"This book is a literary masterpiece that captures the historical, cultural and personal journeys of parents of children with disabilities in the Caribbean island of Trinidad and Tobago. The stories of parents, their children, teachers, and administrators help readers to understand how the historical and socio-cultural context presents powerful barriers to access to inclusive quality education and services for these children."
—Stacey Blackman, *Lecturer in Special and Inclusive Education School of Education, University of the West Indies, Cave Hill, Barbados*

CONTENTS

LIST OF FIGURES

PROLOGUE: WHERE EVERY CREED AND RACE FINDS AN EQUAL PLACE

"Please all stand for the national anthem of Trinidad and Tobago".

As the group of some 80 people rise for this demonstration of respect for their twin-island homeland, all eyes are on the small figure standing on the dais. Daniel leans forward, small hands poised above the shiny steel drum, ready to strike the first note of the anthem. I hold my breath for the first few moments, slightly nervous on behalf of this young musician. I have heard of Daniel's musical prowess and this is my first opportunity to see him "play pan". But in the hands of this slight-bodied 11-year-old, the pan-sticks quickly bring to life the sweet melody of the anthem and, with perfect pitch and timing, the music soars into the warm tropical evening, reminding us of this young nation's commitment to harmony and equality for all its citizens.

Trinibagonians like to sing the words of the anthem, but on this occasion we do not sing, perhaps because we are spellbound by the talent of this young boy whose condition of Down Syndrome in no way defines him. As he plays, his slim frame rocks with the rhythm in total concentration while a head-full of wild curls frame his high cheekbones, chocolate-colored skin, and slightly slanted eyes. As Daniel brings the anthem to an end, the words of the closing stanza are in our minds and hold special meaning for everyone in this small gathering:

> Side by side we stand, islands of the blue Caribbean Sea
> This our native land, we pledge our lives to thee
> Where every creed and race finds an equal place
> And may God bless our nation.

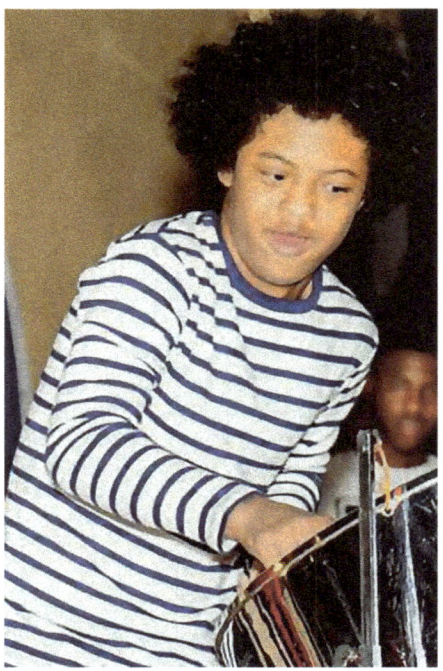

Fig. 1   Daniel Gulston playing the steel pan

THIRTY-FIVE YEARS AND COUNTING

Daniel was a student at the Immortelle Children's Centre and we were celebrating its 35th anniversary. The event also marked the opening of a new life-skills wing for those students who had now grown into adults. These students, about 20 of the total 70 served by the school, would now have the facilities to embark on real career preparation.

Jacqui Leotaud, the principal of the school, introduced me to the gathering as the "founder" of the school and invited me to say a few words about my memories of its origins. I spoke briefly of our humble beginnings in 1978, with eight children in a small rented house on Brabant Street, in Woodbrook, a residential neighborhood in Port of Spain. In recounting the history, I did not have to state that I am Jamaican, as Trinidadians are quick to recognize my accent! My motivation in starting the school was my daughter, Melanie, who was born in Trinidad and was diagnosed in infancy as having suffered brain damage. There were no pre-school programs for children with cerebral palsy in Trinidad and the school for the physically handicapped did not accept children under the age of five. Although I knew nothing about cerebral palsy, as a teacher with 10 years' experience, I knew that age five was too late to start whatever inter-ventions Melanie would need.

My initial plan was to open a playgroup in my home for children with similar conditions. However, I had the good fortune to meet two thera-pists, Joan Knowles and Wendy Gomez, who were providing physiother-apy and speech/language therapy to a handful of young children with disabling conditions who had no school to go to. So, together, we started a little school, which we called the Immortelle Centre.

I described the challenges the school faced when, three years after Melanie's unexpected death at age five, I decided to go to the US to pur-sue a doctoral degree in special education. When attempts to find an act-ing principal failed, I invited the parents to form a non-profit organization and take over the operation of the school.

Jacqui Leotaud, whose daughter, Raquel, had been the very first stu-dent enrolled in Immortelle, agreed to take on the leadership of the school, but only, she declared, "until we find a proper principal". At this commemoratory event, Jacqui followed my comments with her own explanation of how she agreed to take on that daunting job.

> *Jacqui*. I said I will hold on here and I will do everything it needs, because the interest I had was Raquel. I told the board straight, if you're not pre-pared to go the way Raquel needs, I am not taking this on. Because she is my motivation for being here.

Thirty-five years later, with Immortelle still standing tall, it was easy to see that Jacqui was, in fact, the proper principal!

But this is not a book about one school. It is a book about the efforts of many people who dedicated their energies to bringing to fruition the anthem's dream of "an equal place" for all; a place where Daniel, Isaiah, Michael, Tommy, and all the Raquels and Melanies of this small nation can develop their abilities. It is about the love and determination it takes to go against the grain of established social norms; about breaking down prejudices and false beliefs about individuals with disabilities; and about overcoming our own fears of imperfection in our children. It is also about the challenges involved in changing social ideologies and structures as a developing nation struggles to live up to its own vision of equality and take its place among the democracies of the developed world.

THE APPROACH OF THIS BOOK

My main purpose in writing this book is to present a portrait of the challenges and successes of developing and sustaining educational services for children with disabling conditions in a young nation which, despite considerable resources, lacks a legislative structure for including those who do not fit a traditional mold of academic education. I use the Immortelle Centre as an exemplar of such an effort.

The research and writing also served a personal purpose—my own need to understand what it took for the tiny school I started in 1978 to become, over a period of almost 40 years, a highly respected "special school" serving up to 70 children from all walks of life with a range of intellectual and/ or emotional disabilities. I take credit only for planting a seed that had barely begun to sprout when I left it in 1986. This story is, therefore, a tribute to those who nurtured and supported the Immortelle's growth in an often dry and infertile environment.

This book is part ethnography and part memoir. It is ethnographic in its search for an understanding of participants' perspectives on the history and culture of one school, within the context of national disability services and policies. It is a memoir, as my recounting of the history reflects my memory of events that occurred four decades ago. The book is also an effort to bring full circle the work that I began with the birth of my daughter in 1975 and that I continue to the present day.

I conducted the major portion of this research between 2014 and 2016 and analyzed all the interviews and field notes using the coding methodology of grounded theory as described by Kathy Charmaz (2014). I will present some detail on that process in an appendix for those who would like to know more about the research methods.

I held semi-structured and unstructured individual and/or group interviews with approximately 70 individuals across three groups—teachers, parents/family members, and community partners/advocates. At the Immortelle Children's Centre, I observed the summer camp, at least one lesson in every classroom during the 2015 school year, and participated in several social events including PTA meetings, staff meetings, the 35th anniversary celebration, and Carnival and Christmas celebrations. Additionally, I spent uncounted hours at the school observing and participating in the daily flow of activities. I reviewed documents on the establishment of the school's not-for-profit status, letters and reports to parents from the early days of the school and became totally immersed in the many photograph albums that presented a visual history of the school over 40 years. I also reviewed numerous government policy documents and reports from the 1960s onward, newspaper articles about disability issues in Trinidad/Tobago, and brochures, websites, and reports of other special schools. Finally, I observed two community-based events related to disability issues—a meeting at the US Embassy in Port of Spain and a conference led by the Minister of Education.

Shaun Grech (2015), who studied disability issues in Guatemala, has called for research that "prioritizes learning about histories and contexts at the most micro levels, without undermining complexity, heterogeneity, and change, and how these are bound to, and framed by, the geopolitical and the transnational" (p. 268). This study of a small private school and its immediate social context attempts to address that challenge.

Although I write in the first person, I hope that my voice comes through mainly as a conduit for the voices of those who have done and continue to do the work. My hope is that this portrait of Immortelle will be understood as simply one case, whose history can provide a broader understanding of the contextual issues facing individuals with disabilities, their families, and their advocates in this vibrant Caribbean nation. One caveat is that, despite similarities to other Caribbean nations, the findings and recommendations are focused on the specific context of Trinidad and Tobago, and I recommend caution in extrapolating them to other societies.

CHAPTER 1

Historical and Cultural Influences on Education Policy and Disability Services

As the anthem suggests, Trinidad and Tobago, or, as it is fondly referred to by locals, "TT", holds a reputation in the Caribbean as a place of tolerance, multiculturalism, and equitable social relationships. The history of mixed colonial influences has produced a unique combination of cultures from all corners of the globe, and day-to-day life is marked by a tremendous creativity and love of life expressed in its people's quick humor and easy-going ways.

Trinidad was colonized by Spain throughout the sixteenth and seventeenth centuries, and then by Britain from 1802 until the nation's independence in 1962. Tobago, having been settled by an even greater variety of colonists, including the Dutch and the French, was merged with Trinidad as one British territory in 1888. During those colonial periods, French settlers and, subsequently, British landowners developed and maintained economic and social power, buttressed by a "white" or "French Creole" racial/ethnic identity that asserted dominance over the population of African slaves and, subsequently, a large migration of Indian indentured laborers. To this mixture was added immigrants from China, Syria, and Lebanon, groups who, though smaller in number, gained considerable economic success. Out of this complex colonial history grew a culture which, despite centuries of interracial and ethnic inequalities, entered the period of political independence as a nation determined to adopt a stance of mutual acceptance embracing all races, cultures, and religions.

© The Author(s) 2020
B. Harry, *Childhood Disability, Advocacy, and Inclusion in the Caribbean*, Palgrave Studies in Disability and International Development, https://doi.org/10.1007/978-3-030-23858-2_1

The vision of equality has been, to a large extent, enabled by oil and gas resources that have contributed to the attainment of the strongest economy in the Caribbean. With a population of approximately 1.5 million, an official unemployment rate of approximately 4%, and a 99% rate of literacy, Trinidad and Tobago was described by the US Department of State (2014) as "a high income developed country with a GDP per capita of over US $20,000 and an annual GDP of $24 billion" (US Department of State, 2014, p. 1).

A couple of key caveats counter this promising socio-economic profile. First, the poverty rate is estimated at 20% of the population (Borgen Project, 2017; Central Intelligence Agency, 2018), indicating a severe imbalance in the distribution of the nation's wealth. Moreover, the fragility of an over-reliance on energy resources was evidenced in a sharp economic downturn in 2016, in response to changes in the global market for oil.

In Trinidad and Tobago, children with disabilities do not have an entitled place in the public education system. The nation's relative wealth and its high value on education has ensured schooling for all children at public cost, with one exception—those with significant disabilities. As expressed by participants in this study, persons with disabilities have traditionally been isolated by stigma and superstition, yet cherished by those closest to them. In recent decades, the government provided increasing support for private schooling of children whom the public schools are not equipped to serve, but there is still no legal mandate for educational provision for these citizens.

Constructing Disability and Inclusion in the Global Context

The portrait presented in this case study will best be understood against the background of two central conversations related to disabilities: first, the discourse in the field of disability studies regarding issues of identity, self-determination, and the concept of disability itself and, second, the robust global debate regarding the concept of inclusive education for persons with disabilities. An overarching question dominates these lines of discourse: how do culture, context, and identity relate to perceptions of disability and to the meaning of inclusion?

Disability as a Social Construction

First, how is disability to be defined and valued? It is important to note that this study focuses on children with biological or developmental disabling conditions, which, from birth or early childhood, impact the child's ability to participate in typical physical, social, and cognitive interaction. Although I will also refer to the limitations of education policies regarding children with school-based learning difficulties, such as learning disabilities, those are not the children served by the Immortelle Children's Centre.

Defining disability. The United Nations Flagship report on Disability and Development (2018) refers to disability as "an evolving concept" (p. 44). This evolution, though uneven across societies, has been marked by a movement away from a history of rejection and superstition toward the concept of equity and individual rights, and currently highlights self-advocates who emphasize their right to determine their own paths. Articulated most prominently by two groups, those who are deaf and those who have physical impairments, the mantra—'nothing about us without us'—presents a powerful challenge to the assumption that difference is synonymous with deficiency. Addressing this challenge, social theorists, Michael Oliver and Colin Barnes (1998) argued that disability should not be seen solely as an individual characteristic based in biology, but as society's failure to respond positively to human differences. This "social model" of disability sees developmental differences and evident impairments as an integral part of the human landscape rather than as blemishes that detract from its beauty. The "disability", then, lies in society's failure to value and accommodate these differences.

As cited in the United Nations Flagship Report (2018), this debate around individual versus social interpretations seems to have been resolved by the United Nations' (UN) Convention on the Rights of Persons with Disabilities (CRPD). The report acknowledges both intrinsic and social dimensions of disability, defining it as, "the interaction between persons with impairments and attitudinal and environmental barriers that hinder their full and effective participation in society on an equal basis with others" (p. 44). This combination of both views successfully resolves the apparent dichotomy, identifying "impairments" and "barriers" as an interactive dynamic. This conceptualization also supports a long-held distinction between "impairment" as a term indicating a biological anomaly and a "disability", which results from a social environment that does not respect or accommodate the needs of the individual with the impairment. For example, the sociologist Erving Goffman (1963) demonstrated how the identity of individuals with disabilities can be "spoiled", by social stigma as well as by the debilitating realities that mark their daily struggle for existence. Efforts to counter such stigmatization have included the adoption of language meant to highlight strengths rather than limitations, for example, stating the person first—a person with a disability rather than a disabled person, or using terms like "differently abled" or dis/abled.

Several self-advocates, however, such as Tanya Titchkosky (2008), have argued that "people first" language actually oversimplifies the experience of disability by denying the complexity involved in embracing the wholeness of one's identity, including impairments and strengths. Nancy Mairs (2011) and Simi Linton (2006) go further, arguing that recognizing the validity of one's personhood requires authentic and explicit naming of the disability, rather than using euphemisms that avoid stating the facts of their conditions. Thus, these self-advocates refer to themselves as "cripples or crips", choosing to accentuate rather than disguise their physical disabilities. The essence of this argument is that euphemistic descriptions, by avoiding stating the realities, in effect convey a message that the condition is unacceptable.

In comparing the definitions of disability used in the Caribbean nations of Jamaica and Trinidad/Tobago, Annicia Gayle-Geddes (2016) stated that although Trinidad and Tobago's National Policy on Persons with Disabilities (2005) does acknowledge both the biological and the social aspects of disability, both countries "primarily position disability within a traditional medical-oriented model" (p. 130), as seen in the absence of legislation guaranteeing the right to access education and employment. Yet, as many parent narratives in this study will show, the medical response to congenital disabilities in Trinidad/Tobago has continued to be inadequate and inconsistent.

My own view of these contested "models of disability" embraces both. As someone who has experienced parenting not one, but two children with disabling conditions, I am deeply aware of the medical/biological components of most conditions referred to as "disabilities". Neither of my children asked for these identities, nor, to my knowledge, were their conditions created by society. One was born with brain damage that severely restricted her functioning and, ultimately, led to her death. The other enjoyed above-average development until his late teens, when mental illness dealt a harsh blow to his identity. For my daughter, medical care and highly skilled professional therapy was more important to her development than social constraints. For my son, medical science has been the key to moderating his brain chemistry to allow him to be the best he can be. For both, I also saw how societal barriers and lack of responsiveness contributed to negative constructions of their identities, and I continue to challenge the disabling impact of social stigma and limited social services.

In this book, I accept the definition used by the CRPD and will use the terms "impairments" and "disabling conditions" when referring to the children in the study, since all of the conditions experienced by these children are based in biology. While their lived experiences are no doubt in part constructed by social contexts and practices, their physical or cognitive impairments are not.

Valuing disability. Regardless of definitions, I believe that the question of how such conditions are valued reflects societal concepts of "personhood" in the face of the disturbing question: are all human lives equally valuable? If so, in whose eyes? Embracing the lens of the social model, some disability studies scholars have challenged the assumption that mental and physical normative development should necessarily be seen as preferable to developmental anomalies. Nirmala Erevelles (2011), for example, posing the question of whether it is possible to envision a world that "welcomes and desires disability" (p. 27), concluded that such a possibility would require an "engagement with the social conditions that constitute disability" (p. 27). In other words, a positive rather than negative view of disability would depend on the social world in which the person with the disability engages.

Does this mean that, with appropriate supports, the presence of a disability in a newborn or young child should be seen as simply a point along the spectrum of human variation, rather than an anomaly to be mourned, exalted, or rejected? If disability is to be seen as normative, would we then expect the appearance of a congenital impairment to be as welcome as is a healthy body? If so, then should we also expect the occurrence of impairment or illness in a previously healthy body to be just as welcome as continued good health? Memoirs by Simi Linton (2006) and Nancy Mairs (1996), who, respectively, became physically disabled through a car accident and multiple sclerosis, do not present such counter-intuitive arguments; rather, their memoirs poignantly demonstrate the role of both social environments and intrapersonal adjustments in a slow process of expanding their identities to include the painful dimensions created by disability.

Another crucial point in the discourse around valuing and advocating for individuals with disabilities is that the question of self-determination depends to a great extent on the nature of the limitations created by biological impairments. Persons with intellectual or complex multiple impairments will continue to need others to speak for them and act on their behalf, and may depend totally on others for their care. The creation of an equal place for them will be determined by the adults who advocate for them. Eva Kittay (2011), a feminist scholar whose daughter has multiple disabilities, addressed this challenge in a thoughtful discussion of what she refers to as "an ethic of care", which I will describe in more detail in my reporting of the parents' narratives later in the book.

This concern hits close to home for the children and families in this study, as most of the children and adults served by the Immortelle Children's Centre rely extensively on others for their daily functioning and safety as well as for opportunities for personal development and advancement.

Viewing disability through the lens of parenthood. As the parents' narratives in Chaps. 4, 5 and 6 will show, the perspective of a parent whose newborn or young child exhibits debilitating impairments will likely be rather different than the perspective of a self-advocate. First, there is the inevitable shock that contrasts with parents' hopeful expectations of a healthy child. This can be exacerbated initially by medical challenges that may not be adequately addressed, and later by the enduring challenge of finding appropriate educational opportunities for the child. Finally, there is the fear of an absence of support for a child or adult after the death of the parents. All these factors seriously complicate the lens through which disability will be viewed by parents. I think it is fair to say that the narratives demonstrate both individual and social interpretations of disability, illustrating a clear trajectory of parents' journey from shock and fear to a genuine celebration of their children's identities.

The United Nations and the Inclusion Movement

The United Nations (UN) has been the driving force behind the global establishment of rights of persons with disabilities and the vision of inclusive education. In outlining the history of this movement, *The United Nations Flagship Report on Disability and Development* (2018) described the period from the Universal Declaration of Human Rights in 1948 to the Declaration on the Rights of Disabled Persons in 1975 as reflecting a shift from a "medical/social welfare model approach to disability, to a social/human rights model of promoting equal rights and opportunities for persons with disabilities" (p. 47). Over the next three decades, a series of international conferences and policy decisions culminated in the

International Convention on the Rights of Persons with Disabilities (CRPD) in 2006, which "was envisaged from the very beginning as the instrument for inclusive development and for the realization of the universal human rights for persons with disabilities" (p. 50). Article 24 of the Convention (United Nations, 2006) recognized the right of persons with disabilities to an education and called for member states to "ensure an inclusive education system at all levels" (Section 1). Further, the implementation of this principle decried exclusion from "a free and compulsory primary education" on the basis of disability, and called for "reasonable accommodations and individualized supports" (Section 2), as well as the facilitation of alternative modes of communication, orientation, and mobility. The CRPD also called for the preparation of professionals in special education.

In 2015, the year in which the majority of the research in this book was conducted, Trinidad/Tobago joined some 193 countries who had signed on to the CRPD. Also, in 2015, UN Member States adopted the 2030 Agenda for Sustainable Development, which identified five Sustainable Development Goals (SDGs) addressing disability in five areas—education, growth and employment, inequity, accessibility of human settlements, and data monitoring and accountability.

As cited in the 2018 United Nations Flagship report on Disability and Development, Goal 4 of the Sustainable Development Goals (SDGs) targets the development of education systems that will provide all children with disabilities access to education by 2030, and will ensure "inclusive and equitable quality education for persons with disabilities" (p. 97). The report cites 11 distinct international declarations between 1948 and 2015, all of which support the SDG 4 and its core concept of equal access to education for all. Goal 4 also proposes to provide support to developing nations for the production of reliable and high-quality data on disability by 2020. The report specifies nine key actions that need to be implemented toward the attainment of Goal 4. Most relevant to this study are the call for strengthening national policies and legal systems for ensuring access, building capacity and knowledge among policy makers, teachers, and local communities, and adopting a "learner-centred pedagogy that acknowledges that everyone has unique needs that can be accommodated through a continuum of teaching approaches" (p. 29).

Despite these lofty goals, the numbers cited by the 2018 report are not encouraging. Specifically, only 34 of the 193 Member States guarantee, in their constitutions, "the right to education for persons with disabilities or providing protection against discrimination based on disability in education" (p. 29). Further, despite some improvement in recent years, the report states that, "in 44% of UN member States, students with disabilities cannot be taught in the same classroom as other students" (p. 29).

In light of this book's focus on a developing nation, it is instructive to note that disparities in inclusive education among nations who are committed to the goals of the CRPD are not found only in developing or newly developed nations. On the contrary, an analysis of 18 European nations by John Richardson and Justin Powell (2011) showed that rates of school segregation by disability varied widely, ranging from 1% of school children with disabilities in Switzerland and Belgium attending general schools, to 99% in Italy. These authors further related these figures to three basic types of education systems—unitary systems, as in Italy, Norway, and others, in which almost all children are included in one system; dual structures, as in Switzerland, Germany, and others, which maintain two parallel systems for general education and special schools; and multiple structures that offer a continuum of settings and services, as in the US, UK, and others. The authors' analysis of this picture points to the challenge that the inclusive model presents to deeply embedded educational systems:

> Far from being an easily achieved set of goals and changes, inclusive education challenges the long-ago developed structures of education systems, which sort and group students in different ways... (p. 207). Thus far, no international convention or global trend has had the force necessary to lead to convergence, even within Europe. Neither has school integration or inclusive education been achieved everywhere within the United States, although the continuum of educational environments has shifted toward a more inclusive education system.... (p. 231)

Defining inclusion. One aspect of the conundrum of inclusion is that the concept continues to elude one shared definition. Is inclusion to mean that all students should be taught in the same classrooms? In the same buildings? For the entire day or what portion of the day? Should the answers to these questions depend on the nature and extent of the limitations created by the individual's impairments? Or would sorting students by disability categorization limit access to learning and developmental opportunities that the individual might, in fact, be able to benefit from?

It seems to me that the way the concept is interpreted may reflect either social preferences or socio-economic realities. As Richardson and Powell's (2011) comparison of unitary, dual, and multiple education structures indicates, several highly developed European nations maintain structures that serve disabled students separately from their non-disabled peers, although one would imagine that it could be quite feasible for these robust economies to include students with disabilities more fully into mainstream education. On the other hand, differences in application of the principle may also reflect the extent to which a society already includes any and all groups in its education system. For example, it is important to note that the World Declaration on Education for All (EFA), as defined by the United Nations agencies, UNESCO and UNICEF, while including persons with disabilities, was also meant to refer to the inclusion of individuals representing diversity of all types; gender, ethnic affiliation, race, language, poverty, and disability. Thus, countries with unstable economies and less "developed" political and legal infrastructures may interpret inclusion in terms of providing any form of education for those who have traditionally been excluded on the basis of ethnic or economic affiliations, rather than on persons with disabilities.

Several scholars have addressed the principle of inclusion as a "philosophy" rather than a "place". O'Rourke-Lang and Levy (2016), for example, stated:

> Inclusion is not a "place," but a philosophy and practice of affording individuals with disabilities the full range of services and resources needed to access an appropriate education such that they make substantial gains in their lives and contribute meaningfully to society. Unfortunately, the reality is that disparate opportunities exist for individuals with disabilities across the world. (p. 1)

Such "disparate opportunities" are indeed unfortunate, and may simply indicate that we should not be surprised that the implementation of "inclusion" varies widely according to the expectations and resources of each society. Moreover, the foregoing definition does not mention the requirement of students with and without disabilities being educated together.

As this case study will show, Trinidad and Tobago, like the majority of the United Nations member states, struggles to meet its commitment to the CRPD's goal of inclusive education. Specifically, while advocacy is active on a community basis, the government itself does not promote public advocacy regarding disabilities. More importantly, with regard to legislation, while there does exist an "Equal Opportunity Act" that explicitly rejects exclusion from school on the basis of disability, there is actually no legislation that mandates the provision of education to all children regardless of disability.

Does this mean that the society is failing in its commitment to the principle of inclusion? How should disparate implementation be evaluated and how can a developing or newly developed society establish reasonable expectations that honor the principle, while looking very different from the "unitary" or "multiple" education systems in the developed world? This case study provides a view of a society that stands in many ways between the developing and the developed world. As such, I believe that the study will contribute unique insights into the challenges of local versus global perspectives on what might be possible, desirable, and feasible in the provision of inclusive services for children with disabilities.

TRACING DISABILITY AND INCLUSION IN TRINIDAD AND TOBAGO: IDEAL VERSUS REALITY IN DISABILITY POLICY

The provision of education for children with disabilities in the Caribbean is deeply tied to the historical development of the education system. Across the Caribbean, the movement for independence from Britain was accomplished in most territories between the early 1960s and 1970s. Along with sister nations such as Jamaica, Barbados, Grenada, and others, Trinidad and Tobago embarked on its new journey with a focus on extending the base of schooling established during the colonial period. Steeped in a highly academic tradition in which their children competed with their counterparts in Britain for the Cambridge University General Certificate of Education (GCE) secondary school examinations, these new nations created their own version of the traditional curriculum to which they had become accustomed. In 1972, 16 formerly British Caribbean territories participated in the formation of the Caribbean Examinations Council (CXC), which provided the framework of education from that time until the present.

While the vision of education was broadened over the years to include technical and vocational education, children with evident disabilities were simply not on society's radar. Seen as the responsibility solely of their families, with the possible support of charitable organizations, the model for provision of services for those excluded from public schools was what Barbadian scholar Stacey Blackman (2017) referred to as the "charity paradigm".

Trinidadian scholars, Elna Carrington-Blaides and Dennis Conrad (2017), in considering challenges to the development of education for children with disabilities, put the matter bluntly:

> Education systems in the Anglophone Caribbean have maintained the structures of "the mother country"; it is only through radical and sustained nationalistic effort that any change in the typical post-colonial legacy emerged. Unlike Guyana, Jamaica, and Cuba, Trinidad and Tobago have mostly maintained the legacy of its former colonial ruler, a legacy that has handed down an elitist system that is deeply examination-oriented and focused on rewards for small percentages of the brightest citizens. (p. 35)

The Colonial Legacy in Education

A look back to nineteenth century thinking on colonial education reminds us how far we have come in Trinidad and Tobago in a century and a half. I gained a fascinating glimpse into that world on reading the *Keenan Education Report of 1869*, where the author was reporting to "her Majesty's Secretary of State for the Colonies". There was no mention in the report of attention to children with any kind of atypical development, and the tone throughout referenced the superiority of traditional British education, with its focus on academic and religious education. The document was replete with descriptions of the relatively inferior capacities and orientations of "negroes" and "coolies" and the pressing need for schooling to improve the moral fiber of colonial populations.

A century later, a very different tone and vision had emerged. The attainment of independence for most of the British West Indian colonies, coupled with a growing global interest in education, brought special education into the purview of the government. As described by Carol Keller (1993), the year 1962 saw the introduction of World Bank involvement in developing nations and, building on the vision of UNESCO, the Education Act of 1967 came into being. The act's purpose was to "make a better provision for the promotion of education in Trinidad and Tobago" (Government of the Republic of Trinidad and Tobago, 1967, p. 6). Included in government responsibilities were the preparation, remuneration, and monitoring of teachers, the registration and supervision of both public and private schools, and the authority to "assist needy pupils so as to enable them to participate in the facilities offered by the education system" (p. 9).

The Education Act also specified that "in addition… *there may be provided* (italics mine) special schools suitable to the requirements of pupils who are deaf, mute, blind, retarded or otherwise handicapped" (p. 11). While the government was responsible for providing public schools "wholly owned by the government" (p. 13), it also provided for some schools to be run by a board of management but to be "assisted" through receipt of public funds for buildings, equipment, and facilities, and to be fully accountable to the government for all its operations. Private special schools were also required to register with the government and meet the requirements of the Ministry of Education regarding the number of days open per year, the number of pupils on roll and the official registration of teachers. Thus, special schools could be wholly public, assisted, or private, but all were subject to government regulations. These efforts indicated a concern, but no indication of public responsibility for students with specific disabilities or "otherwise handicapped".

A Growing Awareness of Education for Students with Disabilities

The Education Act of 1967 is still the law of the land in Trinidad and Tobago. It was clear in the Act that there was allowance for, but *no mandate requiring* the provision of education for children with disabilities. There is still no such mandate.

In the three decades since the law's enactment, there has been growing concern with the needs of children with disabilities, initiated by individual local pioneers such as, among many others, Dr. Nesta Patrick, best known for her work with children with intellectual impairments at the St. Ann's Hospital, and Errol Pilgrim, the second principal of the School for the Blind at Santa Cruz. These efforts were also fueled by international pressure, particularly the United Nations' Education for All (EFA) in 1990, and the UNESCO Salamanca Statement (UNESCO, 1994), which emphasized the provision of education services to all children regardless of disability, ethnicity, language difference, poverty, or any potentially marginalizing conditions or situations.

Carrington-Blaides and Conrad (2017) offered a succinct history of efforts to develop a policy agenda during the 1980s and 1990s, for children with disabilities. These scholars noted numerous reports by local and foreign consultants, and a turning point in awareness and policy in 1981, with the establishment of a Special Education Unit in the Ministry of Education. This unit would oversee the existing "assisted" special schools, who, run by independent boards, received government subsidies to provide education for individuals with specific disabilities: The Cascade and the Audrey Jeffers Schools for the Deaf, the Santa Cruz School for the Blind, the Princess Elizabeth Centre for the Physically Handicapped, the Lady Hochoy Homes/Schools for the Mentally Retarded, and the Wharton-Patrick School, which initially served children housed at the psychiatric hospital in St. Ann's. In 2004, the Special Education Unit was subsumed under the Division of Student Support Services, which took over the supervision of all public and private special schools. Carrington-Blaides and Conrad also noted a spate of teacher preparation efforts in the 1980s and 1990s, when hundreds of teachers and school personnel gained training and experience through projects such as a collaboration between the Trinidad and Tobago Unified Teacher Association and the University of Sheffield in the United Kingdom, and collaboration with the University of Manitoba and the Canadian International Development Agency.

The Division of Student Support Services continues to provide limited services for children with mild learning difficulties in the public schools. However, children with significant disabilities are not served within the public schools; therefore, private special schools have continued to exist. When the Special Education Unit was established, private special schools did not receive any support from the government but, in 2006, support became available to private schools who met eligibility criteria. The Immortelle Children's Centre is one of the longest standing among this group of schools.

Toward a Mandate for Inclusive Services

There appears to be a paradox in national policy on the acceptance of children with disabilities into public schools. The Equal Opportunity Act of 2001 (Government of the Republic of Trinidad and Tobago, 2001), states:

> An educational establishment shall not discriminate against a person by refusing or failing to accept that person's application for admission as a student… or denying or limiting the student's access to any benefits, facilities or services provided by the educational establishment. (p. 954)

In 2003, a review of the Second Periodic Report under the Convention on the Rights of the Child (Trinidad and Tobago, Ministry of Social Development, 2003), confirmed that the Act included such prohibition, but noted that the legislation was "awaiting implementation" (p. 286). The report further noted that, despite Trinidad and Tobago's participation in international agreements such as the Lima Accord of 1998 and the Kingston Consensus of 2000, progress on the goal of "integration into the mainstream of the education system" was hindered by regional "survival issues" and financial and human resource constraints on monitoring and documenting attainment of the goals. In 2006, the *Ministry of Social Development's National Plan of Action for Children* for the period 2006–2010 (Ministry of Social Development, 2006), acknowledged that the prohibition had still not been implemented.

The concern with "survival issues" as a barrier to inclusive education is not limited to Trinidad and Tobago. Disability scholars, Alfredo Artiles, Elizabeth Kozleski, and Frederico Waitoller (2011), in outlining the history of the inclusion movement, explained that the United Nations' Salamanca Statement of 1994 was the result of the growth of inclusive education philosophies in several European nations in the latter decades of the twentieth century. This model from "developed" nations led to the adoption of the inclusion principle in 94 countries. These authors point out that, although exclusion from the mainstream of public education still occurs in developed nations, including the US, the expectation for inclusion has led to "unintended consequences" for many developing nations who are "still struggling to achieve universal school *access* and *completion*, whereas developed nations are concerned with equity in *participation* and *outcomes* across diverse groups" (p. 5).

As Trinidad/Tobago entered the twenty-first century, global pressure for improvements in the lives of children continued to move the disabilities agenda forward, although in inconsistent waves of effort. Most significant was the Ministry of Social Development's (2006) *National Plan of Action for Children for 2006–2010*, which targeted improvements in a range of circumstances from poverty to environmental safety and stated the intention to designate integration into the mainstream of education as a priority. "Integration" was described as a system in which children "attend the regular school but are provided with special education services delivered by a special educator either in or out of the classroom setting" (p. 53). "Mainstreaming" was described as "the placement of special education students in regular classes on the assumption that these students will demonstrate the ability to 'keep up' with the work assigned by the regular classroom teacher" (p. 53). The report provided a table with specific strategies, responsible agencies, measurable indicators with dates for completion, and means of verification for each strategy.

In 2008, in an important step toward implementing these goals, the Government of Trinidad and Tobago sought funding from the Inter-American Development Bank (IADB) to assist in developing a "seamless" education system encompassing all levels of education (Inter-American Development Bank, 2008). The IADB proposed a pilot plan to phase in new regulations and curricula for Early Childhood Care and Education (ECCE) and for primary education. The new curriculum was to be piloted in a representative group of 60 primary schools and an inclusive model would be implemented in 12 select ECCE and primary "demonstration schools" (p. 3).

The pilot study of the curriculum in 60 schools never took place. Instead, a newly elected government decided to implement the plan in *all* primary schools—a total of 477, all at once. This decision was unfortunate as the resources allotted for a 60-school pilot were totally inadequate to provide for the "seamless, inclusive" system that was envisioned. The sequel to this decision was that, in 2016, when the government changed once more, the IADB was invited back to review and advise on the situation, but it was evident that inclusion was no longer a priority. Rather, by 2018, the focus had shifted to ECCE services, and the IADB was contracted to support the government in increasing and improving the quality of these services (personal communication, AIDB Official).

Overall, this history suggests an ebb and flow of waves of effort, some of which were successful, only to be met with obstacles that diminished or interrupted periods of progress. Most long-lasting have been the establishment in 2007 of a Bachelor's degree in Special Education at the University of Trinidad and Tobago (UTT) and, in 2012, a Masters in Inclusive and Special Education at the University of the West Indies (UWI). Carrington-Blaides and Conrad (2017) concluded their review with a statement on the detrimental role of politics in the nation's disabilities agenda—a statement that will be echoed by participants throughout this book:

> The current situation in Trinidad and Tobago, underpinned by rigid conformity to an inherited post-colonial paradigm, is characterized by policy instability often based on fancied notions of the government of the day... each

time there is political change, there is an equal or greater change in inclusive education policy and provision. (pp. 46–47)

Positive Steps That Made a Difference

Despite all this vacillation on education policy, there were two positive policies that had a powerful impact on families of children with disabilities.

First was the decision by the government, in 2006, to provide a subvention of $1200 per term toward school fees for private special schools that met specified criteria. Because of the high cost of such schooling, most families would continue to pay the difference in fees exceeding that amount. The policy allowed for a means test for financially challenged parents to qualify for an additional $800. Also included were subventions to the schools for ancillary services such as speech/occupational therapy, schools' phone services, grounds and building maintenance, teachers' wages, and payment of water and electricity bills.

The second very helpful policy was the provision of financial assistance for persons with disabilities. This came in two forms: The "Disability Assistance" grant, a monthly grant of $800 for persons age 18 or over who are officially certified as permanently disabled, and the "Special Child Grant", which came into existence in 2008. The latter provided a monthly grant of $800 for parents of children certified as having a mental or physical disability. This grant must be reviewed annually by the local Social Welfare Board and is provided until the child's eighteenth birthday (Government of the Republic of Trinidad and Tobago (2015) TT Connect, https://www.ttconnect.gov.tt).

PURSUING THE DISABILITIES AGENDA: "A BATTLE OF PERSUASION"

This short history indicates the Government's awareness of the continuing dire need for effective implementation of long-proclaimed ideals regarding citizens with disabilities. However, the huge gap between stating a policy and creating legally binding avenues for its implementation was underscored in an interview with Mr. Michael Reid, the Director of the Disability Affairs Unit, which has a small staff of professionals who conduct research, collect data, and coordinate disability policy in TT. In an interview in 2015, Michael explained the 2005 *National Plan* report in this way:

Michael. The mandate of the Unit is to implement the national policy on persons with disabilities. We are also responsible for pushing for legislation for persons with disabilities and for keeping statistics/data on them. Because the policy is a "policy" and not a law, enforcing it is really a battle of persuasion. We have come some way in adjusting so that persons with disabilities could be included, but we still have a long way to go. There are some things that cannot be legislated or forced. Attitudes! It is going to take some time for attitudes to change towards persons with disabilities.

Identifying non-governmental organizations (NGOs) as one of the key channels for effecting attitudinal change, Michael explained that the ministry provides financial support of up to 60% of operating cost for groups that meet the criteria to register as an NGO and whose proposals are approved. These criteria include evidence of their work and its impact, and efforts to raise their own funding. Subventions to such groups could be granted for up to two or three years, after which they would be evaluated for continued funding. The ministry also gives "one-off" grants for special events such as the International Day for Persons with Disabilities, in which various groups participate, and to conferences run by groups such as the Down Syndrome Family Network and the Deaf Empowerment group.

When asked if Trinidad/Tobago might be interested in following standalone legislation similar to the Americans with Disabilities Act, Michael felt that TT would "probably create our own", using different aspects from various models. In contrast to the US model by which much legislation in civil rights has come about through litigation, Michael felt that TT would be more likely to base decisions "on the basis of human rights".

A policy update in June of 2017 by the Ministry of Social Development and Family Services echoed Michael's perspectives. The statement was described as a "revision of the 2005 National Policy on Persons with Disabilities, to reflect the provisions of the United Nations Convention on the Rights of Persons with Disabilities (UNCRPD), which was ratified by the Government of Trinidad and Tobago in June 2015" (p. 3).

As Michael Reid had indicated, the report identified its basis as "the human rights model of disability", with the goal of developing a "more inclusive and barrier-free society" (p. 4), focusing on advocacy, empowerment, and integration into the community. On the thorny question of legislation, this policy statement promised that legislation would be reviewed and, where appropriate, amended, or new legislation enacted as necessary, to address discrimination and prejudice, and to promote equal opportunities for persons with disabilities. This policy statement was met with considerable skepticism by several professionals, who argued that there was little change and no budget for the policy.

I believe that at the heart of the vacillation over special education reform has been a deep reluctance to reframe the concept of education. Whether named "integration", "mainstreaming", or "inclusion", the process of reforming a system not intended to account for children who could not "keep up" continues to be exceedingly difficult. In the new millennium, the education system of this and other Caribbean nations has continued to be defined by a highly competitive academic system in which children are sorted soon after the age of 11, not only into academic and non-academic streams but also into differing levels within the academic stream. Competition is fierce for children to attend kindergarten and elementary schools that will position them for placement in a desirable secondary school. In this scenario, there is little concern about the outcomes for children who will certainly not "keep up".

The TT Model for Service Delivery: Parents, Church, and Charity

One of the themes that dominated the interviews for this project was *parents' individual agency*. Since the 1950s, there have been parents who, driven by an intense need to provide a meaningful life for their children, formed the core of efforts to establish special education services. It was through these parents and their "charitable" allies that services for children with disabilities began.

Religious organizations were essential to the success of these efforts. Leading the way was the Trinidad and Tobago Association for Retarded Children (TTRC), inaugurated in 1958 through the efforts of parent advocates and religious organizations. Prior to that, children with mental retardation who were not supported by their families were accommodated at the House of Refuge and the St. Ann's Psychiatric Hospital. According to a 1984 report of the Trinidad and Tobago Association for Retarded Children, the congregation of Corpus Christi Carmelite sisters engaged in a contract with the TTRC to administer a residence for children which, built on land donated by the government, received two thirds of its funding from the government through the Ministry of Health, and one third to be raised by the TTRC. Initially serving 24 children in 1961, Lady Hochoy soon added a day training program which, after some years, became the responsibility of the Ministry of Education. As the need grew, Lady Hochoy services expanded to include a residence in Gasparillo, a vocational and day training center in Arima on lands leased to the Association by the Ministry of Agriculture, and a day training Centre in Penal with support from the Penal Ecumenical Committee (Trinidad and Tobago Association for Retarded Children, 1984).

Other services initiated during that period included schools for the Deaf and the Blind in 1961 and 1959 respectively, the Princess Elizabeth Centre for Physical disabilities in 1953, and the San Fernando Rehabilitation Centre in 1964, which subsequently became the National Centre for Persons with Disabilities (NCPD). In addition, a unique and long-lasting effort—Service Volunteered for All (SERVOL)—was spearheaded in 1970 by the Catholic priest, Father Gerard Pantin. With a focus on supporting empowerment of low-income communities, SERVOL offered a preschool program and a "Special School" for children diagnosed as "autistic, differently abled, or slow learners" between the ages of six and 17. Unfortunately, when Immortelle Centre opened in 1978, none of the programs noted above served children with disabilities under the age of six.

Seeking Goodness of Fit in Adapting International Perspectives

As argued earlier, I believe that issues of inclusion and the defining of disabilities must have locally crafted answers. Many international scholars have noted that we cannot assume that what is good for developed nations is a good fit for developing nations. This is particularly cogent when the realities of poverty are considered. For example, Maya Kalyanpur (2015) argued that the transfer of such ideals often fails to "mind the gap" between the cultures and traditional practices of "resource-rich" Northern/developed versus Southern/developing societies. Specifying her native India, Kalyanpur referred to two such gaps—a contextual gap, which fails to recognize a mismatch between the "ideal" and local systems and practices, and a "temporal" gap, by which new practices are adopted in developing nations years after they have already been proven inadequate in the developed society. International scholars such as Nidhi Singhal (2013) and Eide Arne and Benedicte Ingstad (2011) have pointed out that disability and poverty are intertwined, each exacerbating the other. Similarly, Shaun Grech (2015) argued that different economic resources must call for different responses and locally determined priorities. For example, Grech's work on disability and poverty in Guatemala represents the overwhelming challenges faced by individuals with disabilities in a developing nation of over 14 million people, marked by vast economic and social disparities.

Nations in the Anglophone Caribbean, despite limited and, as Jamaican scholar Annicia Gayle-Geddes (2015) has argued, inequitably distributed resources, present more hopeful profiles and therefore very different issues as compared to the work of the foregoing scholars. For example, the United Nations Human Development Index (2018) in ranking 189 countries, ranked Barbados in its category of "very high human development" with a placement score of 58, and Trinidad/Tobago and Jamaica as "high human development", with respective rankings of 69 and 97 respectively. In the case of Trinidad/Tobago, the voices in this book suggest that the central issue is not one of resources, but of priorities and of the limited value given to individuals who do not fit the expected mold.

In light of these contrasts, I view Trinidad/Tobago as a nation standing between two worlds, in a liminal space of development with regard to disabilities. With a commitment to many traditional societal values and beliefs, its education policies reflect a continuing tug of war between a belief in equity and an implicit doubt about the value of individuals with disabilities.

References

Artiles, A. J., Kozleski, E. B., & Waitoller, F. R. (2011). *Inclusive education: Examining equity on five continents.* Boston: Harvard Education Press.

Blackman, S. (2017). From charity education toward inclusion: The development of special and inclusive education in Barbados. In S. Blackman & D. Conrad (Eds.), *Caribbean discourse in inclusive education: Historical and contemporary issues* (pp. 3–20). Charlotte, NC: Information Age Publishing.

Carrington-Blaides, E., & Conrad, D. (2017). Toward inclusive education in Trinidad and Tobago: Policy challenges and implications. In S. Blackman & D. Conrad (Eds.), *Caribbean discourse in inclusive education: Historical and contemporary issues* (pp. 33–52). Charlotte, NC: Information Age Publishing.

Central Intelligence Agency. (2018). *The world factbook.* Retrieved from https://www.cia.gov/library/publications/the-world-factbook/geos/t

Eide, A. H., & Ingstad, B. (2011) *Disability and poverty: A global challenge.* Bristol, UK: Policy Press.

Erevelles, N. (2011). *Disability and difference in global contexts: Enabling a transformative body politic.* New York: Palgrave Macmillan.

Gayle-Geddes, A. (2015). *Disability and inequality: Socioeconomic imperatives and public policy in Jamaica*. New York: Palgrave Macmillan.

Gayle-Geddes, A. (2016). A situational analysis of persons with disabilities in Jamaica and Trinidad and Tobago: Education and employment policy imperatives. In P. Block, D. Kasnitz, A. Nishida, & N. Pollard (Eds.), *Occupying disability: Critical approaches to community, justice, and decolonizing disability* (pp. 127–144). New York: Springer.

Goffman, E. (1963). *Stigma: Notes on the management of spoiled identity*. New York: Simon and Schuster.

Government of the Republic of Trinidad and Tobago. (2015). *TT Connect*. Retrieved from https://www.ttconnect.gov.tt

Government of the Republic of Trinidad and Tobago, Equal Opportunity Commission. (2001). *Equal Opportunity Act of 2000*. Retrieved from http://www.equalopportunity.gov.tt/download-act

Government of the Republic of Trinidad and Tobago, Ministry of Education. (1967). *Education Act of 1967*. Port of Spain, Trinidad.

Government of the Republic of Trinidad and Tobago, Ministry of Social Development. (2003, June). *Second periodic report under the Convention on the Rights of the Child*. Retrieved from https://www.ncjrs.gov/pdffiles1/Digitization/203642NCJRS.pdf

Government of the Republic of Trinidad and Tobago, Ministry of Social Development. (2006). *National Plan of Action for Children for 2006–2010*. Port of Spain, Trinidad.

Government of the Republic of Trinidad and Tobago, Ministry of the People and Social Development. (2005). *National Policy on Persons with Disabilities*. Port of Spain, Trinidad.

Grech, S. (2015). *Disability and poverty in the global South: Renegotiating development in Guatemala*. New York: Palgrave Macmillan.

Inter-American Development Bank. (2008). Trinidad/Tobago: Support for a seamless education system project 3: TTL1005. Retrieved from https://www.iadb.org/en/projects.TT-L1005

Kalyanpur, M. (2015). Mind the gap: Special education policy and practice in India in the context of globalization. In S. Rao & M. Kalyanpur, *South Asia and Disability Studies: Redefining boundaries and extending horizons* (pp. 49–72). New York: Peter Lang.

Keller, C. (1993). *Report of the National Task Force on Education, green paper*. Trinidad and Tobago, Ministry of Education, Port of Spain, Trinidad.

Kittay, E. F. (2011). The ethics of care, dependence, and disability. *Ratio Juris. An International Journal of Jurisprudence and Philosophy of Law, 24*(1), 49–58.

Linton, S. (2006). *My body politic: A memoir*. Ann Arbor: University of Michigan Press.

Mairs, N. (1996). *Waist-high in the world: A life among the nondisabled.* Boston: Beacon Press.

Mairs, N. (2011). On being a cripple. *Researchomatic.* Retrieved June 2011, from http://www.researchomatic.com/Nancy-Mairs-On-Being-A-Cripple-75304.html

Oliver, M., & Barnes, C. (1998). *Social policy and disabled people: From exclusion to inclusion.* London: Longman.

O'Rourke-Lang, C., & Levy, R. V. (2016). The global context of disability. *Global Education Review, 3*(3), 1–3.

Richardson, J. G., & Powell, J. W. (2011). *Comparing special education: Origins to contemporary paradoxes.* Stanford, CA: Stanford University Press.

Singhal, N. (Ed.). (2013). *Disability, poverty & education.* Oxford, UK: Routledge.

The Borgen Project: Trinidad and Tobago poverty rate. (2017, October). Retrieved March 29, 2018, from https://borgenproject.org/trinidad-and-tobago-poverty-rate/

Titchkosky, T. (2008). Disability: A rose by any other name? "People-first" language in Canadian society. *Canadian Review of Sociology, 28*(2), 125–140.

Trinidad and Tobago Association for Retarded Children. (1984). *His special children.* Port of Spain, Trinidad: Horsford Printerie.

UNESCO. (1994, June). The Salamanca statement and framework for action on special needs education. Salamanca, Spain. Retrieved from http://unesdoc.unesco.org/images/0009/000984/098427eo.pdf

United Nations. (2006). *Convention on the rights of persons with disabilities.* New York.

United Nations. (2018). *Human development reports.* Human Development Index. Retrieved February 25, 2019, from http://hdr.undp.org/en/content/human-development-index-hdi

United Nations Department of Economic and Social Affairs. (2018). *Flagship report on disability and development: Realization of the sustainable development goals by, for, and with persons with disabilities.*

U.S. Department of State. (2014). Investment climate statement for Trinidad and Tobago. Retrieved from https://www.state.gov/documents/organization/227506.pdf

CHAPTER 2

The Immortelle: Planting, Nurturing, and Sustaining

The Immortelle flower is brilliant orange, and the whole crown of the tree is covered with these outstanding flowers. The view of our northern range at this time of year is one of large bands of orange spread across the deep green foliage. The Immortelle was also known to early cocoa planters as "madre de cacao", or Mother of the Cocoa, because Trinidad and Tobago's very fine cocoa thrives especially in the shade of the Immortelle trees.
(Asa Wright Nature Centre, Trinidad and Tobago)

The Immortelle tree—"madre de cacao"—mother of the cocoa—protects the leafy cocoa plant that withers in direct sunlight but thrives beneath the Immortelle's spreading branches. This expansive flowering tree nurtures the acrid dark brown cocoa that is transformed into a taste beloved across the world—sweet chocolate, so pleasing to the palate. This was our metaphor for a school that would nurture and protect children too delicate or too unique for the harsh realities of a highly academic, examination-driven school system: a system that did not imagine itself responsible for the minority of children who would not fit that mold. On the margins of that system stood a handful of "special schools", offering services to a limited number of children over the age of six. Later in the book, I will discuss possible challenges to the concept of a

© The Author(s) 2020   23
B. Harry, *Childhood Disability, Advocacy, and Inclusion in the Caribbean*, Palgrave Studies in Disability and International Development, https://doi.org/10.1007/978-3-030-23858-2_2

school as a protective environment, but at this point, I state simply that this was our vision of what our children needed.

BETH'S STORY: PLANTING THE IMMORTELLE

The metaphor of the Immortelle was proposed by Joan Knowles, the talented physiotherapist who collaborated with speech/language therapist, Wendy Gomez, and me to start our little school for children with disabilities in 1978. Joan and Wendy were providing therapy on a private basis, but the children they were serving had no school to go to. Prior to this meeting, I had been working on starting a small play group in my home to support my three-year-old daughter, Melanie, whose cerebral palsy rendered her ineligible for any preschool services in Trinidad/Tobago. I already had one potential enrollee for the imagined playgroup—Raquel, the daughter of Jacqui, who was introduced in the prologue. With no clear goal in mind, I jumped at the opportunity to meet these therapists.

Sometime in June of 1978, I visited Joan and Wendy at their practice in Woodbrook, a residential neighborhood in Port of Spain, the capital city of TT. With Melanie on one shoulder and my meager paper credentials in hand, I told these young women about my desire to provide an educational facility for my three-year-old daughter and others like her. My BA in English Literature, MEd, and five years of high school and community college teaching in Canada had certainly *not* prepared me to be a special education teacher. All I really had to offer was a strong sense of myself as a teacher and an overwhelming desire to learn everything I could about adapting my skills to the needs of children like my beautiful baby Melanie. Joan and Wendy, in turn, outlined their professional credentials—Joan had studied physiotherapy with the famous Vera Bobath in London, and Wendy had just returned to Trinidad after completing her master's degree in speech/language therapy at Florida State University in the U.S.

After no more than half an hour's conversation, Joan said, "So, would you like to join us?" I leaped at the offer, an offer that was miles beyond my initial idea of a playgroup in my small living room in Diego Martin. To Joan and Wendy's group of children we would add Raquel and Melanie. These eight children would be our initial students. And that was it. That was how we started.

Phase One: Twelve Kids, Three Therapists, a So-Called Teacher, and a "Babysitter"

The seeds of the Immortelle Center were planted between September 1978 and June 1979. "First to begin", (as we say in TT), we needed a helper—an assistant teacher—and I decided to offer the job to a young man named Gerard Telfer, who, just out of high school, had assisted me very successfully with Melanie and my one-year-old toddler, Mark, during that summer. I knew that Gerard was what we call in teaching "a natural", but, some 40 years later, he told his part of the story this way:

> *Gerard.* Honestly, Beth, you were my first employer, but I didn't start to work with children with disabilities with you. Every year, with 8 of us children in the home, very poor, with one tin of corned beef, Daddy used to bring three children from the orphanage to spend Christmas at home with us. So that helped me to have a feeling for people who were really disadvantaged. Plus, since age five, I was always helping in the church and looking out for the less abled.
>
> When I left school in June of 1977, I was 16 and a half and had just sat my GCE exams. My step-mother, Shirley, came and said, "I have a job for you—babysitting". She told me that you had two children, one with a disability, and that when she proposed me for the job, you said, "But he's a boy!" And Shirley said, "Try him and see if it works out". And it worked out great!
>
> So then, the summer passed, and I was thinking that now I must look for a job. Then you said, "Gerard... I just met two people and we are going to start a school, so you can be my first teacher." I said "A teacher? I know I can babysit!" I was shocked that you used the word "teacher". I said to myself, "Teacher? Desk? Chair? I ain't get no training yet, but I will try!"

We opened our doors in September 1978, and new applications came in quickly through a spontaneous grapevine. By January we had 12 children and the extra help of Deidre, a physiotherapist. Although five adults and 12 children sounds ideal, for us it was overwhelming. We offered the education program from 8 a.m., to noon, leaving the afternoons for the therapists to pursue their private practice. We operated on a rotating structure: Gerard, Deidre, and I worked with eight to ten children at a time, grouped by their perceived abilities, while the therapists worked with individual children. This grouping was really in concept only, as the children's ages ranged from 3 to 14 and their conditions varied widely, as follows: four children with cerebral palsy and varying intellectual levels, two with

Down Syndrome, two with severe language disorder and hyperactivity, two with mild to moderate intellectual disabilities, and two with severe intellectual disabilities, both of whom could walk independently.

While Immortelle struggled to get on its feet, some of the children did so with surprising success. Those with cerebral palsy made incredible strides in response to daily individual physical therapy with Joan. Melanie, for one, transformed from a bundle of floppy little limbs into an excited three-year-old diligently practicing how to move from lying on her side, pushing herself up one slow movement at a time, until she was sitting upright. Intensive speech/language therapy with Wendy also produced wonderful results especially in receptive language for those children who were non-verbal.

In that initial year, we ran a skeletal operation based on fees from parents, which were sufficient to pay each of our portions of the rent, a small salary to Gerard, and a pittance left over for each of us. For my part, it was a balancing act, paying a helper half-day at home to take care of my toddler, Mark, and hurrying home to relieve her in the afternoons. Melanie, meanwhile, was a very dependent little girl, still fed by a spoon and still supremely vulnerable to choking.

I was shaken when, in February, only six months after our opening, my husband Clive, who was an economist with the TT government, was assigned to take up a temporary post in Toronto, Canada. Disappointed as I was, I knew I had no choice but to go with him as it was impossible for me to care for the two children on my own. With a heavy heart, I told Joan and Wendy that I would have to leave at Easter, supposedly for four months, to return in September. And so, it was that, despite our high hopes and the greatest efforts of my partners, the Immortelle's first start was destined to sputter. Wendy described that challenging first year of Immortelle's life:

> *Wendy.* I returned from Florida State University a qualified speech pathologist in August of 1978. I went there when I was just 17 and came back home thinking the government would hire me right away as there was only one speech language pathologist in the whole of TT. I went to the Ministry of Health to present my credentials, which is what people did in those days. The director said, "Fantastic! We would love to hire you. We'd have to create a post and it would take one and a half to two years."
>
> I'd recently gotten married, had no job and I didn't know what I was going to do. Long story short, I got a call from Joan, who said, "I have a little clinic in Brabant Street in Woodbrook. Would you come and join me?" I started in Joan's office, but in those days you couldn't advertise, so I sat around for the first few weeks, waiting to see what would happen.

Then you, Beth, came into the picture—maybe a week or 2 after I started. You said, "I want somebody to help me. I have an Education degree. I have a child with CP, and I need your help". You convinced us. We talked about the Immortelle tree that shaded the cocoa plant. It was Joan's idea, and by the end of that day, we were opening a school! I was like a little girl! I could not believe we were opening a school and my role would be speech therapist! I'd work in the school in the mornings and that would pay my rent. I was excited! "I'm going to be the speech therapist."

A few months later Deidre came to help us. The kids would be with you or Gerard, and Joan and I would pull them out for therapy. It was an amazing idea. It was unheard of here in TT and even though I was young and inexperienced this was how I'd been trained to work—with a team.

Then came Easter. Suddenly, you had to go, and Joan and I were like—how are we going to manage? Because you were very organized. You had that vision and you ran the main classroom. But you left in April. By then Cheryl, the Occupational Therapist, was helping and she said she would try and do the teaching part. But during that last term things were not going well. You had such a personal motivation. There was nobody else to fill your place. I was then pregnant with my first child, Dale, so I had him in August, and I moved my practice to my home. By that time there was no way Joan could continue, so we had to close.

Meanwhile, in Toronto, my heart sank when I received the letter from my friends at home explaining the impossibility of their continuing the school. Yet, I was not surprised, realizing that we were all attempting to do something for which we were ill-prepared. They were not teachers and I was neither a special education teacher nor an administrator by nature or experience. Yet, I could think of no other way to respond to Melanie's developmental and educational needs than to provide the services myself. In September of that year, sensing that Clive's stay would turn out to be much longer, I enrolled in a diploma course in special education at York University. My goal was to learn the basics of the field and figure out how I could build a strong and sustainable Immortelle Centre on my return home.

Phase 2: The Spreading Branches of the Immortelle

September 1980–June 1986 marked the school's second phase. I returned from Toronto in the spring of 1980 with one goal in mind: to re-establish the Immortelle Centre, but in a modified version. In Toronto, I had realized that the model of integrating therapies into an educational program was an ideal that even in a developed society was still beyond affordability. More feasible would be a conventional school model with guidance from therapists on the infusion of key therapeutic principles into our teaching and social activities. Children wanting individual therapies would be referred to the collaborating partners for an additional fee. Fortunately, Joan was now renting half the house on Brabant Street and agreed that I should rent the other half and she would participate as the consulting physiotherapist. Wendy, however, was not available as she was at home, juggling a small private practice and the demands of her new baby.

Of our previous students, only three, including Melanie, were available to return to the school, as some had been enrolled in a small home-based program and the families of some others had emigrated to the US. I set about advertising the program through several medical practitioners and through an interview on a morning TV show by the popular journalist Allison Hennessy, who was herself a wheelchair user. By August, I had six children signed up and several more who wanted to enroll but were unable to pay fees. Relying on the charity model referred to in Chap. 1, through a presentation to the Rotary Club of Port of Spain, I gained four offers of sponsorship for children's fees. This brought our number to 11 for a September opening.

This time, I planned the program in two groups: the nursery section included six very young children whose activities focused on developing fine and gross motor skills and verbal and non-verbal communication. The classroom group included relatively independent children who were ready for some level of academic learning.

Then I needed to find teachers. It was August, and the budding adults of the nation were searching for the next step in their lives, following their high school exams. Gerard was not available as he had taken a job at the Lady Hochoy Home for children with intellectual disabilities. Two wonderful young women joined our staff: Mercedes Telfer, Gerard's sister, and Elizabeth Solomon, the daughter of my close friend, Shielah, had both just completed their O-level exams. Like Gerard, these young women were "naturals" with children, and their contrasting styles proved perfectly complementary—Elizabeth, soft-spoken and low-keyed, and Mercedes, ebullient and engaging.

I have recounted the story of Melanie's life in a memoir, *Melanie, bird with a broken wing: A mother's story* (2010), which includes some detail about the early days of the Immortelle Centre. I will quote here my description in the memoir of the ethos of the school in those days:

> What grew from there were the spreading branches of the Immortelle as our small effort seemed to take onto itself the color and charisma of its chosen symbol. In that first term, days at our little Centre were characterized by the gaiety and energy of my two helpers. Together they exuded all the beauty of youth, the sense of fun and freedom, and the idealism and faith of young people at the brink of adulthood. To them, their charges were simply children, their handicaps incidental, and they approached them with an easy acceptance that allowed neither pity nor condescension. (p. 185)

With this joyful beginning, Immortelle bloomed and thrived, and within a year, we needed more help. We employed two new teachers, Anne-Marie, who had experience working at the Servol school for children with disabilities, and Monica, who brought only her loving intentions and an intuitive knack for creating firm but gentle lines of communication with even the least communicative of children. From these simple beginnings, this phase of the life of Immortelle lasted from September of 1980 until August of 1986. It was, however, a fateful phase, interrupted after just one year by a shocking event that shook me and others to the core.

An Immortelle Tragedy

On July 31, 1981, our little home in Brabant Street was rocked with tragedy when my daughter, Melanie, who had absorbed my life for almost six years, died suddenly by choking. I will leave the details of her passing to those who would like to read the memoir (Harry, 2010) and will say here only that her accidental death was shocking and yet in line with what had been her greatest challenge in life—eating. The brain stem damage she had suffered in utero had resulted in severe dysfunction of the musculature for chewing and swallowing. Indeed, we had discovered early on that the entire process of her peristalsis (by which food is passed through the body in a rhythmic flow), was seriously impaired. Although this had improved a great deal over the years, Melanie's feeding, as is the case with many individuals with cerebral palsy, continued to be a perilous process.

Melanie left us on Friday. It was the Friday before the long weekend marking TT's independence, and we were to begin a two-week summer camp at the school the next Tuesday. Although the day of her death remains vivid in my memory, I remember only a few things about the subsequent three days. I know that Clive, my husband, made all the arrangements to bury Melanie in his family's plot in the San Juan cemetery. On Saturday my mother arrived from Jamaica, and her quiet, stoic wisdom got me back on my feet. On Sunday morning we held funeral services at the small Catholic church in San Juan, and there was one person ahead of us—Veda, the lady who arrived at Immortelle every morning at 5 a.m. to make sure that everything was in place and ready for the children, whom she loved as if they were her own. As part of the service, we read a letter from my brother, Philip, and we sang "Morning has broken". Throughout Sunday night and Monday, our home overflowed with friends and family coming and going with pots of rice and beans and plates of home-baked pastries. This outpouring of caring and support touched our family deeply.

On Tuesday, we opened the Immortelle summer camp as planned. As I stood on the porch welcoming parents, I knew that, truly, the most terrible thing in the world had happened and was overwhelmed by the thought of having to face my many responsibilities. Yet, seeing the familiar faces of the parents, I realized that Immortelle was not Melanie's school. It was a place of love and support for all the children to whom we had promised a happy summer experience, so we had to go on. And we did.

From the time of Melanie's birth until her death, I had devoted all my energies to figuring out, first, how to be her mother and, second, how to provide a place of safety and learning for her and other children like her. By the time of her death, I was deeply immersed, not only in Immortelle, but also in a wide range of disability issues in this small nation that had become my home. In a developing nation, to enter the world of disability is to entirely change your perspective on what you're supposed to be doing with your life. I found that I could not open just one door, because each door led to another and another until I found myself living in an entirely new household.

Going On

In the fall of 1982, a year after Melanie's passing, Immortelle moved to a new location (Fig. 2.1). Student enrollment had grown to about 20 and we needed more space. Fortunately, we found a large old house in Duke Street, opposite Victoria Square, a fenced public park in the heart of Port of Spain.

Fig. 2.1 Immortelle Children's Centre, Duke Street, Port of Spain, 1982–2002

Typical of early-nineteenth-century architecture, the house had a big central room and several small rooms off to one side and at the back. Behind the main building was a large, enclosed yard and a small annex, where we placed the children in the nursery group.

With more students came the need for more teachers. Once more, word of mouth brought us good fortune and, between 1982 and 1985, we added seven new teachers, all young high school graduates, full of the energy needed to respond to the needs of approximately 30 children. The teachers included Charlene, Nicole, Kenny, Cathy, Camille, Marina, and Zorana.

The success and development of Immortelle throughout those years, though exhilarating, gradually took a toll on me. Within a year or two of re-starting Immortelle, I was playing many roles in the disabilities community. I was elected president of the Association for Retarded Children, a volunteer organization responsible for overseeing the operations of the Lady Hochoy Home, whose daily operations were provided by the Roman

Catholic Sisters of the Carmelite Order. I was also a core member of an advocacy organization, "Families of the Disabled", and I served on a Department of Education committee for learning disabilities. Feeling constantly on call, I responded to numerous community requests for public appearances and initiatives related to disability issues.

I was feeling burned out. Melanie's death had taken an immeasurable toll on me personally, and on my marriage, and I was beginning to lose the powerful drive that had brought me this far with the Immortelle Centre.

Along with the constant demands on my time and energies in the community, the intensity of the responsibility for Immortelle was beginning to weigh heavily on me. One episode characterizes a moment when I knew I could not go on much longer. A child in our nursery group, Sherwin, was an energetic and cheerful little fellow whose cerebral palsy impaired his speech and all his movements. He was a joy to work with except for the fact that he frequently experienced lengthy grand mal seizures. Teachers handling Sherwin in a seizure had been taught to see him through these episodes by simply encircling him firmly with their arms, his back against their chest, and wait out the seizure. One day, however, Sherwin's seizure would not stop. After about ten minutes I decided to take him to the hospital. Having no idea of how long it would take to get response from an ambulance, I drove to the hospital, with Sherwin held tightly in the back seat by one of the teachers. Immediately upon our arrival, the hospital personnel placed Sherwin on a bed and administered some medication by injection as we stood by.

Still the seizure did not stop. It must have lasted half an hour, and there was one moment that I will never forget because it emphasized the bizarre nature of this terrible condition: The seizure shifted suddenly to only one side of Sherwin's little body, and, as the right side continued its horrendous shaking, the left side lay perfectly still, so relaxed that, at one point, he brought his left hand to his face and scratched his left cheek in a totally normal movement, while the right side of his face and body was racked with tremors. I was overwhelmed by this demonstration of the inexplicable complexity of the human brain and even more at my own lack of understanding of its nature. I came away shaking, thinking, "What am I doing carrying this kind of responsibility?" I thought of the wonderful services I had observed and been the recipient of during Melanie's visits to Toronto and wept for the absence of support for these children and their families in Trinidad/Tobago. I believe it was soon after this that my level of exhaustion became overwhelming to me.

In 1985, Professor Robert Bogdan from Syracuse University in the US, who had been engaged by the Ministry of Education to advise on matters related to disability services, visited the Immortelle Centre. I found myself asking questions about what would be involved in pursuing a PhD in special education at Syracuse. Professor Bogdan encouraged me with lots of information and an invitation to apply to their program. I applied and received an encouraging response, but with a caveat that I would need to complete six credits of graduate-level work in research methods and introductory statistics, which I had not taken during my master's degree program at the Ontario Institute for Studies in Education (OISE) in Toronto.

I decided to spend the summer of 1985 doing the two required courses at OISE, to explore the possibility of returning to graduate school at the PhD level. That first summer was easy for me to arrange as I had family and friends in Toronto and was able to take Mark with me to visit with his cousins as part of an exciting summer expedition.

I happily made the transition from being a full-time teacher, administrator, and advocate in the field of special education to the carefree role of full-time graduate student. During that summer, and in the subsequent three and a half years pursuing the PhD degree at Syracuse, I frequently marveled at how relative perceptions of stress can be. For my classmates, graduate school was stressful and demanding. For me, being a student was being liberated from responsibility; it was being free to sit back, absorb new knowledge, and explore ideas.

I returned to Trinidad/Tobago from Toronto at the end of the summer of 1985, knowing I had to follow my present need for a break, but struggling with how to create a safety net for those who relied on me through the Immortelle Centre.

Parents—The Safety Net

During the 1985–1986 academic year, with great trepidation and deepest apologies, I told the Immortelle family about my plans to pursue the PhD at Syracuse University. I believe that I framed my explanation mostly in terms of wanting to learn more about special education rather than the fact that I was truly burned out. For the most part, the parents were understanding, and were kind in their responses and promised to support a new principal as best they could.

I also knew, but did not then make public, my intention to leave my marriage. Despite an essentially good relationship with my husband and our shared commitment to Melanie during her lifetime, and to Mark, who was then about 6, Melanie's loss had created a chasm that nothing seemed to fill. My hope was that a new place and new learning would begin to fill that space. Now, from a vantage point of more than 30 years, I would say it did.

In seeking an acting principal, my professional network in TT led me quite quickly to Asha, a Montessori-trained teacher who had recently returned from England. After several visits to the school and meetings with parents, Asha agreed to take the job. Dr. Esla Lynch, a special education colleague who had for some years run her own private school for children with learning disabilities—a school that still thrives to this day— agreed to provide back-up curriculum guidance. We laid the plans as best we could and, in July of 1986, I left Trinidad, after a tearful surprise good-bye at the airport by the entire group of Immortelle teachers.

Despite the best of intentions, that year at Immortelle did not go well and, when I returned to visit at the end of the year, Asha told me she would not be able to continue. I was soon introduced to a Canadian trained teacher who had some experience with special education. She took on the job and seemed to be doing well, but unfortunately, after a year she developed a serious illness that required her to resign.

By that time, I knew that it would take me at least one more year to complete the PhD. I appealed to the parents to propose a solution and they did exactly that. The parents decided to form a not-for-profit and Jacqui Leotaud, Racquel's mother, stepped in, saying that she would "act, until a proper principal came along". The rest of the story of Immortelle's development from 1989 until the present time will occupy the rest of this chapter.

First, however, I will reflect briefly on some of the changes that occurred for me upon leaving Trinidad/Tobago for the US.

Considering Disability Culturally, for the First Time

I started my studies at Syracuse University in the fall of 1986 and became intrigued by the appeal of special education as a field of study and research. At a time when the field was marked by exciting new approaches, I found myself in exactly the right place to embark on a new phase of my career as an educator. Syracuse University was in the vanguard of the inclusion movement. Professor Burton Blatt, the pioneer who had publicized the horrors of institutionalization, had just passed away, and I was working with his peers—leading scholars such as Wolf Wolfensberger, Bob Bogdan, Douglas Biklen, and Luanna Meyer, whose vision of inclusion was on the cutting edge of the movement.

Surprising to me were the considerable differences in cultural perspectives that existed between me and my American professors and colleagues. Yet, my perspectives were readily shared by fellow international students and members of American minority groups, which led me to realize the cultural nature of the way disabilities are defined and treated, something I had not considered previously. There were three key differences that I struggled with: the implications of "the charity model" of service provision, the concept of full inclusion, and the impact of unacknowledged social and cultural biases upon assessment and services.

The charity model I was familiar with did not challenge the premise that these children's disabilities rendered them ineligible for public education. I believe that this acceptance reflected a rationale that went something like this: children with disabilities could not reasonably claim a "right" to an education because the concept of "education" referred specifically to academic learning. There were insufficient funds to support quality education for all those perceived as worthy, far less those perceived to be unable to profit from formal education; therefore, such children were essentially the responsibility of their families. Although I had experienced the injustice of no public support for children with disabilities, I had attempted my own solution by creating an "add-on" to the existing situation. I had not really thought about how the system itself could be changed. My years as an educator and researcher in the US have dramatically changed my understanding of the role of government and the power of public advocacy that can lead to legislation.

Second, and tightly woven into the first concern, was the apparent impossibility of an inclusive model of education. What would education mean for children who can't read and write, let alone talk? How could they possibly be integrated into an academic education system and how could their emotional safety, even their physical safety, be ensured outside of the protective shade of an "Immortelle"? My studies since that time have led me to a position of great respect for the principle of inclusive education, despite a continuing concern that this model is not easily transportable across social and cultural contexts.

Third, I became aware of the socio-cultural biases inherent in the cognitive and developmental assessment of children with disabilities. This was most obvious in the use of IQ tests in which socially and culturally based learning could be misinterpreted as cognitive deficits. But I was shocked to realize that this was also true in the assessment of children with more visible impairments, whereby culturally based behaviors and interactions also might be interpreted through a lens of deficiency.

These issues were new to me and so intriguing that I soon developed a line of research that would interweave my interest in families, culture, and disability. This focus has marked my entire professional life since my departure from Immortelle. The research in this book represents my continuing struggle to figure out how issues of advocacy, inclusion, and equity in the education of persons with disabilities can best be adapted to the contexts of Caribbean nations.

Growing the Immortelle: Jacqui's Story

While I embarked on a new phase of my personal and professional journey, my friends in Trinidad pursued the goal of nurturing and sustaining the work we had accomplished over a period of eight years. This section presents Jacqui's account of how the school moved, over a period of three decades, from a private effort, conceptualized and run by one individual, to the status of a non-governmental organization (NGO) that now receives substantial government subsidies, yet continues to rely heavily upon the charity model. Jacqui's story is marked by personal motivation, imagination, persistence, and social negotiation, revealing the extreme challenge of providing quality educational services on the margins of the society's educational infrastructure.

The entire section is told in Jacqui's own words, adapted directly from approximately 30 hours of audio taped transcribed interviews and innumerable conversations that were partially taped and partially documented in note form. Because this chapter is essentially a history of Jacqui's efforts, I will tell the story mostly as a chronological narrative. However, the themes embedded in this narrative will be echoed throughout the book as I report on my conversations with parents, teachers, and community members alike; themes of individual agency, advocacy, reliance on social contacts, and helpful but inadequate government assistance.

Jacqui: Starting Again

Esla told me she'd hire me until they found a proper principal. She said, "I will look after it for a year but you parents need to form an association or something and take it on."

I had run my own program at home while Immortelle was temporarily closed and I had also run Immortelle for a term when Paula got sick. So I figured I could do it until we got someone with formal training in education.

We started off as a 'limited by guarantee' company. We had a Board of Directors composed of parents and I was the secretary-treasurer. I was instrumental in liaising with the attorney to get all the legal steps done to turn it into an NGO. We changed the name to the Immortelle Children's Centre—new letterheads and everything, because it was a new company. We took over the school in 1988 and it took the year to put everything in place, so we had it registered in 1989. Then we applied for our NGO status and, with the help of Clive Pantin, the Minister of Education, we got that in 1990.

We formed a new board composed mostly of parents of children in the school, and our very first decision, which the school has always been proud of, was that no child who could benefit from the programmes would be turned away because of inability to pay the fees. This policy has never changed.

Stepping Stones: Once you're Known…

With our non-profit status we could then apply to Rotary Club and other corporate and service organizations. I think the first stepping stone was in 1995, when the Rotary Club of Port of Spain West donated $25,000 to open a computer lab. They gave us three computers and this was years before a computer was the thing to have! In those days, none of the private special schools had computers.

In TT the more you're known is the more people want to give you, because when donors find somebody that they feel is using the money for what they've asked for, then they're happy to give more. The TT corporate is very generous. They really are.

But our progress was day to day and we still had to fund-raise. We started very small—a bake sale here and a garage sale there. The Board was very proactive in those days.

In 1998 the petroleum company, BP of Trinidad and Tobago, funded a staff development program for one year. They gave us money to bring in lecturers to train the staff in different areas. Some professionals also donated their services, giving therapy to the students and running workshops to upgrade the teaching skills of the staff.

So we started to get funding, because we started to be known. The professionals in the field could see that we were trying. We were going forward, and it all took on a whole new feeling!

Then *Something Special* Came and We Were Chock-a-block Full

Helen Humphrey had started her own school, called *Something Special*. It was an integrated pre-school, serving regular, typically developing kids and kids with special needs. But then, as the typical students grew up, they went on to regular school and the special-needs kids stayed behind and were getting older. So Helen reached out to Immortelle to see if we could merge.

The timing seemed right, because by then we had a program for teenagers and I had just hired a new teacher who was also qualified as a music therapist. Atlantic LNG (Liquefied Natural Gas) paid for a music therapy program for the entire month of August and they paid the teacher's salary. But it was not only for Immortelle students; they required it to be island wide, so we had to advertise it in the papers. That gave us more visibility.

After we merged with *Something Special* the school was just too full. I took about 15 or 16 kids from them and a couple of their teachers. I think Immortelle already had twenty or more at the time, so with *Something Special* we were pushing 40. The students were teenagers and it was just too many people. We were choc-a-block full!

The Vocational Centre Was My Vision

By that time, Raquel was a teenager and her needs were changing, and I was thinking about her future as an adult. I enrolled in a Special Education program and started to feel more confident in my knowledge and skills. Two other teachers in the school also went to the same programme.

We used to run a lot of fundraisers in the country club and I got to know Joseph Fernandes, so, in 1999, I wrote a proposal for the Joseph B. Fernandes foundation to fund a Vocational Centre and they funded it for a year. We rented a property and bought all sorts of things to outfit the Centre. The Vocational Centre opened in 2000, and the seniors left the Duke Street location and went to the new location in Woodbrook. We had a big graduation with hats and the whole works. But we only lasted a couple of years there, as we just couldn't afford the rent. So we had to bring the seniors back to Duke Street and we re-arranged the annex at the back to become a culinary arts and life-skills centre.

My idea was to train the students for 2 or 3 years and then turn it into a workshop where they would start to produce things. We did green seasoning. The kids knew how to do that and we just churned it out. In mango season, we'd do chutney or anchar. Then, at one stage, just to change, they did buljol and bake, because the students like to bake. Parents and their friends bought the various products. But after a while, parents got tired of buying these things and we did not take it to the next level. To market it, you need labels, food badges for the students, bar codes and so on. Really, we needed a consultant to organize all this for us!

We tried everything. We tried to produce Tobago peppermints. They're long and red and white and when you bite into them they melt in your mouth. You can't get them these days. We made lots of them. We hung them all over the place. No preservatives. We wanted to know if they would get hard, how long they'd last. But they didn't last a long time and they really weren't turning out to be Tobago peppermints, so we just scrapped it.

We made Vetiver sachets and Vetiver Christmas decorations. Vetiver is the aromatic root of the cuscus plant. The Vetiver sachets will sell, but it was hard for the students to make the sachets because you hold it, tie it, then make a bow, so not a lot of the students could do it. We produced them for a while but it turned out the vetiver wasn't always in season and had to be imported from St. Vincent. The ones here in TT weren't plentiful, so it was hard to get.

The Vocational Centre was my vision and it was supposed to evolve into a sheltered workshop. But it never moved forward. The kids and the teachers got bored because they were doing the same thing for 10 years.

By then Duke Street had gotten too small for us. The bigger we got, the bigger the building that was needed; the bigger the expenses, the bigger the responsibility.

We explored several options, including maybe buying the building, but the place was expensive because it was old and needed to be revamped. So when the owners tried to put the rent up, I told them we just couldn't afford it.

Moving to St. Ann's: If You're Not Moving Forward, You're Going Backward

This brought us to the next huge step, which was facilitated by Helen and her husband, John Humphrey. John was a Minister of government and was very instrumental in arranging for us to lease a government property on State lands, for ten dollars per year! That was this building here, in St. Ann's, which we registered in 2003. When I saw it, I couldn't believe this could become a school. It was dilapidated as it hadn't been used in over 20 years (Fig. 2.2).

We were faced with the huge task of raising funds to renovate the building and this is where the corporate sector came to the rescue. Republic Bank gave us $700,000 to start the renovations and then we begged for the other stuff. All the labor for the plumbing in the old wing, the electrics, all the

Fig. 2.2 Abandoned Government property at St. Ann's Gardens, leased to the school, 2002

windows, all the doors were donated by local businesses. It was like $4.2 million in donated stuff (Fig. 2.3).

Republic Bank has a charitable foundation called *The Power to Make a Difference*. That was their first year and we were the first people to get a donation from that fund. They make sure that you spend their money the way you said or else they won't fund you again. The fund administrator would come to check and see what's going on when we started renovating.

When we moved in, we had not even 50 kids. We were not using all the classrooms, so, since the Vocational Centre at Duke Street had not been working properly, we moved those students up here. After a year or two, I decided to pilot a work program. Instead of running the regular program for the seniors, this section would be turned into a work centre. But it must be sustainable. We cannot be begging for money every month. The centre must produce stuff that will sell. It must become a sheltered workshop for the adults. We were able to move forward with this because Republic Bank granted us one million dollars to build a new wing for the Senior Centre!

Fig. 2.3   Immortelle Children's Centre, St. Ann's Gardens, 2003–present

The Cookie Project

So that's how we came to the Cookie Project. There's a place in Texas, a community like ours, that produces cookies by the tin and you can order it online. About ten years ago my sister-in-law went to this place and they had these cookies. When she showed me the brochure, I said, "But we could do that!" I've been talking about cookies for years but nobody would take me on with my cookies!

We are trying to create our own brand. We got the recipe from a lovely parent who's an occupational therapist from Ireland and she has been running our culinary arts department. She and her friend came and tried lots of different cookies and we came up with one that's easy for the kids to make. It's a nice cookie with a little jam in the centre. I told her we need another cookie as well—one with chocolate, or else I'm not buying! Then she came up with another idea to sell cookie dough, to roll it and freeze it and cut it up just like you find it in the grocery. You get the dry ingredients, with the recipe on the outside and make the bottle look pretty, or we can put them in bags that the students make. She said, "We can do that for Christmas". I think that it will work.

We got great help from a group of occupational therapists who came from Toronto to do their internships, and they did a research project to plan the pilot for the cookies. They did a task-analysis of the entire production process and worked out how much the cookies would cost, including the labour charge and everything. This gave me all the information I would need to make a proposal for funding the project.

I thought, this is the last thing I'm doing! I'll open the Assisted Work Centre because that is what these students, and Raquel, need now. The whole school needs it because we're getting fuller and fuller and nobody's leaving. Soon, the Immortelle will be a bunch of old people!

My brother, David, who's the Chairman of the Board, said, "If you're not moving forward, you're going backwards." So I decided this would be the mantra for the school. Every year I feel that the students should be moving forward. They have to be learning something. If you don't learn something new you're going to go backwards.

International Collaborations by Fluke

But, you know, you must also be open to unexpected possibilities. Sometimes it seems like just a fluke that something great comes along! For example, the occupational therapist program and our therapeutic summer camp.

University of Toronto: Occupational and speech therapy interns. Fifteen years ago, a young lady, whose mother was a Trinidadian, was studying occupational therapy at the University of Toronto and wanted to come to Trinidad to do her internship. After some initial explorations, she called her aunt who still lives in Trinidad and said, "Auntie Joan, do you know anyone who has a special school?" Her aunt called me and said, "Do you think you could facilitate my niece?" I said "Of course"! Don't mind I had to go and research to find out exactly what OT is! But I said, "Of course"! So she and another girl came with their internship supervisor, and they found funding for all of this from a local donor.

That was 18 years ago and that is how our OT program started with the University of Toronto OT students. At first, two of them came once a year, then twice a year; then three of them came twice a year, as well as a speech and language intern once a year. We used to have five OTs—one for each group of students. From there, it just continued to evolve.

The OT interns do assessments when their supervisor is here. And they do individual work with some of the students as well as some group work. And they also run a project. For example, the analysis they did of the cookie project, or fixing up the library, or looking at the bag making production to see if more students could learn the skills involved in making bags for the golf tournament. The students make 100 bags for the tournament and it's good advertising for us.

The OT program was our first international project and it has worked beautifully. Really, partnering with an international organization took us to another level. And it all happened because one person wanted to come and do her internship in Trinidad/Tobago.

Seton Hall University: A therapeutic summer camp. That's also how the summer camp started. I met this lady, Dr. Jane Bernstein, who was head of the pediatric psychiatry unit in Boston Children's Hospital. Her husband likes Trinidad, so they spend six months of the year here. Jane told me that she had somebody she wanted me to meet.

Jane arrived with this lady from Seton Hall University in New Jersey, and she said, "So Jacqui, what would you like to see for Immortelle?" I was in the middle of being annoyed by the fact that the summer camp was operating more like a babysitting service, so I said, "You know what I would really like is a camp that is a therapy camp, that does things, that has sports, and that has people who knew what they were doing". (Not that I knew what I was doing, but *people* who know what they are doing!) She said, "Well, I can do that for you". I said, "Wonderful, when do we start?"

That lady was Dr. Laura Palmer, a neuro-psychologist who was a professor at Seton Hall. She wanted her students to experience other cultures. She started bringing five of her graduate students—one for each group of our students. We also used to have five University of Toronto OTs so there was one OT for each group and we had counsellors, who were paid young people, and others who were volunteers. So the summer camp had therapists, supervisors, counsellors and volunteers. There was a year when Laura came here with sixteen people!

This was great for my new students. I interview new students in May, so any student being admitted in September would have to attend the camp for the two weeks and they'd have a neuro-psych assessment by Laura and her students, for free. And that was worth thousands of dollars in Trinidad, eh? I mean, you can get the government to do it, but it takes years.

Laura found that it was wonderful for her students too. It made them better psychologists because they learned so much from the students and teachers here about special education needs. Unfortunately, about two years ago, Laura moved on from her position at Seton Hall so she no longer had students to bring to Immortelle.

We offer a lot of stuff. So, we really offer a lot of stuff! We hold IEP (individual education programme) meetings for every student every year and the parents are required to participate. Then, there are the OTs and the speech and language therapists coming from Toronto. We have a lot of activities: Weekly swimming and horseback riding, a tuck shop, Christmas concerts, carnival events, sports day, an Easter egg hunt with a hat parade. We've also had a music therapist, a cosmetologist, and a certified swimming teacher. The government will pay an amount toward part-time therapists, and some parents are willing to contribute to the difference in the therapy fees. But then, I don't think that the wealthy ones should have therapy and not the ones who can't afford to pay. So I haven't been able to figure that out.

It Hasn't Been Easy! Luckily, the Government Stepped In

It's been 15 years since we moved all the students to St. Ann's. We had a 10 year lease and we've already renewed the lease. But it hasn't been easy. At one point, we thought we might have to decide, either close the school or raise our fees to a price where we could stay open. That would have excluded all the students who couldn't pay the fees. We'd be running a school for the rich and famous. I said that's not a problem—you'll just have to get a new Principal because I'm not prepared to do it.

Luckily the government stepped in about nine years ago and started giving subsidies!

International Persuasion
    The Government had applied to the IADB (Inter-American Development Bank) for a loan to upgrade some aspect of education in Trinidad and the bank asked, "What about special education?" At that time, there were 13 public special schools (for the deaf, visually impaired, physically impaired and mentally impaired), but no support for the private schools. A group of us, representing private special schools, went to a meeting with the IADB and they asked us for a proposal.

Mrs. Manning, Minister of Education at that time, suggested that the private special schools form an organization to present our case to the government as a group, rather than individual schools. So we formed an organization called PATA, which is *Private Special Schools of Trinidad and Tobago*. We sent in our proposal which was that since the government doesn't have schools for our students to go to they need to pay for our students. That is how the government subsidies started nine years ago. But cash flow has been a continuing problem.

So Now We Get Subsidies

Now, all private special schools that are registered with the Ministry of Education receive subsidies. The schools are paid a maximum of $1,600 towards the fees for every registered student. It does not matter to the Ministry what fees you charge. If your fees are less than $1,600 they will only give you what your fees are. If your fees are over $1,600, that's the limit. The students must have a medical report, it must be approved, and they will get the subsidy. But the documents have to be repeated every year: Answer the questions: "Was there a diagnosis? How is the child?" So every year, I put "still has Autism"; "still has Down Syndrome". Whatever the diagnosis was, "still has this"—"still has this". That's how I fill out my documents every year!

Parents pay the difference in our fees, but there's also another $800 that the Ministry will pay for underprivileged students whose families meet the criteria. We have about 22 of those who have been approved and another 10 are on a waiting list. Parents pay varying amounts and several don't pay anything. But I am stricter than I used to be because it's so much more expensive—we have more staff and so much to offer.

Then there are running costs. The government pays our electricity and water bills and a subsidy toward the telephone and upkeep of the grounds and building. We must keep proper accounts.

The government has criteria for the staff, teachers and teachers' aides, and they pay a subsidy toward these salaries. We have a six to one ratio of children to adults. They only pay for one person with a master's degree in the school, so they expect the Principal to have the master's degree. But the amount they are paying for that degree is below what that person can earn somewhere else, so the school must subsidize that. The Ministry also pays for one cleaner and 2 part-time therapists.

The problem is, it's difficult to keep teachers because they are earning less, and after a few years of gaining some experience and skills here, they qualify for jobs in the government schools where they earn more money.

Government Helps, But…

So, sure, the government helps, but for years we were receiving our subsidies later and later and later. Other schools were in this position too and some had to downsize or send their teachers home because they had no money to pay them. For years it would take forever to get the documents and then the cheque from the Ministry. Sometimes our documents would sit there from September and would only get to the cheque payment people in April. Fortunately, this year (2017) they have put personnel in place with specific responsibility for the special school payments and it has been working much better.

So here's how the bureaucracy works. It's really better now, but for years the main problem was that the documents we sent in were sent to three different departments; running costs to one department, student costs to another, staff costs to yet another. The invoices would eventually go back to Student Services, then to Accounts, next to the Chief Education Officer (CEO). This step alone would take at least a week as the CEO was in another building. Next it goes to the Permanent Secretary for his/her approval and finally, to the cheque payment department.

In the 2015 school year, it was drastic! In Term 1, September to December, we submitted our documents within the first 3 weeks in September. We got paid for that on May the 8th, 2016—8 months late! It's not that there were any queries on the documents. They were just sitting there waiting for somebody to work on them!

To bridge delays in government funding we still rely on corporate support and our own fundraisers. We have one big fundraiser every October, which is the golf tournament. We make $100, 000 on it and that used to be our main fundraiser. Recently, the PTA has really pitched in and done a fund-raiser every semester: breakfasts, a curry queue, and donation cards. The breakfast alone pays for the school's stationery for the year.

Contacts Are Essential

A key aspect is the role of the Board of Directors. That is very pivotal. That's part of why we are where we are—because we have a lot of good resource people on the Board. They have good contacts. I can say, "Okay, this is what I think we need, this child needs this, and so how do we get that?" That's how we started the Vocational Centre.

It's really the people on the Board that have accessed the resources for us to keep going and keep growing. And they're always supportive and responsive to my visions. If I had an idea for the school, David would say "Okay, we'll get the money for it".

We have a fixed deposit for the school. How that happened was, I had an uncle who had lots of money and no children. And he used to help the poor. I said, "Uncle Lyn you need to help the school." He said, "What kind of rinky dink school you running, Jacqui?" So I wrote him and asked him if he would help. He gave us a donation every year until he died, at which point we were named as one of several charities to receive a donation from his estate.

Then there's a key school supporter who has been able to fill the gaps. You can't imagine how many times I have called him. But I feel bad to keep going to him because he refuses to take back the money. It's not a loan. It's a gift. But still, it's not right that the school should depend on him. When somebody else takes over from me, I don't know if he'll continue to contribute!

We are working on establishing a funding body called Friends of Immortelle, so that someone other than the principal will find funds to cover all of this. We've been struggling to keep a drive going for standing orders that would generate income that would be there all the time so that we wouldn't have to depend on the Ministry constantly. We need the Ministry money but not the cash flow issue. So far, we have only 13 or 14 orders adding up to $1400 a month, so we'd like to get even a few donors who would give a big chunk.

The 'Friends' is just a small group of people right now. But in my mind it should be the funding agency for the Immortelle. We're looking for young people who can carry it on. The school needs to start functioning without the "Uncles" of the world and without Charles Mouttet being at Republic Bank. It needs to function without us having to always be calling on these people.

Once we can get the funding and we are not dependent on fees, or completely dependent on the government just to survive, there's no reason why we couldn't hire a highly qualified professional in the field to take over the school. Because it will really need an experienced and motivated special educator. That's why everybody laughs at me when I say that I am retiring. Because they ask, who is the next person with the motivation to take this on?

Reference

Harry, B. (2010). *Melanie, bird with a broken wing: A mother's story.* Baltimore: Brookes.

CHAPTER 3

Original Parents' Stories: From "Something Not Right Here" to "She's Wonderful"

Early on in Melanie's infancy, I became intrigued with stories told by mothers of children with disabilities. I wondered if I was the only one who doubted my strength to be a mother to such a fragile child. I wondered how other parents kept their hopes up in the face of harsh pronouncements levied on their children by experts and lay people alike.

As I became immersed in all the memoirs I could find, the majority of which were published in the US, I was struck by one dominant theme: many parents described their experience as a journey from an initial reaction of shock and dismay to a personal philosophy and practice that could accommodate and celebrate the individuality of the child. In many cases, this transformation provided them with the impetus to be of service to others. This positive interpretation of an initially devastating event came through despite the context of the twentieth-century rejection and institutionalization of infants and children with disabilities. I wondered if I, and the other Immortelle parents, could tell similar stories. By the time of Melanie's death in 1981, I was halfway through writing my own account of the experience of learning to be her mother. Before the first anniversary of her death, I had completed my writing. I did not know then that it would be some 27 years before I would have the courage to publish my own version—*Melanie, Bird with a Broken Wing—A Mother's Story*.

In this chapter and the next, I offer the narratives of two groups of parents whose children attended Immortelle—a group I call the "original"

© The Author(s) 2020   49
B. Harry, *Childhood Disability, Advocacy, and Inclusion in the Caribbean*, Palgrave Studies in Disability and International Development, https://doi.org/10.1007/978-3-030-23858-2_3

parents and a group whose children were currently enrolled at the time of this study in 2015–2016. To my knowledge, there are no other published accounts of extended parent narratives from the Caribbean region. Although the stories in this study are briefly told, I hope that sharing them might provide support to those parents who, like me, longed to feel part of a community of parents who have discovered their own strengths through their children's challenges. To set the stage for the stories that I will tell in this chapter and the next, I will provide a quick overview of key moments in the early beginnings of parent narratives published in the US.

THE SURGE OF THE 1950S: PARENTS' POSITIVE NARRATIVES AGAINST THE ODDS

The early 1950s saw a spate of the first published accounts by parents of children with disabilities. At a time when such disclosure was unheard of, two books gained widespread attention in the US, because of the authors' public reputations. First, in 1951, the writer Pearl S. Buck published *The Child Who Never Grew*, which focused both on the sorrow she experienced as a mother and also on the daily challenges of caring for and teaching her child. Like many parents in the US in that period, Buck committed her child to institutional care when she was about 11 years old, reasoning that this was needed to ensure the child's care in the event of her mother's death. Despite her struggles, Buck's message was uplifting: She provided the following encouraging advice for parents:

> There is an alchemy in sorrow. It can be transmuted into wisdom, which, if it does not bring joy, can yet bring happiness… (p. 6)
> Remember this is still your child. Remember, too, that the child has his right to life, whatever that life may be, and he has the right to happiness, which you must find for him. Be proud of your child, accept him as he is and do not heed the words and stares of those who know no better. This child has a meaning for you and for all children. You will find a joy you cannot now suspect in fulfilling his life for and with him. (p. 61)

A book by the actress, Dale Evans, *"Angel Unaware"*, presented a rather different experience, as her child, who had Down Syndrome, died at age two. Evans cast the narrative as a story told from heaven by the child, who explains that her life had been part of God's plan to teach the public about the value of children with disabilities. While this religious framing of the experience was a common theme through subsequent parent narratives, there were also more practical, upbeat accounts, such as *"Karen"*, a story of a girl with cerebral palsy, written by her mother, Marie Killilea in 1952.

A less-known account was published also in 1951 by Dan Boyd. His impassioned description of his personal journey took a step beyond Buck's and Evans' narratives, by outlining a progression from "self-pity" regarding his child's intellectual impairment to concern for his child and then to concern for other children. This simple yet powerful vision was soon echoed by others who described their movement away from self toward advocacy for others. This perspective initiated one of the most enduring interpretations of parents' journey as going through "stages" of adaptation, most of which have invoked concepts proposed by Elisabeth Kübler-Ross (1969) and others, regarding a movement from "denial" through to "acceptance". Unfortunately, this idea was adopted as a simplistic "stage model" by many professionals who tended to view parents more as "patients" needing therapy than as adults in the process of natural adaptation to a life challenge.

Countering Negative Professional Beliefs

Parents writing these early accounts expressed a clear intention to encourage and inspire parents in similar situations. Such positive interpretations were much needed to counteract the many obstacles to transformation and acceptance, obstacles provided not only by the society in which the families lived but, worse, by professionals engaged in disability services, who were producing numerous guides, studies, and psychological interpretations of the experience. Until the 1970s, while parents' stories tended to portray emotional and spiritual journeys from despair to adjustment, the professional literature presented a generally dismal view of the prognosis not only for children's health and life expectancy but also for families' emotional health.

The most devastating aspect of professionals' perspectives was the belief that infants with disabilities should be institutionalized and totally excluded from their families. The role of the medical profession in this was exemplified by an article by pediatrician, Anderson Aldrich (1947), who, in an article in the *Journal of Mental Retardation*, reported that his solution to the "potential family tragedy" occasioned by the birth of a "Mongolian idiot" was to persuade the father and relatives that the infant should be institutionalized without the mother's consent and before the mother had an opportunity to become attached to the child. This doctor argued that his method was "successful" because his advice had "failed" in only two or three cases over a period of 15 years of practice. This kind of approach was supported by publications such as that by John and Nellie Carver (1972), whose study of 37 families who had institutionalized their children demonstrated the emotional wreckage caused by this advice; yet, with a chilling irony, the authors of this study insisted that the families had made the right decision.

Fortunately, as disability advocates in the US gained ground, marked by the passage of the Education for All Handicapped Children Act in 1975, professionals' early negativity gradually gave way to more positive views. This progress has been nicely summarized by Rod and Ann Turnbull and their colleagues (2015) as a progression in perceived roles, moving from early views of the parent as a victim of sad circumstances who needed to be treated as a patient, through the parent as an advocate, and ultimately to the current model of the parent as a "partner" with professionals.

Disability Studies: A Different Lens

By the turn of the twenty-first century, the perspective of disability studies had brought a new lens to the understanding of parents' experiences. As outlined in the Chap. 1 of this book, this view, initially explained by Oliver and Barnes (1998) and increasingly supported by disability self-advocates, challenged the view of disability as a discrete, factual condition inherent in an individual body, and emphasized, rather, the role of society in turning an individual condition into a disability by failure to respond to individual needs. By this view, Oliver argued, disability should be seen not as a tragedy but as an experience of oppression.

The burgeoning literature from disability studies provides extensive philosophical considerations of the implications of this principle, and is well beyond the scope of this brief review. However, Nirmala Erevelles (2011) stated the key principle as follows, that "disability is the embodied experience of social oppression constituted via the inhospitable social, cultural, and economic structures in mainstream society" (p. 181). This scholar also provides a complex analysis of the range of interpretations of disability, which includes a focus on the exploitation of disability through capitalist social and economic structures as well as the question of what constitutes the value of an individual life. For example, is the key to "humanity" the presence of reason? Autonomy? Should a person whose communicative and physical functioning is largely or totally dependent on the support of another be equally valued?

Eva Kittay (2011), while acknowledging the pioneering work of self-advocates and scholars in the disability studies movement, refuted the view that dependency among persons with disabilities is necessarily produced by economic, political, and social forces. Highlighting a need for "an ethic of care", which values dependency as an integral facet of life, this feminist scholar, herself the mother of a child with multiple and profound disabilities, rejected either autonomy, reason, or independence as a central characteristic of human nature. Independence, she argued, should not be seen as "the norm of human functioning... as the route to a dignified life" (p. 51). Rather, dependence should be seen as simply one feature of human experience, in which the provider of care engages willingly, regardless of whether or not the dependent person is able to reciprocate. Describing her daughter as a "sparkling young woman" with multiple disabilities, she says:

> She is fully dependent and while at the age of 40 she (like us all) is still capable of growth and development, it is quite certain that her total dependence will not alter much. I have been learning about disability from the perspective of one who is unable to speak for herself; and it is from her and her caregivers that I have come to have a profound appreciation of care as a practice and an ethic. My daughter's disabilities always threaten her with a life of diminished dignity. It is only with care, and care of the highest quality, that she can be included, loved, and allowed to live a joyful and dignified life. When I speak of disability, I think a great deal about the cognitive disability that marks her life, and my concern is that persons with such disabilities, as well as her caregivers, not be left out of considerations of justice and moral personhood. (p. 52)

All told, Eva Kittay's argument resonates greatly with the stories told in this and the following two chapters. Parents' narratives in this study gave limited credence to the principles espoused by disability studies. While all would agree that social factors exacerbate the limitations their children experience, these parents shared a focus on the built-in nature of their children's impairments and charged society with the responsibility for creating opportunities for the expression and enhancement of their strengths.

Another way in which these narratives differ from the lens of disability studies is the obvious fact that this is the lens of a parent, not that of the individual who is experiencing the disability. In this study, many of the parents' narratives were reminiscent of a theory of parents' reactions that was proposed, in 1961, by psychoanalysts Albert Solnit and Mary Stark. They argued that expectant mothers engage in the "psychological work of pregnancy" as a "preparatory and adaptive process [which] is abruptly interrupted by the birth of a defective child" (p. 109). While I object to the language of "deficiency", my own experience as a mother leads me to see great truth in this theory of pregnancy, and my interviews with both mothers and fathers offered much evidence of similar thinking. In fact, at times, the language used by the parents was strongly suggestive of what Solnit and Stark referred to as feelings of loss of an imagined perfect child—a loss that at times felt like a blow to the parent's self-esteem.

The concept of disability as a social issue, however, was also evident in the fact that parents' feeling of shock was softened by the support of spouses or other key family members and, for most, by religious belief. In all cases, the initial shock was lessened when appropriate medical or other professional help was made available. As the narratives reveal, however, the availability of such help depended to a large extent on families' social and/or economic capital.

Immortelle Parents' Narratives: Transformation and Faith

The narratives by both groups of Immortelle parents echo the themes of initial distress and gradual transformation that have marked the majority of published parent narratives since the mid-twentieth century. This initial distress at there being "something not right here" was reinforced by the absence of supportive and validating health and education systems, with parents often feeling left on their own "not knowing what to do". On the other hand, to experience distress at the diagnosis of a disabling condition did not mean that the child would not be welcomed and loved. In fact, the trajectory of parents' response was an arc marked by love and resilience, ending, in all cases, with a view opposite to the initial one as the children became a source of joy and pride.

This journey was predominantly supported by a strong religious faith that the process was in God's hands and represented his will. Certainly, Immortelle parents' interpretations reflected the deeply cultural commitment to religion that pervades the society of Trinidad and Tobago. While the vast majority of families were of Christian faith, the groups also included Hindus and Muslims, all of whom held that all humanity represents a divine plan that is beyond human comprehension. By this belief, every human being is equally valuable, and the challenge for the believer is to accept that, through faith, the purpose of the child's life will be revealed. Based on faith, this belief is simply not accessible to philosophical argumentation and, in this study, was expressed by parents as a given.

Thus, a predominant theme of the parents' narratives was, "*From 'something not right here' to 'She's wonderful!'*" The narratives, however, do not suggest that they would have preferred this condition if they had been given a choice. For those children who suffered illness and pain as a result of their impairments, there was no indication that the parents would have chosen this condition for their children.

Original Immortelle Parents' Narratives

This chapter highlights the narratives of nine families who enrolled their children in Immortelle between the years 1978 and 1986. Of these, two were still at Immortelle as adult students at the time of this study. Not surprisingly, these narratives echo many of the negative themes from the literature of that time, including concepts of parental "mourning" described by psychologists Solnit and Stark (1961), as well as professionals' negative attitudes and a disturbing lack of clarity in diagnoses. Nevertheless, the concept of parenting as a transformative experience comes through as a central theme.

The original Immortelle families represented the range of ethnic, racial, and religious combinations typical of the twin nation of Trinidad and Tobago. Of African, Indian, Chinese, European, and Middle-Eastern extract, the group included Christians, Muslims, and Hindus. There were, two accountants, three teachers, a nurse, two government employees, a taxi driver, an airline pilot, a businessman, a university librarian, a minister of government, and five mothers who were homemakers. Their children at the time were between the ages of two and about 10. While their disabilities were evident, their abilities were in all cases yet to be discovered.

Let me first introduce Melanie, who was my inspiration. Melanie thrived under the firm and gentle hand of Joan Knowles, an exemplary physiotherapist. Melanie had no speech, but her receptive language was revealed in her use of a picture board and simple non-verbal communications—a nod for yes, a shake for no, and pointing to whatever or whomever she wanted. Because of her tightly clenched jaws, she could not laugh, but smiled and squealed in great joy at the company of her classmates, and especially Mercedes, who was the lead teacher for the nursery group. Mercedes filled Melanie's life with movement and laughter, teasing her with silly games and antics that elicited loud squeals of delight.

Of those who had been Melanie's peers in the nursery group, I was able to find, for this project, the parents of Tommy, Khayam, Candace, Maldon, Vivienne, and Raquel. The diagnoses of these children's conditions varied: Tommy was diagnosed with Down Syndrome; Khayam with cerebral palsy; Vivienne and Raquel with intellectual delay; Candace with multiple disabilities, including hearing and sight impairments; and Maldon, with no clear diagnosis, displayed features commonly associated with autism. Of the children in the "classroom" group, I located the parents of Andrew, a 5-year-old with athetoid cerebral palsy and evident high intelligence; David, a 9-year-old who was born with one leg missing and functioned like a child on the high end of the autism spectrum; and Selris, age 7, who was deaf and partially sighted and displayed high intelligence and artistic talent. Except for David, who in his mother's words, "could speak when he wanted to", and Andrew, whose speech was developing, all the children relied on signs, symbols, and/or gestures for their communication. Their personalities, abilities, and disabilities were as diverse as could be imagined, each one standing out as his/her own person.

I also include brief narratives provided by two families whose children, Lisa and Becky, were enrolled in Immortelle some years after my departure and were adult students at the school at the time of this study.

As the parents described their early years of coming to understand the challenges they faced, I identified five clear themes that resonated across the interviews. This chapter and the next will focus on the first two themes, and Chap. 5 will address themes three though five.

1. Something not right here: facing initial shock and seeking understanding
2. Finding Immortelle
3. Trinidad is nice—Trinidad is a paradise: navigating negativity and creating love
4. Adapting and taking action: avenues of advocacy
5. She's wonderful! Finding meaning and creating purpose

"Something Not Right Here": Facing Initial Shock and Seeking Understanding

For parents in this study, coming to terms with their children's conditions reflected medical, psychological, and social interpretations of disability. The absence of responsive medical and educational interventions intensified parents' shock and anxiety. The phrase, "something not right here", captured the common feeling of bewilderment and confusion that parents experienced as they tried to get a clear diagnosis for the children's atypical conditions. For some, it was a gradual awareness of "something wrong", while others were catapulted into a sudden and shocking medical crisis. For all, there was the challenge of accessing appropriate services to assist in their children's development.

Life or Death Crises

Two stories presented life or death medical crises. Both children were born in countries other than Trinidad and, despite vast differences in available resources in those countries, both families experienced extreme frustration at the diagnosis and treatment of their children.

"The soles of his feet were blue… Navy Blue". Carole Fitt's story of Andrew's birth captures both the period of initial shock and the family's subsequent search for appropriate diagnosis and treatment. Carole is a homemaker with a talent for baking, which she has made into a small business since her four boys have grown up. Her husband, David, recently retired from his life-long career as an airline pilot, and Andrew, now in his forties, completed his Associates degree in computer-based design and engages in his digital art, as shown in an exhibition in 2019 in Port of Spain (Fig. 3.1). Andrew has also published a memoir entitled, *Aching to be* (2015). I spoke with Carole on the family's back porch:

> *Carole.* I married David out of flying school. We moved from Guyana to St. Lucia because he was flying in those days—a light aircraft operation.
>
> So Andrew was born in St. Lucia. Our first child—a normal pregnancy. I headed to hospital about three days before the due date and got to St. Jude hospital and was admitted and induced shortly after.
>
> Everything happened fast. Towards the first hour I was told that Andrew was breached and would have to be turned. It was suggested that a caesarean be done, but by then the labour was progressing and Andrew should have been born but was delayed in the passage because, as we were told afterwards, they were waiting to find an anaesthetist!

Fig. 3.1 Andrew Fitt with his digital art at an exhibition in Port of Spain, 2019

To cut a long story short—they turned him first, then pulled with the forceps. Not realizing that the chord was around his neck twice, the more they pulled, the more he got strangled. They then suggested, because I was hysterical with pain, to give me an epidural. They inserted this needle into my spine and I started to flutter like a little hen. That didn't work. There were no pain killers at that point and I was going through the whole scream-ing process.

Finally they got Andrew out. He didn't cry for the first couple of seconds and then into a few minutes. I looked down when they were suctioning him out and the soles of his feet were blue. Like to the point of navy blue.

The hospital was less than helpful. They put him in an incubator and when my mother went to see him she saw that the incubator was open and his head was arched, he was fighting for breath. She ran to the nurses' station and asked if the incubator was supposed to be open because her grandson was having a problem. With that, a nurse came running behind her. So, it was debatable whether he escaped the brain injury at birth and suffered the brain injury thereafter. We'll never know.

We stayed in the hospital for nine days and it was the worst nine days of my life. In the morning, they kept saying he would make it, and then they would return in the afternoon, and say, "No, no, no, Mrs. Fitt, he will not make it through the night!" Then the doctor would put his head through the door in the morning and say, "Oh Mrs. Fitt you have a little fighter." Then in the night … this went on.

On the tenth day I took him home. They refused to discharge him, so I wrapped him up in a blanket with all the tubes in his nose, because he was being tube fed, and I walked out the hospital and I went home with this child that I had no clue how to take care of! We took him home and fed him with a teaspoon as he couldn't suck at all, so he was spoon fed for a good couple of months.

When Andrew was about six months I looked into his eyes and saw everything that I had hoped to see. Recognizing me. Intelligent. Responsive in every way. Appropriate behaviour. Everything was spot on!

Then I tried to find out what I could do to help him. We took him to Dr. Bertie Graham in Barbados and he diagnosed cerebral palsy. He was the first positive doctor that I encountered. Very positive but very realistic. He said, "This is not a condition that goes away". But he explained that he had met very few kids with CP that had suffered any cognitive damage. It usually is a physical thing. With that, he confirmed what I was seeing with Andrew. He suggested physical therapy as soon as possible.

Back in St. Lucia I took Andrew for therapy three times a week. It was the best thing for him. He was just nine months old and I was thinking, "If I've started therapy at nine months then surely he should be running around the place by the time he's a year!" I really didn't understand this was a long road ahead. Indeed it was.

When Andrew was three years old, we moved back to Guyana for David to get the jet time he needed. Andrew had some therapy down there, but not a lot of positive response. I had picked up what I thought was enough from the therapist in St. Lucia to carry on myself. And that's what I did for the next two years.

Then the seizures started. Grand mal seizures.

In Guyana they weren't sure how to treat it. They were giving him the wrong medication. The first seizure was four hours and ten minutes. Two weeks later, to the day, he had another one—four hours and ten minutes again.

Then I found Dr. Walter Chin, an excellent paediatrician who had TT connections. He said, "This kid needs to go on some medication." Which is what should have been done from the very first seizure.

We had planned to stay in Guyana, but I decided it was time to leave. That created a lot of family problems. Some people's opinion was that I was sacrificing my husband's career to get help for Andrew, which they felt should not even be considered. So that was a tremendous fight. I maintained that's what I felt should happen and we would go forward.

That was a terrible period of my life.

But we got some help from David's uncle and we made our first trip to New York—to United Cerebral Palsy. They did a complete assessment. Speech and physio, IQ, everything from head to toe. What they did was amazing and in the interim David applied to come to Trinidad to fly for Trinidad/Tobago Air Services.

We moved to Trinidad and we continued taking Andrew to United Cerebral palsy every year. They gave me a home programme which I did every single day of life. I did nothing but Andrew. I put everything else on hold. What was wonderful was that Andrew and my second son, Jeffrey were close, so Jeffrey also got a lot of therapy. And, as a result, they grew up very close.

"Candace was normal at birth. Now she's like a light blown out". Rupert and Margaret Jones were living in London, England, when their daughter, Candace, was born. Rupert was a charge nurse at London's famous Guy's Hospital and Margaret was studying for her PhD in Library Sciences. At the time of our interview in 2015, Rupert was the Head of Nursing at Trinidad and Tobago's School of Nursing and Margaret had recently retired from her career as Head Librarian at the University of the West Indies, Trinidad campus.

Candace, age 37 at the time of this study, had multiple disabilities and had always lived at home with her parents. She continued to evidence the same impeccable loving care and nurturing that had marked her life during her years as a student at Immortelle. Every heart in Immortelle was touched as Candace arrived each morning in the arms of her father, whose 6-foot-4 frame filled the doorway of the school as he entered. Despite very limited vision and hearing, Candace participated well in her self-help program and responded with physical movements and a small smile to the voice and touch of loved ones (Fig. 3.2). Seeing her again after almost 30 years, I was gratified that she showed these reactions in response to my greetings.

Fig. 3.2 Candace Jones practicing self-feeding with teacher Camille Kelly, circa 1980

I had always admired this couple's positive approach to Candace's challenges, and was touched when, seated comfortably in their home, they spoke of their initial experience with Candace.

Margaret. Candace was normal at birth. At seven months she contracted pneumococcal meningitis. It was very sudden and quick. You had a normal child today, she came down with a fever. You took her to the hospital, and then…

Rupert. The day she got sick, we were out. We had gone to Dillons bookshop that morning by train. We took her everywhere with us. On the train she'd be jumping from person to person. That was Candace. Now she's like a light blown out.

Margaret. The diagnosis wasn't made immediately, for a host of reasons. It was a weekend. I think there was a junior, inexperienced doctor on duty. One of the first symptoms was vomiting, and lots of children in the hospital had gastro enteritis. So they assumed it was that. They did a lumbar puncture but it didn't show at the time because we had taken her in at the first sign of the fever and the pneumococcal variety does not show in the first twelve hours. So they didn't put her on drips or give her any medication for the first 48 hours or so.

It was Saturday when we took her in. On Monday, after Rupert came in from Guy's, the pediatricians at Guy's called their counterparts at Whittington and told them to repeat the lumbar puncture. And when they did it again, they saw the evidence in the spinal fluid—pneumococcal bacteria. They began to treat her, but by that time, the disease was already ravaging. Then she started to have seizures and they gave her valium and that knocked out her breathing. Then she had a respiratory arrest.

So those are the details. She was in intensive care for about ten days. She was being tube fed and when they took the tubes out, it seemed as if she wasn't breathing on her own, so then they did a tracheostomy.

I don't think they really expected her to live. After about ten days she began to come around. We were almost living in the hospital, watching this whole drama play out. We were back and forth and back and forth. Then they told us that she might be brain damaged. They were then going to do brain scans and so on.

Rupert. Then she was moved from Whittington to Guy's Hospital because I was working at Guys, and when the team realized I was working there, they took over the management.

Margaret. I gave up my studies for the year because I just couldn't leave her. My academic advisor was very understanding. They allowed me to do two of the courses which were to be examined by course work. When I came back in the following year, I registered, and I completed. That was a big help. Candace spent 14 months in hospital and we were up and down with her.

Rupert. Eventually, we decided to have the tracheostomy removed but the doctors were afraid that if they took it out, she would die. So we had to sign consent, and the morning when they took out the tracheostomy Candace just relaxed and went to sleep. They were amazed.

Margaret. She was fine. She's been fine ever since. After that they put in place services for her to go to a nursery near where we lived, free pampers, disability grant, push-chairs, milk…

There's another point that we must make. While Candace was at Guy's there was this Trinidadian pediatric specialist on the ward. She told us that Candace was not going to develop much. She said, "If you all really want to go back home, don't stay in England just because of her. Yes, in England you'll get free services, free pampers, and so on, but in the final analysis the most that Candace will be able to appreciate is your love. And you'll be able to give her that where you are happiest. Don't stay here because of the services. There is a limit to what Candace will become".

I finished my library training the year after Candace came out of the hospital. I was hired by the University of the West Indies and they provided housing for us. I came first with Candace and she spent most of the time with my parents. I would go back and forth and take her on weekends. The next year Rupert came, and then my father found out about Immortelle Centre and Candace started there when she was three, in 1983. And Rupert would pick her up from school and drop her to Daddy in Belmont. Candace was comfortable, because Daddy was retired and Candace was his life. He used to wait for her to come. And he would make her two slices of sweetbread and put jam on it and Candace loved nothing better.

Challenging the Stigma of Down Syndrome

The foregoing narratives represented the most extreme kind of shock, in which parents were faced with crises that meant life or death for their children. Less fearful, but also distressing were stories of newborns not at serious medical risk but identified at birth as having conditions that would limit their development and their social acceptance. Such a child was Tommy Pierre, born with Down Syndrome in the late 1970s, a time when this condition was greatly stigmatized and was referred to as "mongolism". For his parents, Lydia and Tony Pierre, the challenge was partly internal and partly induced by social stigma, but was greatly mitigated by the strength of this couple's relationship, which served to bolster their response to an initially unwelcome diagnosis. Perhaps most important was Tommy's self-confident and joyful personality (Fig. 3.3).

Initial shock: "You think of suicide!" Tommy was diagnosed at birth with Down Syndrome. Almost three when he enrolled at Immortelle, Tommy quickly became the school's heartthrob! Photos of him "playing Indian" in his carnival costume capture the fun-loving, ebullient, favorite of the nursery group. His mother, a teacher, and his father, a government employee, were constant participants in all the school's activities, and quickly took on public advocacy roles that led to the formation of the National Association for Down Syndrome (NADS), the country's first advocacy association specifically for this group. At the time of this study, Tommy, then in his late thirties, continued to live at home with his parents and was a full-time participant in the adult day services operated by the Lady Hochoy Home. His parents' story of his early years took the form of an easy flow of dialogue:

Fig. 3.3   Tommy Pierre
on swim day, circa 1980

Lydia. Tommy was born in a nursing home in St. Ann's. I remember, as soon as I saw him, I realized something was wrong. I couldn't put a name to it, but even before the doctor came in I realized something was wrong.

I remember, you think of suicide! In the nursing home there were bars on the windows. I felt those bars were not just to keep out burglars but to keep in the inmates of the nursing home. The thought of doing something like that crossed my mind but you couldn't because there were bars on the window. I could no longer consider it because it wasn't possible. I couldn't jump through the window. It was barred.

Tony. To me… I thought you accepted it right away! I'm not sure I remember knowing that you had those thoughts!

Lydia. I never told you that?

Tony. No, no, no! I found that you had accepted it very, very well… I couldn't detect anything—to say you were contemplating anything like that!

Lydia. Yes, but that was just a flash! After that, I was just saying "this is my child!" I felt this was our child and in a kind of arrogant way, he can't be so bad if he belongs to Lydia and Tony.

Tony. Your acceptance helped me to accept also. Because we weren't too sure about what to do. He was still a little baby. I kept looking at him and trying to figure it out. I think my mother's sister had Down Syndrome. She lived with us, but I didn't have any details. Nothing was explained so I wasn't sure what it meant.

Lydia. We took Tommy to the health centre for the normal checks, and I remember some doctor told us Tommy would never do this and he would never do that. As time went by, I thought, "I wish I could go back with Tommy and show him what the vegetable could do!" He used that word, a vegetable. I only hope parents don't still go through that now. This is your child. If somebody tells you, you created a vegetable... But, you know, we got through it!

"I think you have a mongoloid baby." The stigma attached to Down Syndrome at the time was also dramatically reflected in Helen and John Humphrey's story of their granddaughter's birth and early years. At the time of Becky's birth in 1986, John was the Minister of Works, Settlements and Infrastructure. Helen was a prominent figure in the social life of TT, well known for her involvement in Carnival as well as in philanthropic activities. Becky was not among the initial group at Immortelle, as Helen herself had started a day program called "Something Special", which later merged with Immortelle. As vocal advocates for individuals with disabilities, and with John's contacts in the government, this couple was later instrumental in the acquisition of the government property on which Immortelle currently stands.

By the time of this study, Becky, then 29 years old, had been a student at Immortelle for some 20 years. Sociable and fun-loving, Becky participated in the senior group along with several others their age. Her grandmother's story revealed both the initial stigma but also the buffer provided to the family by their prominent social status and network, by which they were able to spearhead the creation of a fund-raising effort that helped not only their granddaughter, but many other children in the community:

Helen. Becky, my granddaughter, was born with Down Syndrome. In those days I didn't know what that was. The nurse came to me and said, "I think you have a mongoloid baby". I said, "A what"? I panicked and called Dr. Bratt and, sure enough, he said that Becky had the crease and all the features of Down Syndrome. Now Becky's 29 going on 30 so that was a long time ago and people did not know anything about Down Syndrome. We didn't have the computers where we could go look it up. It was very difficult, but her mother and father took it very well. The father was one of the strong men… he said, "Well, we have a special baby and we will just have to get whatever information we can and see what we're going to do for Rebecca."

Becky had 3 holes in her heart. She had the first operation in Jackson Memorial in Miami. Then she had to go back and do another one. They said one of the holes was not completely closed but they thought after time it would close in. And it did. We did a lot of fundraising because it was very costly, so we went up to the U.S. through Dr. Bratt and the "Heart to Heart" fund. There were quite a few babies who were going away for treatment.

Recognizing Disability—Gradually

For parents whose children's birth did not present with medical crises or immediate diagnoses such as those described above, the early years were confusing in a different way because of an on-going lack of clarity as to the child's condition. Ann and Rud Turnbull and their colleagues (2015), leading scholars in family issues, and who are themselves parents of a child with a disability, pointed out that, despite the intense shock of the unexpected, families whose children present with an obvious disability may be forced to accommodate to the child's needs more readily than families who experience a gradual awareness of ambiguous or fluctuating developmental differences. This situation was evident in the narratives of several "original" Immortelle families.

"We don't have an island scholar here!" Mumtaz and Rita Ali enrolled their son, Khayam, at Immortelle when he was about 3 years old. Khayam's cerebral palsy in no way held him back from making his sweet presence known. Already trying to walk, his sociable spirit made him a great favorite in the nursery group and, being about the same size as Melanie, but with much greater motor skills, he was able to reach out to her as a friendly peer. When I contacted the Ali's after some 30 years, I was sad to learn that Khayam had passed away at the age of 36. Up until that time, he had lived with the family, keeping them joyful company after his sister, Shakira, married and moved on to start her own family (Fig. 3.4).

Sitting in Mumtaz' study in their home, I listened as Mumtaz, an accountant, and Rita, a homemaker, spoke freely of the joys and pains of their life with Khayam, describing their early challenges, as follows:

Mumtaz. The doctors told me that they suspected cerebral palsy. When we realised the implications of Khayam's disability, we were devastated. Our first concern was where to turn to for help. We went to Toronto and saw beautiful facilities, but we couldn't afford to live there. We came back home

Fig. 3.4 Melanie Teelucksingh and Khayam Ali with teacher Mercedes Telfer, circa 1980

and our worry was what to do for Khayam. We saw several doctors. I would say they were very superficial, not interested in Khayam or people like him. One doctor said, "We don't have an island scholar here." That expression was pronounced very harshly on his disabilities.

Rita. They also said that he would never walk.

Mumtaz. Yes. We were recommended to an expert in Ottawa. He came down strongly that our son would never walk. My whole house is carpeted because of that! But one evening while looking at television, Khayam got up and miraculously walked to the television and touched it. Then, sometime later, that same doctor happened to be visiting Trinidad, and my uncle, Dr. Kamaludin Mohammed, invited me to meet him in the hospital. I took Khayam with me!

We had a maid and she would massage his knees every night. I think we went briefly for physical therapy at the General hospital before we came to Immortelle. The maid we had would go and assimilate what was being done and religiously practice on Khayam. Together with Rita, those two gave him a new lease on his life.

"Up to now I don't know what happened". There were also parents who never received any confirming diagnosis for their children's visible conditions. For example, Shirley Clarke's son, David, was born with only one leg and, as he developed, showed communication and social behaviors suggestive of high-functioning autism. As a senior government administrator, Shirley had access to considerable information and yet was never able to gain an explanation of her son's condition. As David grew up, it was evident that he had great academic ability but was hampered by limitations in social interaction and communication.

When I visited them in their home, David greeted me cheerfully and served me a soft drink as I chatted with his mother. I found Shirley in poor health but willing to recount many of the changes that had occurred for David over the years, including a couple of years as a student at Queen's Royal College (QRC), one of the island's leading secondary schools for boys, and a brief period of schooling in Barbados, while his mother was posted there. He currently lives with his mother and keeps very busy participating in advocacy activities of the TT Autism Society. Regarding her initial experience of her son's condition, Shirley said:

> *Shirley.* He was born like that. Up to now I don't know what happened. I remember they gave me some medication during the pregnancy—I was hoarse and the obstetrician gave me 2 things to take and the druggist told me, "I wonder why this man is giving everybody the same thing!" I know I didn't feel well at all after taking that and I always wondered if that is what caused it.

Vivienne: "It was confusing having the label—not autistic." This lack of an explanation was also troubling for Roberta and Patrick White, an English couple who had lived in Trinidad/Tobago for many years. At the time of their daughter's enrolment at Immortelle, Patrick was the Vice Principal of QRC, and Roberta was an accountant with a private firm. These parents were actively involved in all aspects of the life of Immortelle, including Patrick becoming a member of the school board during the period when the school was converted to a non-profit organization.

Vivienne showed signs of delayed development early on. With limited speech but good socialization, Vivienne loved to copy written text and sometimes displayed an inexplicable grasp of written communications. She continued as a student at Immortelle until the time of this study and was then in the senior group of students in the work center. Despite evaluations in the UK and in TT, these parents' understanding of Vivienne's condition was marked by confusion because of the lack of specificity in any diagnosis. As they explained:

> *Roberta*. There was no problem with the birth or anything. She was just slow in starting to speak. She was my first. I just didn't know how a child should be behaving. It was the head mistress of Jack and Jill nursery school who pointed it out. We took her to England for an assessment. They couldn't put a label on it. They said that she was not autistic. But in those days they didn't have that full spectrum that they have now. It was a little confusing having the label "not autistic"!

"We're going to America". Maldon Chappin was another child whose diagnosis remained unclear for many years. His parents, Myrnell and Steve, brought him to Immortelle when he was about 4 years old. Myrnell was employed in the government at the time and Steve had a taxi business. Handsome, polite, and well behaved, Maldon showed no physical signs of disability, but his communication patterns reflected what were by then thought to be signs of autism—notably, stilted, often echolalic speech, and a preference for repetitive routines. Maldon joined the nursery group as one of the most competent children in gross and fine motor skills, which readily contradicted professionals' obviously unfounded opinions of him as a child with cerebral palsy. Despite his limited expressive communication, we often wondered at his receptive understanding not only of language but also of social situations. My favorite memory of Maldon was a day when a classmate, David, whom we also considered to have autism, was about to throw an item at another child, and the normally silent Maldon shouted, "David!" clearly intended as a warning of the present danger.

Maldon left Immortelle shortly after I departed and was enrolled in a private school where he learned to read and write, and later attended SERVOL, a school that focused on vocational preparation. When he was about 12, his parents migrated to the US where, after some frustrations, he finally received an appropriate placement and was able to take advantage of the educational services provided under the law. At the time of this study, Maldon was living with his family in Maryland, had a busy social life, and was actively involved in numerous activities for adults with disabilities. Myrnell and Steve told Maldon's childhood story this way:

Myrnell. When he was born the doctor told me he did not cry and he was a bit blue and they thought he lacked oxygen. Afterwards, they did their testing and so on and they told me they thought he had cerebral palsy because there was some bleeding in the brain, and he didn't breathe as soon as he came out.

I took him home and to me he was a normal baby. But what I did notice is that he never crept. He would just lie down and not move or anything. He was kind of spastic. At one point in time, he would just lie on his belly, but then, one day he just got up and started to walk. He did not know how to bend his knees to sit down, so, after walking, he would fall on his bottom. It went on like that, me trying to find out what was wrong with him, and again being diagnosed with cerebral palsy.

"I said to myself: My mother had six children—I can just wing this!" Among the group of parents whose children's diagnoses came more slowly, Jacqui's story of Raquel was the most extensive. Her narrative offers an example of the challenges facing parents and extended family members of a child whose development is clearly delayed yet who displays no specific neurological or biological markers. Jacqui's easy-going and positive personality comes through as she describes her fluctuating awareness of Raquel's difficulties and the coping strategies she used to "wing this" and even "put it aside" as she responded to the daily demands of her two other children who were born within a four-year span after Raquel's birth. The story also illustrates the reluctance of local doctors to acknowledge an evident but etiologically uncertain problem in the early years:

Jacqui. Raquel was my first child and I didn't know anything about babies. When she was about three months old my mother said, "Raquel's not turning over." I went to my doctor and said, "This child is not turning over yet." He said, "You're gonna look at this cute baby and ask me if something is wrong with her?"

So I said to myself, my mother had six children—I can just wing this! And I left it at that. Over the years you realize nobody wants to know there's something wrong with their child! So if anybody tells you there's nothing wrong with your child, that's what you'll pick up immediately.

When Raquel was 18 months she was not walking yet and she used to fall down a lot. She fell and hit her head so I took her to a paediatrician and I said, "She's 18 months, she's not walking and she fell and hit her head." He said that she seemed fine and she didn't have a concussion. He expressed some concern about her muscle tone, but he didn't say there was an issue and he said she would walk soon.

By the time she was two, she was walking everywhere. So, of course, I let go of that too! But still, Mummy spent a lot of time with Raquel and she kept saying things. I think it's hard to tell your child that something is wrong with their child, so she just hinted.

When Raquel was about three or four she wasn't really talking, just a few words. When she was four, my uncle who was an ophthalmologist in Toronto came to visit and I asked him if he would see Raquel because I thought she had 'cokee eyes' (crossed eyes) I took her to him and he said, "I think there's a little more than just her eyes. Let me arrange for her to come up to Sick Kids Hospital and let's do a battery of tests". I said, sure.

He arranged for me and my grandmother to go to Toronto. And my cousin from North Carolina came and met us and we went to all these doctors. The developmental paediatrician told me that Raquel was mentally retarded and that she would probably never develop more than seven years old. When I told my grandmother this it was very traumatic. She said, "No, we're not taking his word for it. He's old!" She said young people would know new things. She said, "Don't believe everything he tells you!"

I never went back to Sick Kids Hospital. I came home and went to Dr. Bratt, and he arranged for me to go to the Mailman Centre in Miami. That's where I went a few times. The people there verified the diagnosis from Sick Kids, but they were a lot more helpful and Miami was much easier for me to get to. Also my brother lived in Miami so I used to go there. And, of course, I didn't want to go back to Sick Kids hospital because they had told me the bad news!

When I came back from Canada with Raquel, my father and a good friend were sitting having a drink. Uncle Mark says, "Don't worry, Jacqui, if seven years old is what her mind is going to be—do you know how smart seven-year olds are! Don't worry! That's like dealing with adults." I thanked him. That made me feel wonderful!

Gwenie: "I didn't know it was German measles." I close this description of parents' early experiences with the story of Gwenie and Selris James—a story that remains unique among these narratives. It is unique because of the unusual combination of abilities and disabilities Selris displayed from early childhood and until the time of this writing. Unique also, because of the extraordinary efforts and exemplary parenting of his mother, Gwenie, who, only 19 years of age and single when Selris was born, described herself at that time as "just a country girl who didn't know nothing!"

In 1982, Gwenie and seven-year-old Selris appeared on the steps of the original Immortelle building in Brabant Street, accompanied by Bernard Broadbridge, a member of the Port of Spain Rotary Club. Gwenie had reached out to her parish priest, Father Eugene de la Hunte, for guidance with assisting Selris, who had been born deaf and partially blind because of congenital Rubella. After greeting me with a nod and handshake, Selris walked past the group of adults standing on the porch and into the front room of our little school. Placing his face about three inches from the walls, he proceeded to inspect all the photos and wall hangings in the room. Astonished at his self-assurance and curiosity, and learning that he had been refused entry at both the school for the blind and the school for the deaf, I eagerly admitted him to Immortelle, promising to do the best we could despite our own total lack of preparation for teaching this unique child (Fig. 3.5).

At the time of this research, Selris, then almost 40, was still living at home with his mother. I found him as self-assured as ever, although his immense talents have been poorly rewarded, owing to both his family circumstances and the absence of appropriate resources within the society. Here is Gwenie's description of her early experience with him:

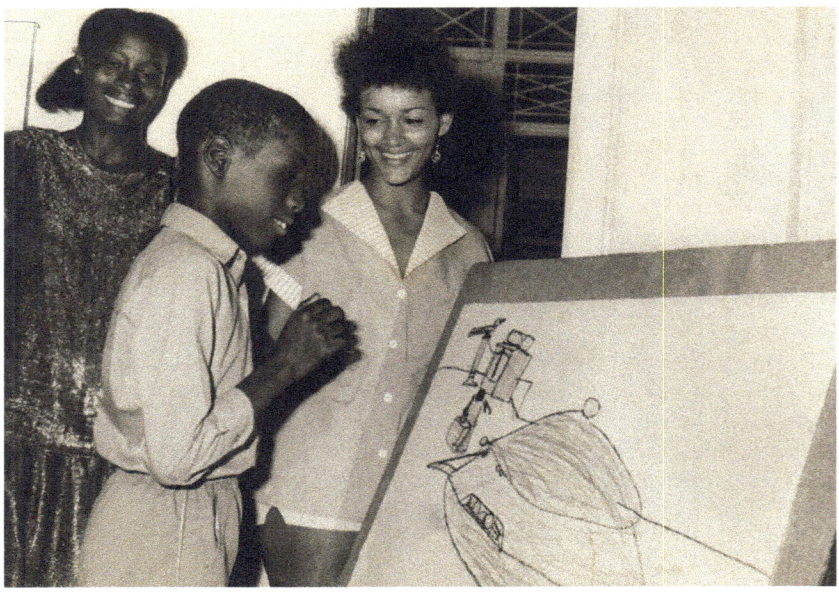

Fig. 3.5 Selris James, his mother Gwenie Gomez-James, and teacher Cathy De Montbrun, circa 1980

Gwenie. I didn't know it was German measles. I had just started to live with Frank and I saw the rash and put Nixoderm on it and because it looked so bad with scabs I didn't tell anybody. I was ashamed to go to the doctor. I was young—just come from the country—and I didn't know nothing.

When Selris was born they said he had jaundice, so they kept him in the hospital for about two weeks. After that, they said he was ok and discharged him to me as a normal child. I didn't know anything was wrong with him till he was almost two because he behaved the same as all the other children and I treated him the same. The only thing I noticed was that he wasn't talking yet and when he walked he would drag his fingers along the wall. When I finally took him to the doctor at about age 2, they tested him and discovered that he was deaf and partly blind. They did surgery to remove cataracts from his eyes and after that his vision improved but was still not normal. Selris used to put his face up against the TV screen and watch Sesame Street and I saw that he was copying the letters so I started giving him paper and he started to write by himself.

By his second week at Immortelle, Selris had learned to write his name in response to the signed question, "What's your name?" and to count to 100 by sorting matchsticks into bundles of 10. During his first year at Immortelle, the Rotary Club funded a trip for Selris to New York and Boston for vision, hearing, and psychological assessments. Finding him to be of high intelligence, Perkins School for the Blind in Boston offered him a partial scholarship and Immortelle embarked on an intensive fund-raising effort in hopes of raising the family's share of Perkins' tuition. Sadly, this effort could come nowhere close to the required amount, so Selris was never able to take advantage of this opportunity. He remained at Immortelle until about the age of 21 and has continued unemployed most of his adult life. His talent, however, still shines, and gained some prominence after eye surgery at Miami's Bascom Palmer Eye Institute in 2015 (Fig. 3.6).

Selris' and Gwenie's journey continued to be a particularly difficult one, marked by greater social and economic disadvantage than most other families in the school. Our efforts to engage Selris in signing were never very fruitful because of our own lack of preparation and the absence of any peers at home or school who signed. Of all the stories in this research, Selris' most closely fits the concept of disability as a social rather than individual challenge. The unwillingness of existing schools in the community to respond to his hearing and vision challenges left this gifted child with only the Immortelle Centre, a willing and loving place that was totally unprepared to give him the kind of specialized education he deserved.

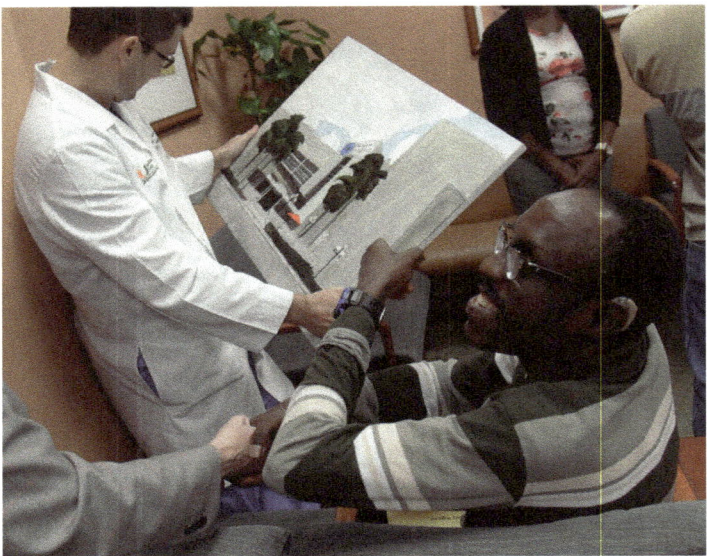

Fig. 3.6   Selris James, after successful eye surgery, showing his painting of Bascom Palmer Eye Institute to his opthalmologist, 2015

FINDING IMMORTELLE: "LIKE A FAMILY"

For all the families, the relevance of a "social model" of disability became evident as the children grew older and the absence of educational provisions became families' paramount concern. As explained at the beginning of the book, there were, at the time of the "first" Immortelle, only a handful of small private programs that were attempting to provide educational services for children with physical and/or intellectual impairments, and none that would address dual sensory impairments such as Selris'. Most importantly, none of these programs accepted children during the most crucial developmental period of birth through age six.

Immortelle families started looking for schooling for their children by the time they were three to five years old. How did they learn about the school and what difference did it make in their lives? How did they afford services that were bound to be costly? Overall, what did it mean to these families to find the Immortelle Center?

There were two main patterns that characterized parents' search for a school placement. For the children who could socialize with peers quite independently, there was a clear pattern of what parents referred to as "trying normal school", before finding Immortelle. For those children whose impairments were much more significant, a specialized setting was essential from the start. For all, finding Immortelle brought a huge sigh of relief partly because of the specialized attention to young children with disabilities, but also because Immortelle provided a haven from the stigma and rejection their children had begun to experience in "trying normal" school. It was, for all the families, like another family. As will be seen in narratives of the current Immortelle parents, told in the next chapter, these patterns changed very little over a period of 40 years.

"Trying Normal School"

Myrnell, whose son Maldon joined Immortelle at age four, displaying features characteristic of autism, explained the typical trajectory for families who started out by "trying normal school".

> *Myrnell: "Immortelle was the answer to my prayers for Maldon."* In Trinidad, children go to the government school at five. So what one would normally do is send the child to a private pre-school before going to the big school. So at least when they get there they know their ABCs, colours, and have the general socialization skills. I was following the same pattern. I have an older son Sean—one year older, so Maldon went to the same program where Sean had gone. But Maldon did not talk early like his older brother. His development was not normal. His verbal skills were not there. Also he was hard to potty train until he was four.
>
> So I kept searching and one day I saw in the papers a place called Immortelle Centre that was offering the things that I needed. I called and scheduled an interview with you, Beth, and I went in and spoke to you and found out that this was exactly what I was looking for. You were offering things like speech therapy, physical therapy and working with children with disabilities. I also felt empathy there because you yourself had a disabled child.
>
> The only thing is it was more expensive than I could afford, but I knew I had to get him in this school because there was nothing else for him. So my family members each decided to contribute $100 to put with what we had so that Maldon could go to Immortelle.
>
> At Immortelle I felt comfortable. You know, in Trinidad if you were different, people would make fun of you and it was always my concern that going to so-called normal school, the kids would make fun of him. I felt better that I put him in an environment where nobody made fun of him and he was able to get the services that he needed. Everything went fine and Maldon started to come out of his shell.

Lydia and Tony, Tommy's parents, told a similar story, but with a few more twists and turns. Knowing that his Down Syndrome would result in continuing delays, Tommy's parents started him at a Montessori school where he did well for a short time, and then brought him to Immortelle at about age three.

Lydia and Tony: Those were fantastic years for Tommy. Suddenly, we saw that he could learn. That he could be happy. That we could get help because there were people working in this area, which we hadn't seen before. It was fantastic. I remember saying, if I had normal children after Tommy I wouldn't mind them coming to the Immortelle at all. Because the child-centered approach was so different to what was happening even in the regular schools for normal children. So for some years Immortelle saved us. Absolutely. They were fantastic years.

When Tommy was about six, his parents once more tried the "normal school" route. As in all the stories of this route, the children were accepted into a "normal" program based on the openness and generosity of an individual school principal. These arrangements lasted only until the school personnel felt that the children were becoming too out of place, partly in terms of socialization, but mainly in terms of the single-track academic curriculum of schools in Trinidad/Tobago. In Tommy's case, his mother explained:

Lydia: "Integration worked because of the personalities involved." So we tried integration at Boissier RC primary school. We paid Mirlin, who used to teach at the National Association for Down Syndrome (NADS), to go part of the day to the school to assist the teacher with Tommy and others in the classroom. Olive, the principal, was so open and lovely and willing to try. The first teacher he had, Mrs. Gellineau, was fantastic. Tommy settled in so well he stayed there for about three years. We were very involved with the school. We met with all the teachers and did workshops with them. It helped the school. And Tommy loved it.

You see, the bad thing about Trinidad is that we don't have policies on the books to help our children. But the good thing is that it's so open! Once a principal is willing to try, the Ministry is so far away, they wouldn't suffer. She could do what she wants! But, remember, they are preparing the children for the Common Entrance. So they can't veer far. If you can't keep up, you're out. Literally, children drop out. So, after about 3 years, Tommy was out-growing the school so we had to find something else.

At that point, Lydia and Tony enrolled Tommy at the Lady Hochoy day school for children with intellectual disabilities and, at the time of this writing, he continued to enjoy that program's adult day services.

"No-one Would Take Him because of the Disability"

The second pattern in parents' accounts of how they came to Immortelle emerged from families whose children "had no choice" from the start. Children with cerebral palsy, such as Khayam, Andrew, and Melanie, were eligible only for the Princess Elizabeth Centre for the Physically Handicapped, but were too young to be accepted there. The situation was similar for preschool-aged children with intellectual impairment and minimal socialization skills, such as Vivienne, and even more so for Candace, whose multiple impairments created total dependence. As Candace's parents said, "Immortelle was unique because it took every child possible. There was no other institution that accepted children with multiple disabilities."

For children with these vulnerabilities, parents sought not only opportunities for their children's development and advancement but, perhaps most importantly, for their emotional and physical safety. Vivienne's mother quickly settled on Immortelle because, "It was a happy place. At one stage when I used to drop her off she would push me back out of the school gate to make sure I couldn't change my mind and take her home!" Similarly, Khayam's parents remembered Immortelle as a social place, with an emphasis on family engagement, sports meetings, Special Olympics, and maybe best of all, participation in the Kiddie's Carnival.

As Candace's parents explained, the most important thing was knowing that their daughter was valued equally with the other children:

Margaret: "I saw Mummy kissing Santa Clause". Immortelle Centre was like an extension of the family for us. It was a place of safety. It was a place of caring and of value. We could go to work and never have to worry about her care or whether she would be ill-treated. I felt very strongly that at Immortelle Centre you were doing all you possibly could to help Candace. I don't think Candace would have been any different if we had stayed in England.

We used to take her to Immortelle for a couple of days a week. And whatever they were doing for every season—Christmas pageant or whatever—Candace was present. Notwithstanding the fact that she couldn't talk, dance or follow an instruction, she had a costume to wear!

I remember the year they did "I saw Mummy kissing Santa Claus" and Candace was Santa Claus. They had her in a Santa Claus suit sitting there, and the choir was singing "I saw Mummy ..." and this other child came up and was kissing Candace. So Candace was part of the performance. Another time she was the reindeer in her wheel chair. Or she would be the Christmas star. She would be something—they never left her out! That applied to every child, and that was one of the very special things about the Immortelle.

Rupert. And Candace benefitted from having other children around her. There was a little boy who used to come to the gate and meet us and he'd take her bag and bring it in. There was another child too who wanted to share the responsibility. It was a big thing when I went to pick up Candace. They wanted to help. That was a type of inclusion.

Candace's story underscores the point made by Eva Kittay (2000): "No degree of impairment is so great that that person cannot contribute to the well-being of those around her—just by being in the world" (p. 74).

Two children in the group—Andrew and Selris—stood out as the most obviously advanced intellectually but were still not eligible for "normal" school. Andrew, after starting off at Immortelle at age 5, was able to go on to the Princess Elizabeth Centre to be prepared for the Common Entrance Exam and ultimately attended Fatima College, a prestigious secondary school for boys, where he sat and passed the CXC school-leaving exams in English and Math. His mother tells the story this way:

Carole: "Andrew was a big fish in a small pond." I found out about Joan shortly after the Immortelle Centre had opened. So I brought Andrew for physiotherapy with her, and Wendy worked out of her home in Glencoe and he was already doing private speech therapy with her. Prior to coming to Immortelle I had tried to find a kindergarten where Andrew could go for a few hours a day. Just to interact with other kids and socialize. But nobody would take Andrew because of the disability.

When I found Immortelle, it was what I was looking for and more! It was small and I felt he would be comfortable in a small environment since he was leaving us for the first time. Immortelle provided all the therapies under one roof—Speech, OT, and Physio—which he needed very desperately at the time.

Most importantly, it felt like he just moved from our home to another home. He was so very happy there. Monica played the biggest part in Andrew's life in those days. I remember Andrew was sort of handed over to Monica and she embraced him with as much love and caring as I thought I was providing.

He was such a big fish in a small pond when he was at Immortelle! When he went to Fatima, he was a small fish in a big pond!

Selris, unlike Andrew, was never given the opportunity to gain the education he was capable of. Despite being born deaf-blind at birth as the result of Rubella in his mother's pregnancy, Selris did gain some limited vision from cataract removal at the age of three. He used this minimal vision not only to learn about the world but also to represent it through his drawings. Selris was a natural artist and an even-tempered, enthusiastic child who brought delight to everyone. His mother told her story of finding Immortelle this way:

> Gwenie: *"The School for the Deaf wouldn't take Selris because he was blind, and the School for the Blind wouldn't take him because he was deaf!"* I went to the School for the Deaf, but they wouldn't take him because he was blind, and the School for the Blind wouldn't take him because he was deaf! But I knew he was bright because he taught himself to copy the letters of the alphabet by watching Sesame Street with his face right up against the TV screen and he used to love to draw things. When he was about six, I was going to get married and I started to worry that I really didn't know how to communicate with him and explain to him what was happening, so I went to my parish priest, Father Eugene de la Hunte, and asked him for guidance. He introduced me to Mr. Broadbridge at the Rotary Club and they brought me to Immortelle to see if you would take Selris in the school. I was so happy when you said yes because I knew Selris could learn!

The Shade of the Immortelle: Protectionism or Opportunity?

Narratives from parents of the "original" Immortelle highlight the family-like atmosphere of the school at that time. As will be seen in the next chapter, current parents described the school in very similar terms, although it now serves about three times as many students and is housed in a sprawling colonial building on the upper end of the city of Port of Spain.

From the perspective of inclusion, however, the very metaphor of Immortelle as a tree that provides shade for vulnerable individuals may evoke unwelcome images of exclusion and protectionism. Indeed, such protectionism might be interpreted as negative in the light of the historical pattern of "paternalistic benevolence", which, as outlined by Richardson and Powell (2011), led to total institutions for persons with disabilities and mental illness and provided the structural bases on which Western special education systems stand today. These authors have argued that it is precisely the depth of this base that makes it so difficult for modern education systems to move toward true inclusion.

While acknowledging the hegemonic power of the historical separate school, I also believe that one size does not fit all persons with disabilities. Nor can models of schooling be evaluated outside of the social and educational context in which the child lives. If disabilities represent a range of points along the spectrum of human experience, then both individual and social experiences must be taken into account in developing educational services. Eva Kittay (2000), in discussing social justice for persons with disabilities, argued this point in the following way:

> The paternalism of a protective environment that may be irksome to a person with blindness who is in all other respects fully able to participate in employment and community life stands in contrast to the goal of integration into the community. Such integration is achieved in an independent home for adults, and a family for a child, settings that would be properly characterized as "least restrictive". For someone like my daughter, however, a protective environment is more crucial than many other considerations. (p. 73).

Another consideration is the point in the trajectory of personal development at which a person may need more or less protection. For example, in this study, Andrew's mother, Carole, in reflecting on her decision to move Andrew on to full inclusion at the high-school level, credited the caring and protected environment of Immortelle in Andrew's early days, with his confidence in being able to be the "lone star" person with a disability when he entered high school:

> *Carole.* What Andrew gained being at the Immortelle Centre was responsible for giving him the confidence to be able to cope going on to

Princess Elizabeth Centre and into Fatima College. I'm not sure if he could've gone straight into mainstream in those days, because there was no one else like him. Being alone might have been too much for him to cope with. When he did go there, it was with the confidence that started in his home in the way we brought him up and then was continued in Immortelle.

As I will show in later chapters, while the majority of parents in this study approved of the principle of inclusive education, some actively wished for such opportunities although most expressed satisfaction with the safety and individualized opportunities for learning that Immortelle provided for their children. The most typical response to the question of inclusion versus separate schooling was that "it depends" on the child and on the quality of the opportunity being offered. Certainly, though, for the "original" parents of children at Immortelle between the 1980s and 1990s, the predominant view was of great appreciation of the family-like atmosphere that Immortelle provided for their children.

Mrs. Maraj's Fridge

The spirit of Immortelle in those days was evident not only in the daily curriculum tailored to individual children, but also in the extra-curricular activities that engaged all children and family members to the fullest extent possible. The small paved, enclosed patio at the back of the house was our community area that housed children's activities, parents' meetings, Carnival rehearsals, and Christmas concerts. Although most were working parents, all were welcome in the school at any time, and several who had the time would come to help with various activities. High points in the year were Carnival and Christmas. For Carnival, the lead teacher, Anne-Marie, arranged for her mother to sew the children's masquerade costumes, and all families were encouraged to bring siblings and extended family members. We "played mas" (masquerade) in Kiddie's Carnival several years in a row, costumed as pirates, freshwater tourists, and several other amusing characters. For Christmas, as Candace's mother emphasized in her interview, every child had a place in the concert, and the back patio of our little corner of Woodbrook was alive with Christmas carols and shouts of laughter as the children practiced their songs and dances, each one performing to the best of

Fig. 3.7 Immortelle students masquerading as "sailors" in Kiddie's carnival, circa 1984

his or her own abilities, cheered on by their families, friends and teachers (Figs. 3.7 and 3.8).

One day that stands out in my memory as symbolic of the mutually supportive atmosphere of the school was the day Mrs. Maraj donated a fridge. Sanjeev Maraj came to us the year after Melanie died. Only two years old, his small stature and physical fragility had quickly earned him the status of the baby of the school. The Maraj family owned a prosperous business in Port of Spain and were very active in their financial support of the school. One morning, I returned to the school from running errands in town and was greeted at the gate by a shout from children and teachers alike, "Beth! Come and see this!" At about 9 a.m., a couple of men had arrived in a small truck and rolled a brand-new fridge up the steps and into the school building, announcing "Mrs. Maraj say you-all need a new fridge!"

Fig. 3.8 Immortelle Special Olympics team, circa 1984

REFERENCES

Aldrich, C. A. (1947). Preventive medicine and Mongolism. *American Journal of Mental Deficiency, LII*(2), 127–129.

Carver, J., & Carver, N. (1972). *The family of the retarded child*. Syracuse: Syracuse University Press.

Erevelles, N. (2011). *Disability and difference in global contexts: Enabling a transformative body politic*. New York: Palgrave Macmillan.

Fitt, A. (2015). *Aching to be.* Toronto, Canada: Ponies + Horses Books.

Kittay, E. F. (2000). At home with my daughter. In L. P. Francis & A. Silvers (Eds.), *Americans with disabilities: Exploring implications of the law for individuals and institutions* (pp. 64–81). New York: Routledge.

Kittay, E. F. (2011). The ethics of care, dependence, and disability. *Ratio Juris. An International Journal of Jurisprudence and Philosophy of Law, 24*(1), 49–58.

Kübler-Ross, E. (1969). *On death and dying.* Routledge.

Oliver, M., & Barnes, C. (1998). *Social policy and disabled people: From exclusion to inclusion.* London: Longman.

Richardson, J. G., & Powell, J. W. (2011). *Comparing special education: Origins to contemporary paradoxes.* Stanford, CA: Stanford University Press.

Solnit, A. J., & Stark, M. H. (1961). Mourning and the birth of a defective child. *Psychoanalytic Study Child, 16,* 523–537.

Turnbull, A., Turnbull, R., Erwin, E., Soodak, L., & Shogren, K. (2015). *Families, professionals, and exceptionality: Positive outcomes through partnerships and trust* (7th ed.). Boston: Pearson.

CHAPTER 4

Forty Years Later: Current Parents' Stories— From "Something Not Right Here" to "We Need Systems!"

Forty years later, the narratives of parents of children currently enrolled in Immortelle were strikingly similar to those of the earlier group. From interviews with 13 "current" families, most of whom had enrolled their children between 2000 and 2014, the same five themes were evident, with one additional theme—"We need systems!"

1. "Something not right here": facing initial shock and seeking understanding
2. Finding Immortelle
3. Trinidad is nice—Trinidad is a paradise: navigating negativity and creating love
4. Adapting and taking action: avenues of advocacy
5. She's wonderful! Finding meaning and creating purpose
6. We need systems!

The similarities in the two sets of parents' accounts were uncanny, especially considering the significant improvements in the economy of Trinidad and Tobago over three to four decades. There were two "current" families for whom this similarity in views was not surprising since their children were in their thirties at the time of this research so their experience had actually begun around the same time as the "original" group. One of these, Lisa, had started attending Immortelle around 1995 and the other,

© The Author(s) 2020
B. Harry, *Childhood Disability, Advocacy, and Inclusion in the Caribbean*, Palgrave Studies in Disability and International Development, https://doi.org/10.1007/978-3-030-23858-2_4

Candace, began in 2000. (I will refer to this second "Candace" as "Candy" to distinguish her from the daughter of "original parents" Rupert and Margaret). However, the other 11 "current" children were younger, ranging in age from Sarah, age 6, to Dimitri, age 23, all of whom enrolled in Immortelle between the years 2000 and 2014. Across this broad spectrum of time periods, the stories of these two groups of parents struck dramatically similar chords.

Despite improvements in educational policy and provisions for children with disabilities, and despite the tremendous progress in the economic status of the nation, these parents' narratives were marked by a similar sense of confusion and frustration regarding appropriate diagnoses and treatments, social and logistical challenges, and the unavailability of appropriate schooling. Public policy decisions had certainly made a difference, including the provision of grants for families of young children with disabilities and for adults aged 18 and over, and, of course, the subsidies to private special schools, which made education somewhat accessible. However, with higher expectations for public support of their children, the unpredictability in the implementation of these policies left parents frustrated and dissatisfied. The discrepancy between official policy and actual practice was so evident to parents and teachers that the theme "*we need systems*" overshadowed all positive descriptions of the current policy situation.

One area of improvement in the social context was greater acceptance of disabilities. However, this varied with the disability, with Down Syndrome appearing to be better regarded than some other visible disabilities. Despite these difficulties, parents exhibited tremendous agency in responding to their challenges and presented a hopeful and positive outlook.

FACING INITIAL SHOCK AND SEEKING UNDERSTANDING

As with the "original" parents' narratives of their children's early years, I will group the current parents' narratives of initial shock into two groups: those that described critical medical challenges at birth and those who experienced a more gradual process of recognizing the children's disabilities. Of the 13 current parents I interviewed, 6 children were identified with what seemed to be life or death crises at birth. The other 7 families described a range of issues that began early and gradually became evident within the first few years of the child's life. I will begin with the former group.

Life or Death Crises: A Tale of Two Daniels

The narratives told by the parents of two very different "Daniels" captured the essence of the shock parents experience when disability and severe medical issues present together at a child's birth. Both these children had a diagnosis of Down Syndrome and, despite the aforementioned improvement in public attitudes toward this disability, both families reported inadequate, even unkind responses from medical professionals regarding the needs of these infants. These stories demonstrated the "social model" of disability at work.

Both these families demonstrated the strong reliance on faith that characterized all the interviews. One mother, Renata, reported that she and her husband immediately accepted the diagnosis, attributing it to the will of God. The other mother, Diane, experienced it as a "hard" blow, but "drew strength" from her husband and her faith. For both, however, the health challenges were greater than the disability itself. As is not uncommon among newborns with Down Syndrome, both babies were born with "holes in the heart" and, despite their parents' experience of rejecting attitudes at the hospital, both found very different solutions to their infants' medical problems. Both interpreted their children's progress and health as God's work.

Daniel: "A gift from God". At the time of my interview with Renata, her son, Daniel was an affectionate 9-year-old, with light skin tone and a charming smile, whose small stature made him appear several years younger (Fig. 4.1). As a student in Monica's kindergarten group, Daniel was learning elementary-level academics as well as self-help and social skills and was much loved by everyone for his friendly personality. Renata's story of Daniel's birth and early development revealed a family very willing to accept the diagnosis but sorely distressed by poor initial health care and the absence of inclusive education opportunities for their son.

Renata, Daniel's mother. Daniel was diagnosed within 45 minutes of birth. We didn't care. I loved him from the second I knew I was pregnant. He was born with liver failure and while he was in the nursing home, he wasn't waking, just sleeping right through. He wouldn't even eat. I told his paediatrician I didn't understand why Daniel was not waking up. He said, "Oh your son is Down Syndrome. Your problems are only now starting."

My husband and I held Daniel's hand and we prayed and rebuked the doctor's words in the name of Jesus. My husband prayed over Daniel that he would be in life what God designed him to be. No health issues, no

Fig. 4.1 Daniel Texeira with his parents, Brent and Renata

challenges that we couldn't overcome as a family. We brought him home unconscious after four days, not knowing if he was going to die. As we got home Mummy said, "Something is wrong with him!" So we took him to the paediatrician next door (who is now his paediatrician) and she took one look at him and said, "His liver isn't working".

His liver was swollen and about to burst. He had been critical for 5 days and nearly died. But the first doctor didn't care. This doctor re-admitted him to hospital right away. She said he would not last the rest of the day. But he recovered, and in two weeks, when he was totally recovered, she told us we had another obstacle to overcome—he had multiple holes in his heart and she realised we hadn't been told this either.

We went to a paediatric heart specialist and that too was a nightmare. We tried to see her at Mt. Hope, which would've been free of charge. He was born in February and they gave us an appointment to do the ECG and other tests not until September of that year! By that time he would've been dead! We were treated with hostility. I think they took one look at us and assumed we had money to pay. I said to the nurse, "You saw us as white. Not as human beings with a new born baby that needed your help!"

We left and went to the doctor privately when she would have seen him for *free* at Mt. Hope. We saw her privately almost immediately. Her prices were extremely high—in the thousands. We took a loan and did what we had to do. She confirmed that he had two large holes and he needed surgery. It was frightening! The surgery would cost US$250,000." So instead, we took him to church and the pastor and the church prayed for him. Within the first three months the first hole closed. Every six weeks he had to do tests. Somewhere between three and nine months the second hole closed!

My son's paediatrician treats him as if he's just as important as any other child. Any parent of any special needs child will tell you that's all we want. That they're just as valuable to us as other people's children are to them. I don't see Daniel the Down Syndrome child. I see Daniel the sweet adorable child that I love to death, who just happens to have Down Syndrome.

Daniel the pan-player: "It had to be God"! Dane and Diane were the parents of Daniel—the boy whose pan-playing opened this book. Daniel was a slim, attractive 11-year old with velvety dark brown skin and a wild, shimmering Afro. I observed Daniel in his "Junior" classroom, where he seemed to show little interest in the basic academic skills being taught, but was always ready to join in a group game, or perform in some musical mode (Fig. 4.2).

Like Renata, the mother of Daniel in the foregoing tale, Dane and Diane told a painful story of uncaring and hurtful treatment at their son's birth and through his early medical needs. Diane is a police officer and Dane and their older son are musicians, Dane being well known in Trinidad and abroad for his innovative pan-playing skills. Because Dane had a work permit to perform in the US, the family was able to take Daniel to the US for surgery and access Medicaid support. Talking in tandem, they told the story this way:

Diane, Daniel's mother. From day one it was hard. I couldn't bring myself to accept the fact that I had a child like that. He went to full term and when

Fig. 4.2 Daniel
Gulston with his parents,
Dane and Diane and
brother Denilson

he was born the nurse said there was something strange about this child. His skin. He was looking like a normal baby at the time. Fat and everything. And when the doctor came in he didn't know what was wrong. He called for the doctor in the ante natal unit. I started to panic because I thought something was wrong. When the doctor came it so happened that she was my first son's doctor. When she saw Daniel she said, "My goodness, Diane, we have to talk!"

I said, "Doctor what's wrong?" She said, "As far as I'm concerned nothing is wrong, this is God's work." She explained that Daniel would be diagnosed with Down syndrome. She spoke about Trisomy 21 (which

I didn't understand). She said, "Diane everything is going to be alright." Really, at the time I didn't understand everything she said because I just held on to her and started to cry.

I was feeling down. I looked at the parents around me with their babies and everybody was looking healthy and happy. And still, at the time, he was looking like a normal child.

But my husband, I pulled strength from him.

Soon after the birth, we went to the doctor because Daniel had a heart murmur. He had 3 holes in his heart. Each time he bathed, he would turn blue. The doctor suggested we take him to Mt. Hope hospital. That was an experience! They said he was too young to do open heart surgery and we would have to bring him back in a year because he was so small.

Now, my husband had contacted a Trinidadian doctor he knew in New York. He told us to get a recording of the sound of Daniel's heart and send it to him so he could see what's happening. So when the hospital told us it would take a year, Mr. Man here [my husband] started to get on bad! I'm crying and he's getting on! He says, "All I want is a tape to take to New York. All I want is a tape of my child's heart! Film it!" A doctor at the hospital asked if we were citizens of the US. I said no, so she said, "Well, if they don't do the surgery, don't come back here and beg!" Eventually, we got the tape and took it to New York. Daniel was a baby so we had to get him a passport, my husband had to get a work permit, and we had to go to the US embassy (and you know how they give trouble).

But everything worked out so fast. It had to be God! We went to the U.S. when Daniel was 2 1/2 months old. He had the surgery at 5 months. We were scared, but they were really nice. They started occupational therapy and physical therapy right away. We stayed almost a year. I sent a letter to my job through the Trinidad Consulate in Manhattan. I'm a police officer. My boss told me stay as long as I want until the child is ready to travel. It had to be God! They took good care of him and good care of us.

Dane. I think what the person at the hospital here said about us not getting the surgery in the U.S. inspired us to make sure that it happened. You know how things are when you're bitter! I remember a night my cousin, CJ, came to the house and Diane was feeding Daniel and he said to me, "You're going to America with this child! OK!"

I knew Diane was scared because she hardly talked about it. Pride. People feel like it's a kind of embarrassment to walk with the child. But that really wasn't my thinking at all. God is good. I really didn't see the difference at first.

Diane. In my mind, my husband was only living in denial. Anywhere you go, people would be bending the corner! Or you go in the supermarket—people staring. This was mostly when he got bigger—when he started to run about.

Dane. And now it's totally the opposite. Daniel is a star. If you go anywhere, even in South—It's "Look meh boy!" We don't have a clue who the person is, but they're seeing him all the time. Because he performs.

Life or Death Crises: "Nothing Prepared Us for This!"

Sarah and Isaiah were classmates in the preschool classroom, which focused on basic developmental goals such as eating, toileting, verbal and non-verbal communication, and perceptual and fine-motor tasks. Both children needed intensive one-on-one attention to participate in group or individual activities. Both came into the world in crisis, obviously at risk, both for initially inexplicable reasons. Their conditions were, however, very different. At the time of my interviews with their parents, Sarah was about six years old and Isaiah about nine, but both were small for their age and looked a couple of years younger,

Sarah: "In the first hours of her life she stopped breathing." Sarah's chocolate-colored skin and shiny black eyes and hair reflected her Indian heritage. Although she showed no physical signs of a disability, her limited communication and motor skills and extremely non-compliant behavior made her stand out. Although she could walk, she preferred to sit or lie on the floor, frequently using this to refuse to participate in an activity. She would often find her way to the locked gate of the school building and would be literally underfoot as adults attempted to enter or exit.

Sarah lived with her paternal grandparents, her grandmother, Sharmain, being the primary caregiver, while her mother was gradually becoming more involved. Sarah's grandmother described her as "spoiled" and determined to have her own way, and she found it difficult to elicit compliant behavior from her. I interviewed Sarah's grandmother and mother together at the school and learned about her birth:

> *Sharmain, Sarah's grandmother.* In the first hours of her life she stopped breathing. They had to resuscitate and they incubated her for a while. While in incubation we realised there were problems. She was born at 38 weeks. She weighed like about 2lbs 2oz. They did a CT scan and saw there was a little bleeding in the brain. So from then we knew something was wrong. Initially we didn't realise the sort of damage because at the hospital they said the bleeding cut down and everything should be okay.
>
> But she wasn't growing as she was supposed to. At age two, she was not walking, not crawling. She used to drag on her butt with her feet under her.

She had no strength in her legs. Her Mummy was not able to handle the situation, so I took the lead role.

"Isaiah came out—He wasn't breathing. He was blue." At the time of this research, Isaiah could walk with assistance, though with unsteady gait. On mornings he could be seen heading eagerly for the front door holding on to his father's hand. With several physical features that indicated developmental anomalies, Isaiah also needed intensive individualized attention to participate in activities. In the classroom, he often sat in a triangular shaped chair designed to provide some containment for children with poor balance or children who just needed to stay put to pay attention to a task.

The family, a typical Trinidadian mixture of African, European, and Chinese origins, comprised Isaiah's father and mother, Francis and Lisa Escayg, and two children younger than Isaiah (Fig. 4.3). Francis and Lisa were both professionals in the arts, Francis a filmmaker and public relations specialist, and Lisa a popular singer and music composer. Francis served on

Fig. 4.3 Isaiah Escayg, with his parents, Lisa and Francis, and sisters Roxy-Moon and Phoenix

Immortelle's Board of Directors and was working on an exciting vision of spearheading the development of a rurally located center that could provide adults with disabilities with a livelihood in agricultural production. I interviewed Francis at Immortelle Centre and he spoke of his son's condition and of his own conflicts in coming to terms with this unexpected challenge.

> *Francis, Isaiah's father.* Nothing prepared us for having Isaiah come this early. This was my fourth child, but my first with my new wife. We had just come back from Tobago and he wasn't due for another six weeks. My wife went into labour and Isaiah came out—he wasn't breathing. They put him in the incubator where he warmed up. This was very new to me because of how he looked. He was six weeks early and he was looking like a plucked chicken! A lot of skin! He had no muscle tone and he wasn't nursing. We had to feed him with all different size droppers. One night we gave him a medicine for gas, the usual stuff they give kids for colic, and he stopped breathing. We had to rush him to the hospital. Dr. Bratt was monitoring his development and he recommended us to TIBS, who would help us find a way for him to breastfeed.
>
> We went there and they helped us and he was able to pull with the help of an attachment. It was like a nipple over the nipple and he was able to grab on to it. It was amazing and then he started growing. But for the first nine months Isaiah didn't meet any of his milestones and Dr. Bratt told us to try not to worry. Some kids meet their milestones later. At nine months he wasn't rolling over, he wasn't holding up his head. At that point all kinds of things were going wrong with him. He had eczema. He had a lot of allergies, a lot of restrictions on what he can eat.
>
> The diagnosis was Incontinentia Pigmenti (IP). It's an in utero condition. Usually males don't survive it. My wife went into immediate—"How do we fix this?" She started to mourn—those were her words. She formed CKFTO (Caribbean Kids and Families Therapy Organization)—an organization that gives occupational therapy to children with disabilities.

At the older end of the spectrum of current students who had experienced severe issues at birth, I interviewed the parents of Michael, and Dimitri. Once more, these students' conditions were very different, with poorly understood etiologies, and very different initial treatments and developmental outcomes. Michael, age 19, and Dimitri, age 23, were in Charlene's class, where a focus on basic academic and life skills along with adult socialization reflected the higher developmental goals expected for these two young men.

Michael: "Everything made sense when you got to Dr. Bratt."
Michael's mother, Alberta, was employed at Immortelle as an office assistant. She spoke with me about her experience with Michael and her tremendous dissatisfaction with the lack of information or guidance she had received. As her description of her son indicates, Michael, a sturdy, dark-skinned young man of predominantly African descent, had unusually shaped eyes and a somewhat asymmetrical shaped face. I observed him frequently in Charlene's class, where he proved to be courteous, sociable, and on target cognitively, often helping other classmates with their work or with following the rules of a game.

Alberta, Michael's mother. Michael's syndrome is very rare. He has AASKOG. It happens in one in three million kids. It's inherited. With AASKOG, your body doesn't develop the way it's supposed to. When he came home from hospital, I realised he wasn't breathing properly—kind of gasping. The doctors were not telling me anything. This was new to me so I'm like, "What's wrong?" His eyes were always puffy and swollen, always red and bulging but the doctors didn't care. At first, they wouldn't give me advice, just, "Something is wrong with your child, check with this person". A referral. You don't know what to do!

His face didn't form so they had to put tubes in because everything was flattened. They had to put, like drainage to the eye, to the ears, to the mouth. So we joined the eye clinic and they had doctors looking at it. They tried surgery but it just didn't work. They attempted six times and then the doctor gave me a referral to go to a private specialist. I had to pay for the CT scan. It's like $1200 every time you go and do stuff. It's really sad because when you have a child like that, you must pay for everything. It's only nowadays that you're getting things free. When that doctor did the surgery, it took about four and a half months to see results—before his eyes stopped draining.

Everything made sense when we went to Dr. Bratt! He was the one that recognized the syndrome. He explained so many things. And he sent me to Immortelle, because Michael had a behavioural problem too. I didn't know how to cope with him. He used to roll on the ground because he couldn't speak properly. He was trying to express himself but he couldn't.

Dimitri: "We give thanks every day. Every minute of our lives."
Dimitri, at age 23, was a slim, courteous young man of predominantly Indian descent, whose father described him as also having some Chinese ethnicity. In Charlene's "senior" class, Dimitri was serious and attentive to his work, doing his best to follow instructions. He did, however, exhibit

severe anxiety, which was sometimes a precursor to a seizure. Consequently, his teacher and classmates paid close attention to his mood, making modifications to requirements when necessary to give him individualized support. I interviewed his father, Robert Thomas, at Immortelle Centre. Although he did not mention a diagnosis of autism, Dimitri's repetitive verbal style and physical mannerisms were suggestive of a person on the autism spectrum. As his father reported, Dimitri was a devout Catholic, always in possession of his rosary, and frequently offering prayers and religious wishes for his teacher and peers. His father was at the time retired from a long-standing career as a bank official.

Robert, Dimitri's father. Dimitri will be 23 in November coming. He is the last of 4 children. We lost the second child 14 hours after he was born. When Dimitri was born, my wife asked the nurses why the baby was not crying. The nurses gave some lame excuse. The doctor checked the child and said he was fine. My wife still was not satisfied. She said call Dr. Bratt, who was our paediatrician. Dimitri was born sometime in the night and Dr. Bratt came in early that morning and checked him out. He came shortly afterwards and said he didn't like Dimitri's skin colouring, it was kind of greyish, which meant lack of oxygen. And he had some blotches on his hand. He arranged for him to be transferred immediately to Mt. Hope hospital where he was in charge of the paediatric ward. He had a team of doctors working on Dimitri. His blood count was very low and they gave him 3 blood transfusions. Dimitri remained in Mt. Hope hospital for 2 weeks. My wife and I slept up there with him.

Three blood transfusions and the blood count went up and then went back down. The doctors did not know what the cause was. They took x-rays and found that the forceps had caused some damage. I saw the x-ray and learned that Dimitri had severe brain damage. The first 2 days he was home from the hospital, his head started swelling. We took him to Dr. Bratt who sent him back to Mt. Hope. They did more tests, trying to figure out why his blood count was so low.

Next, they wanted to do a bone marrow test. I told Dr. Bratt if it was that kind of test, I wanted to take the child away to the U.S. Dr. Bratt knew a doctor in Jackson Memorial hospital in Miami so he made arrangements and we took Dimitri there the week before Christmas or the first week in January. We stayed at Ronald McDonald House. The following day we went to the lab to get the blood tests done and it turned out that he had Thalassemia. There are two types of Thalassemia—major and minor. Dimitri had Thalassemia minor, thank God. They explained that with the major type, he would have had to have a blood transfusion every month.

At Mt. Hope, after the x-rays, Dr. Bratt was very despondent and didn't give Dimitri much of a chance to survive. And then he started to get seizures at age 8.

But now, Dimitri is 23, so we give thanks every day! Every minute of our lives.

A Gradual Awareness: Coming to Terms with Disability

As with the original Immortelle parents, this group of current parents included some whose children, despite displaying developmental anomalies, were not initially marked by severe medical crises. Rather, for these seven families, learning about and responding to the children's challenges was more of a gradual process.

Three of these students were in Immortelle's work center for adults: Darren, who was on the autism spectrum; Candy, whose combination of mild hearing and vision impairments made it difficult to know the extent of her cognitive abilities; and Lisa, who had Down Syndrome. Candy and Lisa had both started school at *Something Special* and had stayed when it merged with Immortelle. The other four students were Shekinah, age 21; Corey, who was in his teens and on the autism spectrum; and Nathaniel and Christopher, both about 12 years old and had Down Syndrome. These boys were in the same class as Daniel, the pan-player.

Christopher: "I treated him normally, as I did my other children." Christopher, age 11, was in Reynaldo's class, and was best friends with Daniel the pan-player. Slim and of a light-skinned ethnic mixture, Christopher was most noticeable to me at school social events such as Carnival and the Christmas concert. On both occasions, he performed "rock star" roles in which he pretended to play the guitar, dancing and singing animatedly in time to the music. In class, he and Daniel liked to share activities, so I understood why his mother said Christopher's love of music was inspired by his pan-playing friend.

Allison, Christopher's mother. When I had him it was a challenge for me. I quit my job and stayed home. I made sure he got all the attention he needed. I did pre-learning at home with him so that when he starts school the teacher wouldn't have to teach him everything. I did my own charts that were stuck all over the house to teach him what's a chair, table, bed, flowers, trees. He got familiar with what he was seeing and he knew his colours. He knew the basic things—how to put his clothes on properly. If something is on the wrong side, to turn it. I treated him normally, as I did my other children. I never treated him like he couldn't do anything.

Then he had a little brother, and he was thrilled that he did. He took care of him. The little brother grew up knowing him as the big brother, and as he started walking and talking he referred to him as his best friend. Up to today they're best friends.

Shekina: "She took over a year to start to walk and talk. But talk she did!" Shekinah, then about 21, was a dark-skinned, out-going young lady of predominantly African descent, who had a good memory for people. While one might be struck initially by her unusually shaped facial features, her friendly personality would quickly initiate a positive social dynamic. Despite some distortion in her speech, Shekinah used short sentences to convey relevant information. With medical complications of her kidneys, Shekinah was receiving kidney dialysis three times a week and attended school on the other days. In the afternoons, sitting in her wheelchair at the doorway to the school as she waited for her mother to pick her up, she would often strike up conversations with me and was always willing to share information about her family, such as the fact that her brother was studying to be a doctor and that she wanted to be a doctor too.

Perceptions of Shekinah's level of development differed rather sharply between her mother and teachers. Her mother emphasized Shekinah's visual skills, for instance, her ability to complete complex jigsaw puzzles of up to 300 pieces, working methodically from the perimeter to the internal patterns. Her mother felt that her most urgent need was more challenging instruction as well as speech therapy. However, at the time of the study, Jacqui was considering moving Shekinah to the Ruby group, which included young adults with the most significant disabilities, whose curriculum would be less, rather than more cognitively challenging. Cheryl gave me a detailed account of Shekina's development:

Cheryl, Shekina's mother. Shekinah is my third child. She was twenty one in December. She is brave, loving, teachable, observant and alert. When I was seven months pregnant with her they saw that the foetus appeared small for the age of the pregnancy.

She was born, full-term, in December, and at birth, the doctors gave a very negative prognosis. She took over a year to start to walk and talk. But talk she did! We never did any chromosome studies to know what the disability was. It's definitely not Down and one doctor suggested CP. When she was a baby I took her to Mt. Hope developmental clinic but nothing much happened there and I stopped taking her because I wasn't getting support.

When she was 10 we saw challenges in walking. They started doing a study on her spine but they never got to finish it because they realised there was something wrong with her kidneys, and that took precedence over everything. In 2008, Shekina had a kidney transplant. I am the donor. After that, there were great medical challenges with a lot of infections, UTI's and other challenges, which caused the transplanted kidney to be lost after one year. That's why since 2009 she's been on dialysis three times a week. So they didn't go back to see what happened with the spine—that would be major surgery there and it is not recommended.

Candy: "I said to myself, her development is slow—something not right here." Candy, a quiet, dark-skinned young woman of African descent, was 32 years old and a very active member of the work center. Serious and attentive, she participated fully in the cookie-making routines of her class and displayed all the competence her mother described in her interview with me. Assisted by glasses with thick lenses, Candy's visual impairment did not seem to hamper her much, and the only sign of hearing impairment was in the halting lilt of her speech. Her mother described the long and complicated process she went through as she sought explanations and treatments for her daughter, finally enrolling her in Immortelle at about the age of 17:

> *Glenda, Candy's mother.* She's 32 now. I had two sons before. I had noticed that she was slow in doing things. Like moving around and such. She was missing out on things that I'd seen the other children develop at age two and three. Like her speech. I'd encourage her to say "mama', but that wasn't happening either. I said to myself, something is not right here. Her development stage is slower than normal, although she did not look like she's differently abled.
>
> I took her to the doctor and after some tests they gave me a letter to take to the hospital. There she was diagnosed with a cataract in one eye and a heart murmur. The hospital visits came on and then I realised she has a condition. But still her development was slow.

Corey: "People thought he was deaf." Marie (pseudonym), warm and expressive, told me about the relationship she had built with Corey (pseudonym), her stepson. At age 13, Corey was in the junior classroom taught by Reynaldo, focusing on basic academics and social interaction skills. Corey loved to write and would learn best when information was written as well as spoken. He was particularly fond of geography, always eager to name countries on the map and recognize their flags. Diagnosed as being on the autism spectrum, this slim, dark-skinned young man displayed repetitive mannerisms and social interaction styles typical of this condition and functioned best in structured situations where he could anticipate the rhythm of the activities. Marie said:

> *Marie, Corey's step-mother.* Corey is my step-son. I met him at age 4. We connected from the first day. He was like a child lost. He just made noises, running, running, running. People thought he was deaf. Everyone used to be shouting at him. I think his father knew he was autistic, and thought that he was also deaf. But I discovered that he wasn't deaf. I didn't know anything about autism, but when I met him, we connected and I started to work with him. About three weeks after meeting him and having him around me, one night something clicked and I wrote about four lines: "*My name is Corey; I live at ... my daddy's name is ... He has a white van.*" I taught him to say these words and read them. After doing it for like fifteen minutes, he read it for himself. And when his father came and I showed him what this child had done, he cried. He couldn't believe that this child could have even spoken.

Darren: "They didn't know what was wrong. I was the one to ask them." Emil was the very first mother to volunteer for an interview with me. Warm and open in her manner, she described the difficulties of getting a clear diagnosis of autism for her son, Darren, who, at age 24, currently participated in the school's work center program. His mother described him as participating well in the cookie project but with limited ability to follow instructions independently. She explained:

> *Emil, Darren's mother.* My son began his special education at *Something Special.* At first the doctors didn't know what was wrong, and I didn't know either. I was the one to ask them. Finally, a doctor at the Port of Spain hospital said it was autism and I didn't know what that was.

FINDING IMMORTELLE: YOU FEEL LIKE YOU'RE COMING HOME

After the initial shock and confusion brought on by medical crises or ambiguous developmental delays, by the time the child was four or five years old, these parents began to search for educational services. The process of finding an appropriate school was surprisingly like the experience of the "original" parents some 40 years prior.

You Don't Know What to Do!

Alberta's exclamation, "you don't know what to do" captured the angst felt by all the parents as they tried to figure things out, with minimal or no support. There was no central location where information could be provided on special education services, so parents were on their own.

Similar to the original Immortelle parents some 40 years prior, these parents' searches reflected three main scenarios: most commonly, they would "try normal school", arranging to enroll the child in either a private or public school or preschool that served typically developing children. Having much empathy but no specialized skills or programs, the personnel in charge of these programs would take the child in, simply trying to help. In some cases, the parent and/or school would make some special arrangement for the child. These arrangements worked well for a while in some cases, until the school's curriculum could no longer be adjusted to meet the child's needs. An alternative approach was to try to enroll the child in a special school geared for children with a specific disability, such as the school for children with physical disabilities, but these did not usually prove to be appropriate, for various reasons. Finally, most parents found out about Immortelle Centre by serendipity or by a referral from a doctor or therapist who knew about the school.

Alberta: "They wouldn't even give you advice. You don't know what to do!" Only the children with the most obviously disabling conditions came directly to Immortelle, and that occurred typically after some years of "not knowing what to do". The search prior to finding Immortelle was distressing and frustrating, as in the case of Alberta, whose son, Michael, had AASKOGs syndrome.

> *Alberta, Michael's mother.* You don't know what to do! You have Michael and you take him to all these different clinics in the hospital, and they wouldn't tell you that there is a special school. You just hope that someone sees you and helps you. Finally, when you reach to Dr. Bratt—like half the problems that you have disappear. When Michael was about six, Dr. Bratt referred him for evaluation and Dr. Robin the speech therapist, worked with him and he made one year's progress in three months!

Growing "Too Big for Normal School"

These families' search for Immortelle was almost identical to that of the parents 40 years earlier. The majority started out by enrolling their children in "normal" schools or preschool programs and most told a similar story of children doing quite well until their peers outgrew them cognitively, and the curriculum became impossible for them to "keep up".

Glenda, Candy's mother, recounted a history that spanned both groups of families and revealed a roller coaster of frustration, temporary success, renewed frustration, and finally, an appropriate program at Immortelle. Thirty years old at the time of this project, Candy was born in 1985, during the years that the Immortelle was struggling to get on its feet. However, she did not get to Immortelle until about 2000. Fortunately, Glenda's search up until that time proved quite successful when she was admitted to the School for the Deaf, but on Candy's graduation in her mid-teens, she had nowhere to go. Glenda described her search:

Glenda, Candy's mother: "*Normal school, the School for the Deaf, and then what?*" At five years she was still small for her age. I got her enrolled in a normal school—Malabar Government School. She went there for about two or three years but during that period I did these researches and I read about Dretchi and I took her there to run certain tests for hearing impairment. With all the tests they had done in the hospital, nobody had told me she had a hearing problem. At Dretchi, they said she had lost a certain amount of hearing in one ear but the other ear was more or less okay, but it had affected her speech. Dretchi recommended that she go to Cascade School for the Deaf. When I went there, they told me they couldn't take her because she's not deaf. But luckily the principal spoke with me and I told her I didn't know what to do. Finally, she decided to accept her. So Candy spent some years there and graduated at fifteen.

But where could she go from there? I was going to work so I couldn't just leave her at home alone. At the School for the Deaf she had improved a lot, but I felt it was not enough. There was a little school in Arima called the Deaf Pioneer that she went to but it was just three afternoons a week and I wanted her to be in an environment where she would be all day, so she could interact more with people. She had gotten into the school for Differently Abled People in San Fernando, but that was much too far—as we were living at La Horquetta at that time.

So she stayed home for a while. Then I heard about Immortelle just by reading. Pronto, I said, "This is my chance!" I took her and the rest is history. I took her like today, and two days later she was at Immortelle!

"*Now she's wonderful!*" Now, she's at the St. Ann's location and the facilities are so much better. She's A class! When we're at home, I say, "Candy, you almost own the house!" She packs cupboards. She cleans the stove. She cleans the fridge. She keeps her room A-class. She's neat. She's clean. She makes her breakfast. She puts away the laundry. She's organized. She sits at the table with her napkin. When they send the end of term reports they show what the children learned, and she does these things at home too. She irons her own clothes. She sets her own hair. She hems her own clothes. She's wonderful!

Glenda's story captured the essence of the frustrating search for a school and the ultimate sense of "feeling at home" upon finding Immortelle. This pattern was echoed by Lana and Allison, mothers of children with Down Syndrome. Like Tommy Pierre in the original Immortelle group, privately arranged inclusion in preschool or primary schools for a few years resulted in pleasant socialization until, in Lana's words, "she grew too big for that school". Regardless of the children's disabilities, the stories were all similar. Dimitri's parents tried "a little school in Woodbrook". Emil tried a nursery school in St. James. Sharmain placed Sarah in a daycare where, she said, "they weren't feeding her properly" and finally, upon her joining Immortelle at age two and a half as "the baby of the school, she started to progress in leaps and bounds after Roxanne and Val took her under their wing". Cheryl tried "three different normal schools" for Shekina and finally turned to a special school in Arima, which she described this way: "It was isolated, far from home, dull, dreary, with sad students. My heart broke. One day after prayer I looked in the phone directory and saw Immortelle. I called the school and went in and talked with Jacqui."

Renata, Daniel's mother, told a story in 2015 of attempted inclusion that was strikingly similar to that told by Lydia Pierre about Tommy's inclusive placement some 35 years before. Ironically, the main difference in the placements was that Tommy had actually been accepted into a regular classroom in a government primary school, based totally on the kindness of the principal. Daniel's inclusion, on the other hand, followed the more similar pattern of placement in a private school. Another difference was the extreme heartbreak Renata expressed when she had to decide that his placement in a "normal school" was no longer working. As the only mother in both groups who explicitly stated a strong preference for full inclusion for her son with Down Syndrome, she described how conflicted she was about the decision, being a firm believer that children with and without disabilities should be in school together. Daniel's inclusion was facilitated by a friend of Renata's who had a private preschool.

Renata, Daniel's mother: "The down side was there was nowhere to promote him to!" One aspect of it was great, which was that he was learning to mimic normal patterns and normal behaviours from the normal kids. But there was the downside of it where he could not do the class work and the activities. So after about two years we realised that each September when the children would be promoted there was nowhere to promote Daniel. He kept seeing his friends moving on and he had to make new friends with younger children. We saw him going from a happy child to confused, and then he did not want to go to school because his friends kept moving on and he kept being left behind.

I moved him and sent him to a special school but they didn't have the facilities. The children went from five or six years old all the way to 21, 22. It was extremely overwhelming for him and he wasn't happy at all.

The therapist who was working with him recommended Immortelle for him. We came with Daniel and did an interview with Jacqui everything was going well, but when Jacqui took us on a tour of the school—I'll be extremely honest with you—I freaked! I went from class to class and I saw all these special needs children, and I thought, my son does not belong here. He went from being in a normal school where socially his behaviour was totally normal because he was learning from normal children. When he went from that to a school with just 12 special needs children, I had already started seeing his behaviour retarding.

Then, here, in my mind, it seemed like hundreds—even though it wasn't hundreds—of special needs children. I said, "Oh, my Lord!" I just didn't believe in my heart that it was the right thing for him.

But he wasn't happy at the other school. He was crying to go to school and crying to come home. So, after another six or eight months, his occupational therapist said to me, "Renata, Daniel can do better than this. I'm begging you to take him back to Immortelle."

I sucked up my pride and embarrassment and came back. Jacqui was fantastic. She never made me feel bad or said, "I told you so". When Daniel came the first day, I was so nervous but it was as if God knew my fears because as soon as Daniel walked in, he ran off in joy. Now, nearly three years later, I have the happiest child under the sun in this school. My son has not cried a day in here. I drop him in the morning and he goes his way. I return for him in the evening and he's in no rush to leave, I have to call him and say, "It's time to leave."

Inclusion? "It Just Depends"

As Renata's story indicates, inclusion is where her heart was. Her decision to place Daniel in a separate special school came after much resistance and facing the total absence of other appropriate options. As overjoyed as she was to see her son happy and loved at Immortelle, this was not her vision of the best situation. Moreover, she also tied her concerns to social interactions outside of school, pointing out that separate schooling leads to separate social lives for children with and without disabilities.

> *Renata, Daniel's mother: It's a compromise.* Immortelle is the best that you're going to get in the system that we have. But our children need inclusion. They need to learn alongside normal children and nothing will tell me that's there's anything better than that. But if we don't have that choice, then we must take what's best after that.
>
> For inclusion to work, the curriculum would have to be adjusted for our kids. They need trained special needs teachers. But at least there would be activities that the children could all do together—physical education, choir, gym, music, art, dance, all the other extra curricula activities. And this would be an education for the normal children too, to mix with other children.
>
> Where we live, the normal children don't have anything to do with Daniel. When they have birthday parties, he's not invited. He sees the balloons and all the children in the yard playing, and he looks at them, and even though he can't talk, he would point. As a mother it breaks my heart!
>
> I think its ignorance and a lack of education on the parents' part. Children are more open, more accepting. They need to take on the role of teaching their parents. But how are they going to do that when, in our system in Trinidad, our children are kept on two different sides of the pole?

I asked both the original and current parents about their views of inclusion. Although Renata's views echoed the wishful sentiment across both groups, most were less enthusiastic than she was. For most parents, inclusion in schools was an ideal that seemed out of reach with the negative social attitudes toward disability and the nation's continuing commitment to a traditional, academic focused curriculum. The majority expressed significant reservations about inclusion, and those who supported the concept did so with many caveats on the nature of schooling, appropriate teacher preparation, and social attitudes.

Among the "original" parents, Tony and Lydia Pierre supported the ideal of inclusion but focused on the role of the government in moving the educational system forward.

> *Tony, Tommy's father: Our political system has failed us.* We haven't made the kind of strides we should have. Every time a government changes they

throw out everything whether it's good or bad. Every five years it's a whole political upheaval.

If the children went to school together, by the next generation they would have grown up accepting this as the norm—knowing that these children are just like you and me. But it has all been individual. Like the individual Primary school principal who included Tommy. But when she is replaced, the next one might not do it. We feel it is time for government to put systems in place so that it isn't a parent fighting all the time to get something for their child. There should be systems! A strategic plan for five or seven years that would be in place and would go on regardless of who's in charge.

This country has so much potential—all these resources! All this money! Creative people! There is a lot going for Trinidad and Tobago. All the energy that people like us put in for years and years and once you move off, unless some other individuals pull it up again, it just dies. Because no system was put in place to support it. Lots of countries suffer because they don't have the finances, or the human resources. But in Trinidad you have it all. Educated people, and plenty of managers!

Helen Humphrey, who, with her husband John, had been a key figure in the establishment of NADS, along with Tony and Lydia Pierre, expressed grave reservations about the feasibility of inclusion in schools:

Helen, Becky's grandmother: "Inclusion would have to be very gradual." Not just impose it, because we need special teachers. I think Glen, at the Down Syndrome Family Network, is going to have a problem trying to get that because the children are special and there's no way they could completely fall into the regular school system. Don't care how they try. But I think he would not agree with what we're trying to do. One of the problems is the curriculum. We need special teachers, but also a flexible curriculum. The one we have is one tracked.

There were several parents in both groups who were unequivocal in their support of separate schooling. These parents had no faith that they could trust their vulnerable children to the public educational sphere. For example, Rita, speaking of her son who had been in Immortelle 35 years before, felt strongly that children like Khayam would "get lost" in an included setting.

Emil, whose son, Darren, had autism, shared the view that normally developing children need to be educated about their peers with disabilities, and suggested that the book that would come of this research should be included in schools as part of the curricular reading. Nevertheless, she did not see inclusion as appropriate for her son. For her, it is "an individual thing that depends on the child". Diane, Daniel's mother also feared that her son would be "set aside" in a regular primary school. However, toward the end of this research, she reported that they had moved Daniel, at age 14, to the Goodwill Industries program, where he was learning a range of trades and could work on his music. Glenda, Marie, and Lana held similar views. Lana's words were typical:

> *Lana, Lisa's mother: "I'm okay with it here."* Here she can go at her own pace and do things to suit her abilities. Whereas in another school she would be left behind. You've got to be real. She can't read or write like a normal child or a woman of her age, 31. I have no problem with her being here. My thing though is how much longer is she going to be here? I suppose it's my choice if I want to keep her here. But when do I stop?

Carole's story of inclusion. Across these two groups of parents, there were two whose children left Immortelle to attend the regular public school system, to prepare for the Common Entrance Examination and, ultimately, for a secondary education. Shirley, whose son, David, had autism, saw her son shine academically but experience total exclusion socially. She felt that he had gone as far as he could in that system. Carole, whose son, Andrew, had cerebral palsy, was very vocal on this issue, saying that she had no option but to provide her son with that opportunity but that the social effects were in many ways detrimental to him. When asked if she would again place Andrew in a fully included setting, she replied:

> *Carole, Andrew's mother.* Absolutely! But not as a lone star. It is too much pressure. I think what Andrew gained being at the Immortelle Centre was responsible for giving him the confidence to be able to cope going through Princess Elizabeth Centre and into Fatima College. I'm not sure if he could've gone straight into mainstream in those days, because there was no one else like him. Being alone might have been too much I think in coping.
>
> I've never thought, Andrew would have achieved more if he'd been in the regular school from a younger age. No. Because he would have been the pioneer, the only kid in a normal school. When he did go there, it was with the confidence which started in his home in the way we brought him up and then it was continued in Immortelle. So he came there a very confident person with a disability. It was a new thing for Fatima College. They'd never

taken a kid like him. They have a couple other kids now. But not nearly as involved as Andrew in terms of his cerebral palsy.

But there was a lot of negativity. "Exactly why is he here? There's a place for him! Why do they have to bring him here?" That was a big thing for everybody to deal with.

I will go to my grave with this wonderful experience that I had: We were at a PTA one afternoon. We were sitting in the hall and Andrew was at the door waiting for me, looking in every so often to see if I was ready. In front of me were these two mothers sitting together who started to discuss Andrew. "I can't believe what this school is coming to! Imagine they have this retarded boy coming to the school!" I'm sitting there and I'm not saying anything.

So one of them got up and went up to speak with the teacher and apparently her kid wasn't doing so well. So she turns to the lady she had been talking to and says, "I don't know what to do with this boy. He just failed his English class!" So my turn comes, I get to the teacher and she tells me Andrew got 98% in his English. I went and sat behind the two ladies and said, "Excuse me ladies, I just thought I'd let you know, you see that young man at the door? That's my son. These are his results—English—98%. What were you saying?" I just enlightened them!

"You Feel Like You're Coming Home"

In the face of a generally unwelcoming educational environment, all the parents emphasized the need for a safe and supportive environment for their children. Renata's statement of confidence in Immortelle was expressed unanimously across the interviews. This feeling of comfort echoed the words of "original" parents, such as Carole's "you feel like you're moving from your home to another home", or Margaret's "a place of safety and value". While a couple of the current parents expressed wanting more from the curriculum, on the question of school climate there were no dissenting voices: Immortelle had, they said, "an atmosphere of love"—"like a family". Sharmain, explaining her fears for Sarah's safety, concluded:

> When you walk in here, you don't feel like you're going to school, you feel like you're coming home. When I'm leaving, I don't feel like I'm leaving her in a school. I feel confident and safe.

CHAPTER 5

"Trinidad Is Nice, Trinidad Is a Paradise": Navigating Negativity and Creating Love

As described in the foregoing chapters, parents of the children enrolled at Immortelle generally viewed the school as a safe haven for children whose vulnerabilities were exacerbated by the realities of inadequate medical and educational services in the society at large. These realities also included more ambiguous yet no less discriminatory attitudes that affected children and families' daily lives. In this chapter, I use the voices of both groups of parents to paint a picture of the social and cultural context regarding disabilities. Their views, spanning a period of 40 years, acknowledged significant improvements, yet signified a wistful sense of the saying, "the more things change, the more they are the same".

Trinidad is not alone in this. Caribbean scholar Annicia Gayle-Geddes (2016) provided a comparative analysis of the situation of persons with disabilities in Jamaica and Trinidad/Tobago. Based on both qualitative and quantitative data, she concluded that, despite increased social acceptance, the socio-cultural environment for persons with disabilities in these two Caribbean countries remains "generally restrictive", marked by institutional, environmental, and attitudinal discrimination that "affect all aspects of the lived experiences of disability" (p. 132).

© The Author(s) 2020
B. Harry, *Childhood Disability, Advocacy, and Inclusion in the Caribbean*, Palgrave Studies in Disability and International Development, https://doi.org/10.1007/978-3-030-23858-2_5

A COMPLEX PARADISE

The title of this chapter suggests an ironic view of this island paradise, known for its calypso music, pre-Lenten Carnival, and light-hearted personal style. The fluidity of the culture is reflected in the ethnic mixture of the population which has, for many years, been officially estimated as approximately 45% of African descent, 45% Indian descent, and 10% other, which includes people of French, Portuguese, or other European, Middle-Eastern (colloquially referred to as "Syrian"), and Chinese origins. The reality is, however, that many people in these categories also represent racial/ethnic mixtures across any or all of the groups in an on-going process of "creolization", which Caribbean literature scholar, Paula Morgan (2014) has described as yielding "multifarious prolific and creative intersections [and] ethnic signifiers" (p. 51). The society prides itself on this unique version of diversity.

The "Trini" casual, humorous approach to serious topics is a popular stereotype across Caribbean cultures. "Trinis" are known for a unique style of social teasing and joking, referred to as "picong" or "fatigue". This is famously reflected in the lyrics of the annual calypsos, in which the calypsonian deftly weaves pointed, often risqué caricatures of prominent personalities and current events. Thus, the calypsonian attempts to cloak his/her critique in a humorous vein that softens the potential offense to listeners.

Calypso also includes serious satire, and the title of this chapter is taken from a calypso first performed in 1975 by Brother Valentino, at that time a young man with dread-locks whose serious facial expression and minor-key compositions provoked a feeling of deep unease that contradicted the light-heartedness of the culture. As observed by calypso scholar, Gordon Rohlehr (1990), Valentino's use of the "potentially melancholic quality" (p. 84) of the minor key, and the words of the calypso's opening verse point to the pains behind the "Carnival mentality" of the culture. The subsequent verses go on to provide an intense critique of the island's colonial history and the continuing influence of a powerful minority supported by "oppressors and foreign investors". Brother Valentino's concern is so great that he anticipates a possible "revolution" as he sings in a prophetic tone, "change is on the way". I will quote here an excerpt from the first verse and the ironic chorus of the song, which juxtaposed the voices of female back-up singers repeating the vision of an island paradise, while Valentino spells out his concerns about the lack of serious "consciousness" in the culture:

Trinidad is nice, Trinidad is a paradise
You talk 'bout a place

Where the people are carefree living
It is such a place
Of fun loving, spreeing and feting
Tis the land where people...
Have a Carnival mentality
They are not serious, very few conscious
So I cannot agree with my own chorus
Trinidad is nice, Trinidad is a paradise

Valentino's critical view of the society was reflected in many of the situations described by parents from the 1980s and 2015 alike. Yet, perhaps typical of the generosity and possibly fatalism of Trinidad/Tobago culture, most parents told their stories without rancor. Moreover, they often juxtaposed the positive with the negative, on a spectrum that ranged from descriptions of the society as "not nice!" to a place where there is "so much love".

NAVIGATING NEGATIVITY

Earlier chapters outlined the initial reactions of shock and confusion experienced by both groups of parents as they began their unexpected personal journeys. Compounding these challenges, and not unlike many other societies in both developed and developing economies, was a general ethos of negativity and superstition on issues of disability. The gap of some 30 years between the times of those experiences did not make much difference in the societal attitudes the two groups faced. Despite these challenges, parents presented a buoyancy and resilience that led them to focus on their children's strengths and the joys and rewards brought by their challenges. All the parents reported having deliberately taken a stance to challenge the common assumption of shame or embarrassment by insisting on bringing their children into the society, although with stringent protections for their physical and emotional safety.

Three key themes echoed across the span of decades of experience: *parents navigating the social/cultural context of the time, advocating and taking action,* and *ascribing meaning to children's lives.* The only notable difference between the stories of the 1980s and 2015 was that improvements in social and educational policies generated higher expectations which, unfortunately, were often not met. Echoing Jacqui Leotaud's caveat—"government helps, but...", these parents' concerns were expressed in the cry, "*we need systems!*"

Not Nice!

The theme of negative social attitudes was reflected in concerns about the ostracism that children with disabilities might experience, and in the dangers of possible abuse. Descriptions by Lydia, whose son, Tommy, was 38 years old at the time of this research, were typical of parents' views:

> *Lydia, Tommy's mother.* People would stare. Trinidadians can be so crass and so rude. So unmannerly. And the adults! I have stared down so many adults, and children, who kept staring at him or making snide remarks. I can't remember anybody asking [about him]. They just stared. And remember, at that time, these children were hidden. But Tommy was going everywhere. So he was one of the few who were seen in public.

Thirty years later, despite their own involvement in intensive advocacy as Tommy was growing up, this family still maintained a protective approach to Tommy's social independence. Tommy was then in a day program at the Lady Hochoy Home, which included social outings and activities that he enjoyed and that provided him with a place of belonging in the community. However, in discussing possibilities for accessing supported employment placements, while Lydia thought this would be a good idea, she expressed grave doubts about being able to trust people in public situations.

> *Lydia, Tommy's mother.* Trinidad is not a nice place. We're a very complicated people. People think we nice—but we not nice! We only *look* nice! The general population I don't trust. I don't think that we're civilized enough to see the person in disabled persons. As a parent I would be loath to put Tommy any and everywhere—in terms of his safety, his comfort, and my peace of mind. There could be sexual advantage taken. There could be abuse and he wouldn't be able to talk and tell us. I think we very quietly decided a long time ago, that we wouldn't make a fuss about employment.
>
> It breaks our heart. All the dreams we talked about in NADS (National Association for Down Syndrome) among us parents, where we wanted to go, what we wanted to see happen, what could happen right here in Trinidad. A lot of it hasn't come about at all.

Several parents told stories that echoed Lydia's description of "crass" and "rude" comments, usually focusing on the child's appearance. For example, both Michael and Shekina had facial features that indicated some medical anomaly:

Alberta, Michael's mother. They would say, "What's wrong with your child?" My own family would say, "You're so nice and look at the kind of child you make!" That is so upsetting! It's really sad that they look at children like that.

Cheryl, Shekina's mother. When I'm out with her in public the children stare. They're not taught that these are children too, to appreciate and love. They are either afraid or it's still a stigma in our culture. Corporate Trinidad has opened up a bit. Buildings are now being built with ramps. Massey Stores will hire people with disabilities to do menial jobs. But so much more must be done to integrate persons with disabilities.

In addition to physical features, it seemed that socially unusual or unacceptable behaviors provoked particularly negative responses. Sharmain, Sarah's grandmother, described unkind treatment in public because of Sarah's behavior. For example:

Sharmain, Sarah's grandmother. Sarah does not like crowds or elevators. She reacts badly. She will start screaming, pulling, biting, pushing. So whenever I'm taking her out, I say, "Sarah, we're going to the mall. Sarah we're going to Granny's house" and so on. People don't ask questions, but they look at her. "That child has no behaviour! That child ..." They do not understand. At Christmas time if I take the children to the mall and the store owners realise Sarah is a special child, they close the door of the store. I explain. "Okay, she's a special child. I'll be very careful around your things. I won't allow her to break anything." But they shut them out. I'm still learning how to deal with Sarah. It has opened my eyes.

Emil spoke of negative public attitudes toward her son, Darren, who has autism:

Emil, Darren's mother. My son, I take him all about. It took some people a long time to accept the fact that, as a person with a disability, he is out in public. He has gestures, and the first time I was with him going to and from school on the bus or taxi, there were a lot of adults who were so ignorant. It's not the children—but the adults who would stand up and laugh. But, I will admit that before I had Darren, I had never really paid much attention to people who have disabilities.

Emil's admission that part of the problem was simply lack of familiarity with disabilities was echoed by several parents. Candace's parents, Rupert and Margaret, described it this way:

Rupert. I look at Trinidadians as a kind of frivolous, easy going type of people. And we may not pay the same type of attention to less fortunate people as we do to those who can be in the mainstream of life. There is a lot of ignorance. And the ignorance has led to non-acceptance. When we lived in St. Augustine we used to take Candace to the market every Saturday and she used to enjoy being out. One day a lady said "Why you bring this child here? This is not the place for this child!" I said to her, "Who knows whether you have a grandchild at home and you're afraid to take her out." After that, she tried to put twenty five cents in Candace's hand.

Selris: "Deaf and dumb". Selris James, despite a dual disability of deaf/blindness, nevertheless had enough vision to use his artistic talent to relate his experiences. Using a comic-strip format, Selris drew pictures of some of the hardships he endured growing up in poverty in a society where someone with his disability is still described as "deaf and dumb". Despite having the benefit of a close and loving family, Selris' pictures tell the tale of being taken advantage of, even physically abused by people in his neighborhood. Below are two of these narratives, the first, showing him working all day for minimal pay (Fig. 5.1), and the second showing a young man throwing a beer bottle at him because he was looking at the man's girlfriend (Fig. 5.2). His sketches tell his story in a more emotive manner than could be evoked by words.

Positive Trends

Despite these negative experiences, there were some positive trends. Most notable were reports of improved social attitudes in the narratives of parents of four children with Down Syndrome, as compared with those whose children had other equally visible, but less well-known conditions. Parents attributed the positive vibes they received partly to a better understanding of Down Syndrome, which had received considerable public prominence over the years, but also to the children's friendly nature, physical appearance, or appropriate socialization in public.

One particularly positive story of social attitudes, past and present, came from Helen and John Humphrey, whose granddaughter, Becky, was born with Down Syndrome in 1993, at a time when the condition was still generally reviled. As well-known political and social figures, this family enjoyed a high-profile reputation that seemed to enhance their decision to "go public" with Becky's Down Syndrome.

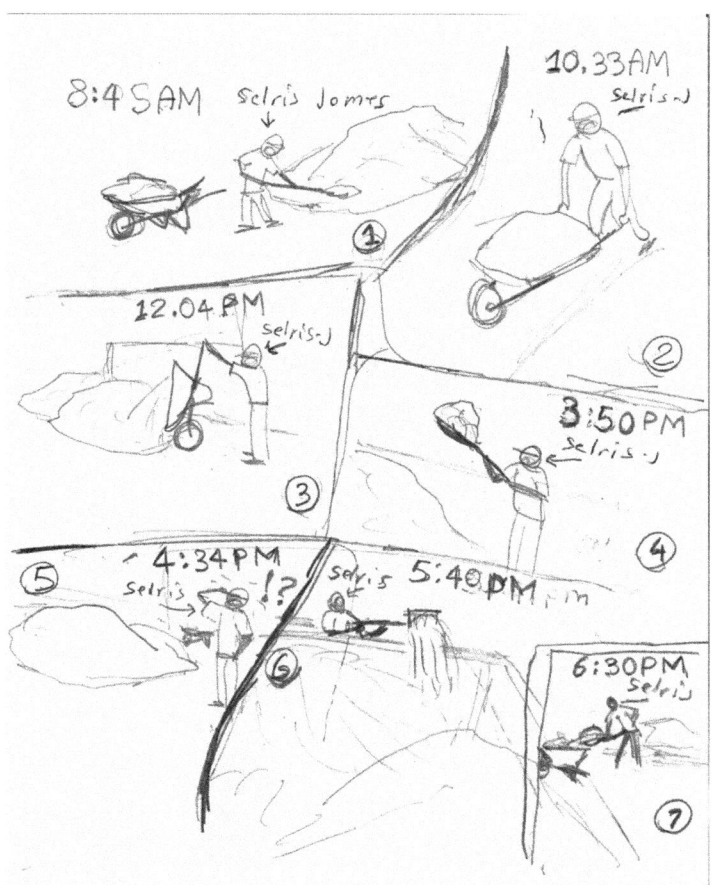

Fig. 5.1 Selris James at work, circa 2007

Helen, Becky's grandmother: Even in those days we took her everywhere. At that time, parents hid their children. Why? So we used to dress Becky up as cute as ever and take her everywhere with us. There were very few negative reactions. One woman came to me one day and asked, "you're sure it's not contagious"? That's to tell you how uneducated people were. She didn't mean any harm. But most people were excited that we were bringing this baby with us everywhere. Becky was always in the newspapers. We had all these fundraisers so she was always in the public eye—Carnival, Special Olympics, everything.

Fig. 5.2 Selris James under attack, circa 2007

Fig. 5.3 Lisa de Gannes as bridesmaid at her sister's wedding, with her parents Lana and Martin, and the bride and groom, Amanda and Kerry

Recently I went to a seminar with Glen Niles, Leader of the Down Syndrome Family Network. The younger parents wanted to interview those of us that had children from the early times for us to tell them about it. One woman said, "Mrs. Humphrey, I want to let you know that so many mothers seeing you taking Becky out, gave us the courage to take our children out!" I cried!

Lana de Gannes, whose daughter, Lisa (Fig. 5.3) had attended Immortelle from the early 1990s, spoke of more mixed experiences, but noted a gradual improvement:

Lana, Lisa's mother: "I think it's improving—more awareness, acceptance." Thirty one years ago it was very difficult; and I suppose thirty one years prior to that it would have been even worse. I found at that time people told you to hide these children. Keep them away from the general people. We chose not to do that. As parents we decided, "No! This is our child!" Lisa has a bigger sister and a younger brother and she's one of ten cousins so she's always made to be a part of the family—never excluded from anything. Even as a child, we would go to a restaurant and her table manners were very

good. We'd see people looking at us and waiting to see what mess she's
going to make. Hello! She would correct you! Elbows off the table, cross
your knife and fork!

Among the parents of younger children with Down Syndrome, there
was a common theme of family inclusion, which also noted positive, even
caring responses from strangers in public settings:

> *Renata, Daniel's mother: "God didn't give Daniel to us for us to leave him at
> home."* We go everywhere with him and people do not treat him funny. If
> we get invited somewhere and Daniel is not invited, we don't go. We move
> as a family or we don't move at all. He's so friendly. He would shake your
> hand and hug you. And I guess his physical appearance too. He's cute! Of
> course, that should not play a part, but I guess a lot of people don't realise
> anything is wrong with him.
> *Allison, Christopher's mother. "Wherever we go, he goes—the cinema, dinner,
> the mall."* He's very well behaved. I've never had the problem of him mis-
> behaving in public. I never got any negative feelings from the public about
> him. Strangers would look at him but a lot of them would show kindness
> toward him. He's warm and loving. We would take public transport and he
> would always acknowledge the person sitting next to him. He might smile
> or caress them on the hand. People would know by looking at him that he
> has Down Syndrome. It is visible, but some people say they can't see it
> because he has a Chinese look anyway.

Beyond the group of children with Down Syndrome, the importance of
appropriate socialization seemed to be the common denominator for positive public reactions to children's disabilities. Typical of this view was the
statement of Mumtaz and Rita, whose son Khayam, had mild features of
cerebral palsy and intellectual delay. For them, Khayam's personality and
social behavior were the key component of the treatment he received in
social settings: "Everyone took a liking to him because he was very
sociable".

Adapting and Taking Action: Avenues of Advocacy

Against a background of negativity, parents must often create their own
paths to improving the situations for their children. Literature on the
development of services for children with disabilities points consistently to
the central role of parental advocacy in countries as disparate as India (Sen,

Goldbart, & Kaul, 2008) and the US (Turnbull, Turnbull, Erwin, Soodak, & Shogren, 2015). Citing Samuel Kirk, a foundational scholar in special education in the US, Turnbull and colleagues highlighted the impact of parent advocacy on the creation and implementation of the legal mandate for education for all children with disabilities. In giving credit for the advancements that have been made in the education of exceptional children, Kirk stated, "I would place the parent organizations and parent movement in the forefront as the leading force" (Kirk, 1984, p. 41, as cited in Turnbull et al., 2015).

The influence of parents in that movement resulted in legal requirements not only for educational services to children with disabilities but also for the engagement of parents in educational decision-making for those children. As Colin Ong-Dean (2009) pointed out, the main role of parents of children with disabilities in the US became one of participating in school-based processes to ensure that children receive appropriate services.

In this study, parents' advocacy continued to be at the level of initiation and pursuit of services, since there was no legal mandate for such services. In this chapter, I will highlight parental advocacy on a personal level by parents at Immortelle; in a later chapter, I will provide a broader view of advocacy as a public movement.

Across both groups of parents, their narratives indicated a range of types of advocacy that made a difference in large and small ways. There were several kinds of advocacy: personal confrontations or sacrifices like Cheryl's and Diane and Dane's to gain medical services for their children; continuous, everyday advocacy without which children's needs could not be met; advocacy that broke social barriers to children's opportunities; and advocacy that literally created a public voice previously unheard or muted.

Everyday Advocacy

The "everyday" advocacy in which parents engaged included a range of changes to their work and living situations. Some offered their services voluntarily to Immortelle, such as Emil offering dance classes for the students and trying to organize a transportation support system for families, which would include parents volunteering to stay with children until their parents could come for them. Sharmain quit her job and started a small business out of her home. Allyson quit her job and stayed home to prepare her son for school. Marie and several other parents gave examples of their own quiet advocacy for their children, often on a one-to-one basis in trying to educate individuals in public. An in-depth view of one mother, Glenda, represents how the taken-for-granted work of parents is also advocacy.

Glenda, Candy's mother: From "something not right here" to "she's wonderful!" This theme in the study was generated by Glenda's words in her interview, which were echoed in various ways by both groups of parents. She expressed great joy in her daughter's development over the years, but her story of advocacy did not become fully clear to me until I went to visit her at home almost two years later. I knew that Glenda's journey as a parent had been one of energetic agency, from the early days of receiving unsatisfying, incomplete diagnoses of Candy's hearing, vision, and intellectual challenges. Like most parents in the study, finding and pursuing appropriate services for her daughter was the essence of her long-term advocacy.

In 2017, in writing the first draft of the book, I reached out to all interviewees to seek their consent to use direct quotations from interviews. Glenda readily agreed to meet me and gave me detailed directions to her home, as Candy was no longer a student at Immortelle. Following her directions, I took a winding, uphill road through a neighborhood on the hillside that was quite unknown to me and that friends later told me was known to be an unsafe area. I, however, did not feel unsafe and, upon arriving at the corner Glenda had specified, I almost missed the house, which, like many houses along the way, was built into the hillside. Glenda came out to meet me and escorted me up the slanting steps at the side of the building and into her impeccably kept home. As we sat side by side on the couch, Glenda reviewed the quotations I had brought for her and looked at me with a smile, saying:

> *Glenda.* You know, when you called me saying you wanted to bring some quotes to show me, I couldn't remember what we had talked about in that interview. But now I see it all here—yes—that's exactly how it was. And you know you can see right here all the things I told you about that Candy does here at home. She's really wonderful!

Glenda had recently retired and had decided that Candy, then 40 years old, was so self-sufficient and such a good homemaker that there was no need for her to go to school any more. Nor was there any reason for her to go out to work; rather, she and her mother would enjoy their "retirement" together. They had celebrated the start of this period with a vacation in Tobago.

Marveling at the distance that this trip had taken me from the main road, I asked Glenda how she and Candy had traveled to Immortelle Centre for all those years. "Three taxis", she said, "One from here to the Main road, one into town, and one up to St. Ann's." If they set out at the right time, the trip would take them about an hour and a half each way. Although Candy had, on occasion, taken a taxi by herself for short trips, there was no way her mother would have considered it safe for her attempt this journey, so it was always a trip for two.

Jacqui, Raquel's mother: If I didn't keep taking her, then people would feel she shouldn't be invited. Another version of parental "everyday advocacy" was present in Jacqui's description of how she handled social attitudes during Raquel's early years. In her usual emphatic style, Jacqui shared the following stories:

> If somebody didn't treat Raquel properly, I couldn't stand them eh! It was difficult to be among people when she was young, but I was prepared to bite the bullet and go out with her, so people would get accustomed to her. Some people were very, very open to her. Some people were not. But if my friends had a party and other kids were at the party, it was difficult. Do you know how many cakes she put her hands in? But if I didn't keep taking her, then people would feel she shouldn't be invited. So I always made it clear that she was part of my family. She was one of my children. If you wanted any of them, you have all.
>
> Sometimes I wondered if it was fair to Michelle and Giselle, but I decided if it's unfair, I'll be unfair! I remember someone having a party for one of her kids and she only invited Michelle and Giselle. I was in a rage! I called my mother and vented, and she said "Jacqui, maybe she can't cope". I said, "If she can't cope, she not coping with any of the Leotauds!" Mummy said that wasn't fair to Michelle and Giselle, and I said, "I'm going to have to be horrible but I am making a stand here". So my children didn't go. The lady called and apologized and I told her next time she should come upfront and say it. I am touchy about it and emotional. I pretend I'm not, but there are some things that are very hurtful.

Breaking-Barriers Advocacy

Two parents engaged in advocacy that broke established social/educational barriers as their children made the journey to full inclusion. The children, Andrew and David, both had the unique experience of being enrolled in prestigious high schools in Trinidad and Tobago. As a brilliant teenager with autism, David's high school experience at Queen's Royal College (QRC) was not particularly successful, partly because of the poor fit between the school's traditional ethos and his social demeanor and learning style, and partly because of the teachers' lack of understanding.

Andrew, despite his more evident disability, had not only outstanding intellect but also excellent social preparation and personality for an inclusive setting. His parents, Carole and David, effectively broke an unspoken barrier at Fatima College when Andrew became the first student with cerebral palsy ever to be enrolled. Both Andrew and his parents, toughened by years of other people's misunderstandings of the meaning of his cerebral palsy, learned to weather the storms of stigma that he faced in his pursuit of a normal life.

To prepare for a high school diploma, Andrew left Immortelle and went to the Princess Elizabeth Centre for the Physically Handicapped. This school prepared him for the entrance exam to high school, then on to Fatima College. Many years later, Andrew's family was able to send him to the International School for the Arts in Miami, where he completed a two-year Associates in Arts degree, living on campus with appropriate physical supports.

Creating-a-Public-Voice Advocacy

Most dramatic in terms of advocacy were those efforts that became lasting national movements. This kind of advocacy among the parents who participated in this study was surprisingly robust for such a small group. Among the original parents, the Pierre, de Gannes, and Humphrey families initiated the National Association for Down Syndrome (NADS) during the 1980s. Among the current families, Francis and Laura Escayg, Isaiah's parents, created two such efforts—Cause an Effect, a non-profit dedicated to using film media to create public awareness, and Caribbean Kids and Families Therapy Organization (CKFTO), an organization providing private therapy services.

Beyond the Immortelle families, other parents in the study included community advocates, such as Rosanna Trestrail, who established the Life Center serving children with autism, Teresina Seunarine, who initiated the Autistic Society of Trinidad/Tobago, and Glenn Niles, who initiated the Down Syndrome Family Network (DSFN). Unique among the stories of advocacy was that of Crystal Jones, the mother of a son with cerebral palsy, whose public shaming of the Minister of Health led to the formation of the Cerebral Palsy Association and of a self-help group by which parents could become self-supporting by creating and selling a range of products. I will save detailed accounts of these efforts for Chap. 8, in which several community advocates tell their stories.

"She's Wonderful!" Finding Meaning and Creating Purpose

In addition to parents' visible and public efforts to counter the absence of societal supports, there is also the invisible question of how parents make their peace with the pain of seeing their children suffer physically or emotionally, and with their own disappointment at not having the healthy child they dreamed of. In stark contrast to the general context of negativity and the images of loss and despair that some professionals evoked when pronouncing prognoses for the children, all the parents echoed Glenda's exclamation of, "She's wonderful!"

"This Is the Same Child You Sat and Waited on for Nine Months"

Carole, Andrew's mother, explained the tremendous impact professional pronouncements could have on parents' view of their child. For her, the question was how to develop a realistic grasp of the child's needs while never forgetting his/her value as an individual.

> *Carole.* When this child is diagnosed with a problem, whatever it may be, this is the same child that you sat and waited on for nine months, just like everybody else. You've got to remember that and not listen to what you're being told. Because the child then is defined by what is wrong with the child and that introduces a lot of negativity.
>
> For example, after we went to United Cerebral Palsy for the first time, Andrew was about five or six years old. The doctor examined him and said, "Mrs. Fitt, I think you need to buy a wheel chair for Andrew. I'm a doctor in the field of Cerebral Palsy and I am going to tell you that Andrew will never walk". I said, "I don't agree with you." And, of course, Andrew did walk!
>
> On the other hand, as happened to us at one point, you might get desperate for a positive diagnosis. I remember we heard about a doctor in Puerto Rico and so we went off to Puerto Rico. We sat there waiting for three hours to see this doctor. Finally we saw him and he examined Andrew and said "Don't worry about what the other doctors tell you. By the time

he's nine years old he'll be running and playing football!" Of course, I held on to that! We left there and I thought—this man is brilliant! We've been going to quacks! That's one of the first times David and I ever totally disagreed on something. I was hearing what I wanted to hear but he was hearing what he knew was not the truth! And of course it turned out to be absolutely false. I had enough time with the help of David over the years to move forward with what I was told, trying to make it a reality. Trying to assist Andrew to be the best he could be with his cerebral palsy.

God's Grace as the Source, the Support, and the Solution

Across the board in this sample of parents, faith was at the center. For some parents, like Renata, the role of faith was in the foreground of their narratives, while for others it appeared as more of an assumption, though always explicitly stated at some point in the interview. Several parents described positive social experiences to which they ascribed spiritual meaning. These meanings reflected a sense of gratitude that their children's lives had served to touch another human heart, or to educate and inspire someone who had not previously given thought to disabilities. The following statements typify this belief:

> *Lydia, Tommy's mother: "We always said we knew there was a reason Tommy was born."* Eventually we came around to realizing that Tommy was born so that we could do the work we did for Down Syndrome and disability. He was able to inspire it. He was the motivator. It was inspirational for other parents to see him because he was so lively and personable.
> *Lana, Lisa's mother: "Little do you know you're giving someone encouragement. If I did that, thank you dear Jesus!"* I think that, through NADS, we did something! Hopefully somebody will benefit. And people have, although you don't always know it. But people obviously observe you, and you get a call here or there; someone might say, "Lana, you're an inspiration to me". I say, "I'm just going about my own business". "No, the way you are with Lisa and how you're managing with everything!"
> *Dane, Daniel's father: "This is real inspiration here".* After the first gig, when Daniel performed on the pan, a buddy of ours took Daniel and me where people organizing the military Tattoo could see Daniel perform. I carried a recorder with the song and set it up in a corridor in somebody's office. A police officer in plain clothes started taking pictures and was crying. He said he deals with people in all kinds of places and doing all sorts of things but saying—this is real inspiration here.

Rupert, Candace's father: "If that is the reason why Candace is living, so be it." Once, I was in a public place with Candace and there was this young man who was looking at me. He looked at how I dealt with Candace. He came over and he said to me, almost in tears, "You have taught me to go home and look after my little children." I said, "If that is the reason why Candace is living, so be it."

Margaret, Candace's mother. "I am sure that God, in His high heaven, took note of the interaction." We sit in the last row of the hall where our Church meets. Rupert sits on the end and Candace is in her wheelchair close to him to his left, slanting towards the row of seats in front of us. There was an older man who sat in front of her for years and Candace was always stroking his head with her hand and he told us to just let her be. He eventually passed away, so then she would stroke the head of Annette, the lady who sits there now. Then, one day, Annette was not at church and another young woman, Juliet, who normally sits in front of me, was sitting in that end seat when Candace reached out her hand. When Candace reached forward and touched Juliet's head, she smiled. Juliet responded and stroked Candace's hand in return. Candace just remained with a pleased look on her face. It was obvious from her expression that she knew it was not a familiar touch, but she appreciated Juliet's stroking her hand in response. Juliet told me that she felt the connection and she knew that Candace was at ease. I am sure that God, in His high heaven, took note of the interaction.

In addition to these social experiences were religious interpretations of how a powerful faith provided solutions to challenges, or the strength to go on in the face of intense adversity. The belief that God was in charge was a central theme. For example, Renata, Daniel's mother, saw this as extending even to the provision of an excellent teacher, like Monica, and of Immortelle itself:

Renata, Daniel's mother: "God worked that out." Daniel went straight into Monica's class. God worked that out. Monica is the best teacher I have ever met in my life. For someone who has never had children of her own, I tell her all the time that the reason she had no children is because God had a purpose for her. The Immortelle children are her children. I honestly believe that Immortelle has something extremely special. Jacqui being the mother of a special needs child—God gave her her daughter because He had a plan for these children in this school. This school would not be what it is today if Jacqui didn't have her daughter. She lives it, and that's why this school is how it is.

Robert, Dimitri's father: "Through the power of prayer, he survived." Dr. Bratt said we should try and prepare ourselves that it was a 50/50 chance for Dimitri to survive. But through the power of prayer, he did. We hope that Dimitri has a comfortable life for whatever span God allows him. That's all we have ever asked for. Thank God Dimitri has developed. He works well with the other children and gets along with them. The teachers like him. He helps with things. So through our faith, our trust in God and our prayers, God has extended Dimitri's life.

Diane, Daniel's mother: "The experience in all of that was God." Daniel was a baby, we had to get a passport, my husband had to get a work permit, we had to go to the embassy—and you know how they give trouble! Everything worked out so fast. It had to be God.

Cheryl, Shekina's mother: "God has given her grace to endure." So there have been all kinds of very, very severe challenges. But by the grace of God Shekina has been very good. Smiling, happy. God has given her grace to endure.

Mumtaz and Rita. In Chap. 3, I reported the experiences of the Ali family, whose son, Khayam, was a great source of joy to the family until his unexpected illness and death at the age of 36. His father's description of this loss echoed the theme of religious meaning but with a different twist, as the Ali's were the only Muslim family among the group of original parents. In the quote below, Mumtaz described his feelings at the time of Khayam's death and since.

Mumtaz, Khayam's father: "As a parent you have to decide that this is God's gift." I knew my son was dying so I tried to get things in place and there was a song I wanted to be sung at his funeral. I felt that would comfort me to share with the people who were there how I feel about my son. It's in Hindustani. The words tell of a farmer's legacy to his son. The farmer is saying you will take my name to the stars, and that kind of thing. But the Imam did not think the song appropriate because it was in Hindi not Arabic. Which I find is so stupid! Why should something have to be in Arabic? Why couldn't it be in French or Greek or whatever? I didn't want to be controversial but my annoyance still resides within me.

Now, every night when I'm going to bed—I look down the corridor, and wish I could see Khayam peeping out as he would do in those days. I don't know if the experience will make me stronger or weaker but it was something inevitable, and I hope I could see only the love that emanates from it. It has been an experience that perhaps I have been richer for having gone through. So indelible has it been that I cannot leave the house without going to his room and virtually talking with him. When I'm working or in my study he would sit here or there. Then after a while he would say, "Dad, it's time for me to go".

Testing Faith

While some parents hinted at temporary struggles to keep their faith in the face of their child's disability, Francis, Isaiah's father, described a severe internal struggle that tested his faith. I will quote extensively from his story as he speaks of his wife's initial practical response and his own hidden struggle.

Francis, Isaiah's father. My wife, Laura, went and she formed CKFTO—Caribbean Kids and Families Therapy Organization—an organization that gives occupational therapy to children with disabilities. They're now a full-fledged clinic. She was the chair of the board. And she and an Occupational Therapist, Sara Stephens, who was a visiting therapist from the U.S., started the organization. In the first three years she and Laura gave Isaiah all his therapy.

I was just being the strong guy—"Don't worry—everything will work out!" But I was bottling up a lot of anger and this affected me for a few years. I was angry at God. Because when I looked down the road I realised that I would have to deal with this for the rest of my life. That was upsetting to me and it just threw my life off.

I'm a film maker and a published author. For my first feature I got $1.3 mil from TV6. At the same time, McMillan Publishers released my book and I was just about to go on tour marketing the film and the book when Laura basically lost it. She couldn't go any further. She was burnt out from dealing with Isaiah for these three years. I just had to stop and jump in to help him. That made me even more angry, because I was doing all these things with the hope that we could keep moving forward.

So I had to jump in, and in dealing with Isaiah I had to learn quite a few lessons. I realised that I was going at a pace and I had to slow down, even go into slow motion mode to deal with Isaiah and try to understand what was wrong with him. A friend who is a yoga instructor taught me to do some deep breathing relaxation sessions with her. This is when I realised how angry I was. For years I had recurring nightmares of lions snarling and I knew that it was Isaiah in the middle there.

I walked into the church one day and cried out to God and asked him what was going on. I was in a battle with the TV company and all the actors were calling me about the film. I was angry that my work was falling through. I was angry at having to leave all of this to deal with Isaiah. I was angry with my wife. I was angry with everybody. And I cried out, "God, I just cannot carry this. Help me!" I'm telling you just as I saw it. Two angels came and looked at me and I saw concern in their eyes. They came and tapped me on my shoulder twice. I started seeing everybody in the church as if their skin was stripped. I was seeing their sinews, muscles. I was seeing their torment and agony. I was able to see that everybody else was having some kind of problem and that I was not unique.

I walked out of that church feeling light. I couldn't wait to go home and tell my wife what I had just experienced. And that started a journey of self-realization. I had been on a fast track, not in touch with what was really going on and I had to stop and deal with everybody and everything.

You would not believe that was the last day the phone rang with problems! Everybody stopped calling. I had the opportunity to go out there in peace and try to solve the problem with the TV company, and I got the time to do that. After that the film went into the festival and won awards. And since then I have been even closer with Isaiah.

Moving forward, Francis was developing a vision of a unique kind of advocacy based on entrepreneurial efforts rather than service provision. Placing his hope in his own entrepreneurial drive and professional skills, Francis envisioned using his media company to engage in an on-going campaign of consciousness-raising regarding disabilities and to provide a productive working and living space in which individuals with disabilities could produce agricultural products that could be marketed to the larger society.

Visions of the Future: What Will Happen When I Die?

For all the parents, the main hope was for their children to attain as much personal independence and adequate socialization skills as possible. For many of the current group, a major concern was for an educational and vocational curriculum that would provide opportunities for some amount of independence and/or income for their adult children. All supported the idea of Immortelle's "cookie project" and hoped that the products could be marketed to large outlets like the Massey stores. Some parents, however, felt that the cookie project alone was not enough and wished for more expansive, more diversified vocational opportunities.

Above all, though, was the haunting fear for their children's safety after the parents' death. All expressed fears of abuse in an institutional setting and most expressed either confidence or hope that family members would take full responsibility (Fig. 5.3). Two families stated this view with great confidence:

Lana, Lisa's mother. No! I will not put Lisa in that! No, no, no! Lisa will live at home. When we are no longer here, her sister and her younger brother are fully aware—"She is your responsibility! It not this one of you, then that one. However you'll work it out but *you all* are responsible for Lisa". They are both married. They have their own families and their respective spouses. There is no choice in the matter! If you like my son or my daughter, it's a package you're getting. Accept it or make your decision before you get started. And they both accepted it and they get along well. Whatever they have to do, it will be done. Thank God for that!

Robert, Dimitri's father. We know that we will have to cater for Dimitri for the rest of his life and we have told the other children that when we pass, they must take care of him because we do not want him going into a home. We are setting aside funds for him. Whatever assets we have will go to our children. "We are giving you our assets, whatever property we have, but you must take care of Dimitri." That's our condition. That is our will. We have brought up our children in our faith. Thank God for that!

Of the total of 22 parents across the two groups, only 2 expressed an explicit hope that institutional residential care could become available. Nerissa (pseudonym) stated that she felt there should be a range of options, since family support could not be guaranteed. In discussing the possibility of an assisted living facility, she put the matter plainly:

Nerissa, Norman's mother. I'm 43. If something, God forbid, should happen to me in my 50's, my mom is not around. What happens to my son? As a mother, a parent, you make a will and put things in order, but you could make a will and say I want John or Mary to see about Nathaniel but if they respond no, what happens then? Or, they may say yes at the beginning, but when reality requires you to put a signature on a will—not everyone will want that responsibility. It is hard. We must have options! Like there are senior citizens' homes—we need a facility like that for our disabled children Whether we get help from private sources, or from the government, or even as parents ourselves to come together.

Improving Public Awareness

All the parents lamented the lack of public awareness of disabilities. A frequent suggestion was that the government should support the use of public media to address this concern.

Allison and Renata felt that, although public awareness of Down Syndrome had improved, there was still a long way to go in people's active support of the cause. They also saw this issue as indicating insufficient support from families of the children themselves. For example:

> *Renata, Daniel's mother.* We have the DSFN—Down Syndrome Family Network—which Glen Niles started. So we have the Down Syndrome walk, every October when it's Down Syndrome day around the world. And we have workshops every three months. But even the Down Syndrome walk in October might get 30 seconds on the news; it just might—if at all! It's by the way! The parents of the same kids show up at Special Olympics. Brent and I and half the family were there. We spent the entire day with Daniel but we were the exception to the rule. There's no advertisement on television, nothing on the radio or newspaper. Maybe 30 seconds on the news again. And the government doesn't see it as a priority to give it funding. So everything we do we're scraping for pennies.

Likewise, Nerissa, whose son, Norman, also had Down Syndrome, was very vocal in her expression of dissatisfaction with public awareness and public policy. She also emphasized that the lack of funding made even the best intentioned advocacy efforts inaccessible for many parents.

> *Nerissa, Norman's mother.* Before I got the grant, or entrance to the school, I asked, "How do we get grants? How do we get our children into schools?" Lots of parents don't want or can't get their children in Lady Hochoy or Princess Elizabeth. So I'm looking through the yellow pages, the newspapers to see how, if I have a special needs child, how do we get our children into other schools, any programs, any assistance? No information. We need workshops in Trinidad. We lack that. For all parents of special needs, not just Down Syndrome.
>
>   We need programs before news, during prime time. From 6:00 to 7:00 that is a prime time—even if it's half hour, say six thirty—when people know for a fact that news is going to come. In between, educate the public, and inform them this is what it is—so that people can become aware. If we could come together as parents of all disabilities and form a team and have a spokesperson, one spokesperson that can go to the government—the Ministry of Social Development.

Government Helps, But...

Current parents in the study echoed the theme, "*government helps, but...*", which was expressed strongly by Jacqui in Chap. 5 and, more implicitly, by the group of "original" parents. For the group of current parents, however, the level of frustration seemed greater, if only because, in these times, parents knew that their children were entitled to certain benefits and had greater expectations of more expansive services that they felt ought to be available. Awareness of the lack of services or the inadequacy of policy implementation was foremost in these parents' descriptions of the challenges they faced. They identified numerous components of services that were missing, including efficient medical and therapeutic support, transportation, and two overarching concerns—systematic availability of government grants to which families were entitled and the lack of a mandate for the provision of education to children with disabilities. In Chaps. 8 and 9, I will use the voices of community stakeholders to detail the basic issues with the first three components and will focus here on the last two.

How do we get grants? Nerissa's complaint about the difficulties in accessing grants represented a particularly sore point. There are two kinds of government grants related to disabilities: first, the provision of grants for families of children under age 18 and, second, individual grants to adults upon attainment of that age.

Generally, the grant for adults at age 18 seemed to work reasonably well, although even this was by no means a smooth process. For the family grants, however, there was an inexplicable level of confusion regarding eligibility. Although I was assured by Michael Reid, a senior official in the Ministry of Social Development that the only criterion for eligibility was a medical examiner's proof of the child's disability, and although the website for Social Services included no reference to an income criterion, parents told a different story.

One issue seemed to be the bureaucratic structures for implementation. Worse, was individual mean-spiritedness exercised by public servants responsible for making decisions about eligibility for disability grants. These episodes highlighted the abuse of power exhibited by some individuals who seemed to hold a negative view of individuals with disabilities. In some cases, parents themselves were unclear as to what their children were really entitled to and, when faced with arbitrary and unfair decisions, many retreated, feeling helpless. Moreover, the power of "contacts" and "status" were evident in many of the descriptions of who did or did not receive benefits to which they were entitled.

Several parents reported having their applications rejected because the family did not meet a supposed financial need criterion for eligibility. Some parents reported that they were only able to access the grant through the assistance of a "contact" who had some clout in the public service:

> *Cheryl, Shekina's mother.* I was able to access the disability grant for Shekina from age 18. Although it doesn't depend on the parent's income once she's 18, we were still fortunate to get it because of her being managed by social workers in Mt. Hope. They had their contact with the branch in Tunapuna. It is through their communication she was able to get through. But the average person on the street, they don't get it easy. And these are people who really, very much need it.

Alberta, Michael's mother, told an equally distressing tale of the arbitrary nature of the process and the dependence on the whim of personnel in the government service.

> *Alberta, Michael's mother.* There's a disability benefit, but I don't get it. When I was staying in Port of Spain I was working for a family and when social services came and saw the house, they said I'm not qualified. But the house was not mine! I was working there and living there too. The family had their grandmother and I was taking care of her. I think the social service people looked at the environment and that's why they turned me down off the bat. She was just flat—"Not qualified. No you're not!" So I must wait until he's eighteen to get eligibility.

A year after my initial interview with Alberta, she reported that when she did apply for the adult disability benefit after Michael turned 18, she was finding the process very difficult. She was told she needed to go back to the hospital for all of Michael's records.

Nerissa's report indicated an equally arbitrary, even hostile, bureaucratic process which, in her case, took a rather unique turn. Certain of her rights, she showed the kind of persistence and self-assurance it took to pursue the application in the face of intense pressure and unconscionable manipulation of the grant eligibility process:

> *Nerissa, Norman's mother.* I got through with the grant for my son because God was at my side. I went in and explained my situation. They gave me a document with all the things I had to get and I went and got everything. The procedures are that you cannot go to a private doctor. Everything is

through the government. It's free. But you must go to the health office in the area where you're living and get a letter from Social Welfare. The doctor will assess the child, stamp the application, and then you must verify whether or not you are employed, and if you'll get any money from NIS (National Insurance). You have to go to NIS, sit and claim that you're not working presently, get a bank statement, and all these things. It's a lot to do, but you get a package, then you get a social worker to come to your home to assess.

If one lives in Woodbrook or St. Clair and you want assistance from the government, and they see that you're in a nice home and they assess that you don't need the support, then they will call you back and deny the application because of address and the nice home. Now, suppose I'm begging a lodging by my mother because of my special needs child! My mother has taken me in because she's helping me with my child. Social Welfare comes to my doorstep. They don't know about my situation, they go back and inform NIS that I am living in St. Clair. But I'm not! And, in fact, by law, each disabled child is due a grant and support from the government. But everything is backward!

In my case, they assessed the situation. I explained why I was in St. Clair living with my mother. Separated from my husband, I couldn't live on the street. I had to come here.

The case worker said he understood. I was then called by another officer who was reviewing the application. She asks: "Tell me about your son. What do you do? Which doctor does he see?" Then I was told that I had to submit proof that he was undergoing speech therapy. What she was saying made no sense! I told her, "You're saying that for me to receive money from the government I have to submit receipts verifying that I'm paying $500 to a therapist, so you all could see I'm paying something? I'm not working anywhere. Where am I getting $500 to pay a speech therapist to provide a receipt? How could you ask me a stupid question like that? I'm going through a divorce, my husband doesn't want to see about his son. If I have to come out and protest, I will! I have rights. My son has rights to obtain the grant. It is not ethical for you to call me and say this!"

She responded that I was right. She said she was also going through a divorce with children (not special needs). She gave me a month to come up with any sort of receipt. But I told her I decided to leave it right there. If the government would not help, I will protest. I left it at that.

A month after that, I received the cheque for Norman for $1700!

In a stunning contradiction to the oppressive experiences of the mothers above, Roberta told exactly the opposite story of accessing the disability grant for her adult child. Roberta features in this research as one of the few parents who was both an "original" and a "current" parent, as her daughter, Vivienne, then age 32, had been at Immortelle almost since its inception. Roberta and her husband, Patrick, hailed from the UK but, by virtue of over 40 years in Trinidad/Tobago, identified as true "Trinis". While living in a modest neighborhood, this couple nevertheless held considerable social status based both on their British origins and their educational and occupational status. Roberta was well aware of the irony of her situation, although it's also true that she was mistaken in thinking that eligibility was to be based on financial need. She described her receipt of Vivienne's disability grant as follows:

> *Roberta, Vivienne's mother.* When we were getting the disability grant for Vivienne, one of the things we had to do was get a letter from National Insurance to say she doesn't have an NIS number because it's means based— on the individual. It's a grant for an adult. She has no income of her own. As soon we took her in, before they tried to assess her or anything, they took one look at her and they didn't test the family means, which to my way of thinking they should have done. I feel a bit of a fraud claiming it. On the other hand, I'm supporting an adult and I don't get any tax relief for her. So I decided, you're not taking tax allowance, so I'll take the grant!

After all the errors, abuses, and complications that parents experienced in getting the disability grants, the final blow came when they found they had to repeat the application every year. Renata's account of this typified the frustration expressed by many parents:

> *Renata, Daniel's mother.* The government's way of assisting is through grants. Which takes two and three years, mind you, to obtain! And then, when you get it, every single year you go through this ritual as if the child is a new child all over again! Every year they want a letter from the school saying he's still in the school. So to get Daniel's disability grant, every year I must go in to the Ministry and apply, and tell them he's still Down Syndrome! Every year I tell them Down Syndrome is constant. It's not a sickness he will get better from. This is his life. This is who he is going to be. Why do I every year have to go through this? How could there be so much ignorance even on the State level!

Education Should Be Free for All!

Current parents in the study were sharply aware that their children's schooling continued to be an "add-on" to the education system. They realized that this had a negative impact not only on the availability of schools, but on the quality of teachers that could be employed, on teacher satisfaction, and, consequently, on the nature of the curriculum and instruction that would be afforded to children. Robert put the argument plainly:

> *Robert, Dimitri's father.* The government is not doing enough. I retired as a bank manager. When I consider the kind of taxes I paid—the kind of taxes that are still being paid, to think that the government is not funding these institutions. Because they fund the other schools that are run for normal children. So what is the difference? This is a school as well! It's just the students are different. Most of the parents who would send their children to these schools can't afford it. The main source of funding should come from the government. In my case we can support Dimitri. But what about those parents who can't?

REFERENCES

Gayle-Geddes, A. (2016). A situational analysis of persons with disabilities in Jamaica and Trinidad and Tobago: Education and employment policy imperatives. In P. Block, D. Kasnitz, A. Nishida, & N. Pollard (Eds.), *Occupying disability: Critical approaches to community, justice, and decolonizing disability* (pp. 127–144). New York: Springer.

Kirk, S. A. (1984). Introspection and prophecy. In B. Blatt & R. J. Morris (Eds.), *Perspectives in special education: Personal orientations* (pp. 24–55). Glenview, IL: Scott Foresman.

Morgan, P. (2014). *The terror and the time: Banal violence and trauma in Caribbean discourse.* Kingston, Jamaica: University of the West Indies press.

Ong-Dean, C. (2009). *Distinguishing disability: Parents, privilege, and special education.* Chicago: University of Chicago Press.

Rohlehr, G. (1990). *Calypso and society in pre-independence Trinidad.* Port of Spain, Trinidad: Gordon Rohlehr.

Sen, R., Goldbart, J, & Kaul, S. (2008). Growth of an NGO: The Indian Institute of Cerebral Palsy from 1974–2006. *Journal of Policy and Practice in Intellectual Disabilities, 5*(2), 105–111

Turnbull, A., Turnbull, R., Erwin, E., Soodak, L., & Shogren, K. (2015). *Families, professionals, and exceptionality: Positive outcomes through partnerships and trust* (7th ed.). Boston: Pearson.

CHAPTER 6

Sustaining the Immortelle: "You Have to Love What You Do"

The focus of this book so far has been on the history of the Immortelle Children's Centre and the parents and children it has served over a period of almost 40 years. However, the soul of the school lies with the teachers, whose hearts, minds, and hands create the spirit that is felt throughout the school. To capture the ambience that continues to inspire Immortelle, I would emphasize that the school reflects the spirit of joy that pervades this Caribbean nation.

Trini Joy at the Immortelle

The joyfulness of the culture that is Trinidad/Tobago is evident in the number of annual holidays recognized by the government. Obligatory holidays reflect both the multicultural nature of this society and a strong sense of pride in the nation's independence from colonial rule. Four key religions are officially recognized—Christianity, Islam, Hinduism, and more recently, the previously much maligned, African-based Spiritual Baptist religion. Each of these religions has designated holidays and there are also holidays commemorating historic moments in the nation's development, such as Emancipation Day (from slavery), Independence Day, and Indian Arrival Day, the latter commemorating the arrival of the first indentured laborers from India.

© The Author(s) 2020

B. Harry, *Childhood Disability, Advocacy, and Inclusion in the Caribbean*, Palgrave Studies in Disability and International Development, https://doi.org/10.1007/978-3-030-23858-2_6

While all these celebrations are honored by at least some groups in the community, there are two days that cut across the many groups and subgroups of this superbly diverse society. In February of every year, two essential days are set aside for what I can only call a celebration of life, the annual "Carnival". These two days immediately precede the Wednesday that marks the beginning of Lent—40 days before Easter Sunday. However, the "bacchanal" spirit of the Carnival seeps steadily into the society long before the actual Monday and Tuesday of the Carnival, and weeks, even months, are marked by private and public fetes and competitions for costumes, calypsos, and "Panorama", the much loved steel-band competition.

During this intense build-up toward the Carnival, many schools create opportunities for their students to engage in their own competitions or be treated to special Carnival performances. And so it was that, about two weeks before the Carnival, as I approached the peach-colored wall at the entrance to the narrow lane marked "St. Ann's Gardens" and turned into the school's large, gated entrance and paved driveway, I was greeted by the blaring sound of "soca" music coming from inside the building. Hurrying through the oval-shaped gate, under the scripted sign *Immortelle*, I recognized the calypso that came blasting from the large back patio:

They callin' me a hoo-li-gan! A hoo-li-gan! A hoo-li-gan!

And sure enough, there on the back porch, was the popular calypsonian, Ricardo Drue, performing his current hit song for the entire school of students. Big and small, verbal and non-verbal, on their feet, on the floor, or in wheelchairs—all were transformed into a sea of bobbing heads and waving arms, as they sang, shouted, or jumped along with the chorus. Drue, in shimmering black and gold, pranced across the front of the room, engaging eye-to-eye with the students, at times pulling individual members into the center to dance with him. All was joy, and, for the moment, everyone was "a hooligan, a hooligan, a hooligan"!

Two weeks after the hooligan performance, on the Friday before the Carnival, I had the further joy of participating in the students' costume parade and competition in the school's large backyard. Again, neither age nor disability could diminish the excitement of the day as students, transformed into gypsies, aristocrats, traditional dancers in flounced skirts and frilled blouses, robots, and insects, took turns showing off their costumes. With Jacqui's voice announcing the various "bands" and individuals over a loudspeaker, there were several winners and really no losers, as everyone received recognition for their costume. The king costume went to an unrecognizable robot, and the queen to a stunning Cleopatra.

No Hooligans Here!

In the regular, day-to-day existence of Immortelle, life went on as normal, with a climate of devotion to providing personalized education and socialization for the children and adults served by the school. Indeed, it is safe to say, there were no hooligans here!

Mixing traditional and modern lifestyles, social interactions in Trinidad/ Tobago are marked by a remarkable combination of casualness and formality. For example, traditional courtesies continue to include the following: obligatory greetings of "good morning" or "good afternoon"; an agreement that the sharing of meals is a social rather than an individual event; and the use of titles when addressing elders or persons of notable status in the community. Within these quite strict parameters, individual social interactions tend to be light-hearted and friendly, with an expectation that humor is always acceptable, even desirable.

One clear thread that ran throughout the school was an emphasis on maintaining these and other social norms of the society. There was only one exception to the usual norm—that all teachers at Immortelle were known to their students by their first names. Jacqui explained that this was a deliberate policy, since teachers' last names were usually more difficult to pronounce than the first names, and she did not want the students to revert to the easiest abbreviation of "Miss", which Caribbean children often use for their teachers. So, for example, Jacqui was "Jacqui" to all at Immortelle, students, parents, and visitors alike. For me, this informality added to the relaxed and friendly atmosphere of the school.

As Jacqui said in an earlier chapter, the school offered "a lot of stuff", constructed to meet the widely varying needs of a population that ranged from age 4 to 54 and from mild cognitive and communicative impairments to complicated neurological, intellectual, and/or physical anomalies. To give a rough idea of the range of diagnoses, I would say that in just about every classroom there would probably be two students with Down Syndrome, two who displayed autistic-like behaviors or communication, and two of unspecified or rare etiologies. Most students were ambulatory, except four who were wheelchair users.

With this incredibly diverse population, although curriculum planning included the development of IEPs (Individualized Education Plans) in which parents were required to participate, limitations in the number and the qualifications of the staff made consistent implementation of these plans very difficult. In this chapter, I will rely on teachers' descriptions and my own observations to represent the main strengths and challenges of this ambitious educational program.

Upstairs and Downstairs

The two-story colonial style building with its long hallways and numerous rooms of varying sizes housed basically eight groups of students sorted roughly by age range but mainly by their developmental and skill levels. Each classroom had a lead teacher, an assistant, and at the best of times, one or two volunteers.

Classes for students between the ages of 4 and about 24 included 2 "preschool" classrooms, a "junior" classroom, 2 "intermediate" classrooms, and 2 "senior" classrooms. Of the two preschool classes, the "A" group included the more advanced students, while the "B" group included the more delayed and more dependent children. The junior classroom served six children between the ages of about 8 and 12, and was described by Jacqui as offering "something like an advanced preschool" curriculum. The two "intermediate" classrooms aimed to move students from early childhood developmental and academic tasks toward readiness for functional literacy and numeracy. Intermediate "B" generally served younger children, while Intermediate A prepared the children to move on to the senior classrooms. Similarly, the two "senior" classrooms represented increasing levels of social and academic competence.

The older adults worked in two groups—those in the "work center" which included the Cookie Project, and the "Ruby" group, who, with multiple disabilities, engaged in a basic program of cognitive and sensory stimulation. Both of these adult groups were housed on the ground floor in a large wing that effectively separated them from the preschool and junior classrooms on that floor. That wing included a large classroom where these adults engaged in bag-making and other fine motor activities, and led at the far end to the large, fully equipped kitchen that housed the culinary program.

In addition to these groups, there were two or three adults with disabilities who were employed as "OJTs"—"on the job trainees"—who performed basic assisting functions, such as greeting visitors, taking messages from one classroom to another, helping with delivery of lunches, and so on.

Teachers' Views: "The Strength of the School Is the Level of Caring Amongst the Staff"

My research into the current Immortelle Children's Centre was enlivened by the teachers' descriptions of their work as well as my own observations of a wide range of activities. The staff were a microcosm of Trinidad's diversity in all aspects—age, ethnicity, gender, and religion (Fig. 6.1). I will not say that I found perfection in the school. But, without a doubt, I found love.

"Wanting to Make a Difference in Children's Lives"

Two of the teachers had been at Immortelle from the very start. Charlene, the vice-principal of the school, had been hired by me in about 1982. Having taken a few years off to raise her young children, Charlene retained her love of the work and returned to Immortelle when her youngest started school. She described the teachers' caring for the children as the greatest strength of the school. Looking back, she spoke of her own passion for the work and of the dominant climate of the school in this way:

> *Charlene.* I was looking for a job, and I remember asking someone I knew and they said there was an opening at Immortelle Centre. I came in and spoke with you, Beth, and I said, "Yes! This is where I want to be!" I had absolutely no exposure to special needs—none at all. But because I felt I didn't know, I wanted to know! And the school had such an environment— it was small, it had about 20 something students, and the teachers and everybody were focused on one goal, and that left no room for me to think otherwise. I signed up for every special education opportunity. I did a two-week this—a six-week that—a weekend something! Because I wanted to know. I paid for it out of my own pocket, and I soaked it up like sponge.

Charlene described her greatest reward in this work as seeing the children progress. She was, however, very modest in her estimation of her own influence, saying:

Fig. 6.1 Immortelle teachers, 2018. Front row (right to left): Charlene Gittens, Penny Munro, Ann Marie O'Brien, Joanne Ramsaran, and Jacqui Leotaud. Behind Jacqui (left to right): Nehanda Fraser, Val Nelson, Michael de Gannes, Arlene Sealey, Colette Browne, and Joshua Warde

Charlene. I guess I came in wanting to make a difference in children's lives. A lot of it is just observing where they're at and then moving from there. Sometimes observing can have you waiting a long time, you know? But their growth, whenever it happens, is what is extremely satisfying, extremely rewarding. And you realize that sometimes it doesn't really have anything to do with you. Sometimes it's as if you're just in the path of their development. When you're in the middle of it and it takes place, it's really gratifying.

Monica, another veteran teacher hired by me the year before Charlene, spoke of the many lessons she learned during more than three decades at Immortelle. Like Charlene, her comments revealed a great humility about her own power as a teacher:

> *Monica.* To look at the children's physical appearance—sometimes you wouldn't know if some children really have anything wrong with them. Because we have a few in school here that, if you just watch them, without them talking, you wouldn't know. So for me, I learned not to judge! And then just think that, I might call myself normal. I might be going down the road and I get into an accident and I might become like them, you know.
>
> And sometimes when you have a good rapport with the parent, they can tell you about something that you didn't realize the child already does at home. The parent might come and say, "You know, the child is doing that". You might be teaching him to tie the laces, and no matter what you do, he's not doing it for you. Then one morning he's dressing, and suddenly he will tie the laces or put on the shoes or the shirt. And the parents will come and tell you he was doing it all along.

"It Brings a Joy"

A focus on the intrinsic rewards of the work pervaded my interviews with the teachers. Avian was introduced to Immortelle by a teacher who invited her to volunteer for a while. Knowing nothing about special needs, soon after starting at Immortelle, she enrolled in an Early Childhood Care Program offered by the government. She also participated in several workshops over the years. Avian spoke enthusiastically of the enjoyment she experienced in this work:

> *Avian.* I volunteered for a few months and after that I fell in love with the field of Special Education, so I stayed. I've been here for the past eight, almost nine years. I loved it because it was different—totally different compared to the mainstream schools. A lot of the things are challenging but to see a child move from one point to the next—a simple thing like writing the letter A. Saying a few words at a time. It's amazing. It takes longer for them to learn and it might seem frustrating at times. But at the end of every day, you always have something to look back at. To laugh at. To reminisce on. It brings a joy!

Autism fascinates me. Each one of them is unique in their own way. The spectrum is so broad. Their reactions to say—light. Sensory issues. Touch. Scents. Simple things. That's what intrigues me. There is one child who I had to carry to his first Christmas party because he didn't want his feet to touch the ground. So when he came out of the taxi I had to lift him straight into the building and into a chair. So we would have him touch certain things to get a feel of different textures—gently touch the soles of his feet with your hands or a feather. Different things to let him know this is the ground—it's not going to harm you. Gradually he was able to transition from not wanting to touch the ground to now he's running! He's skipping! Hopping! He takes part in everything! So from that point to where he is now, is fascinating.

My advice for new teachers would be—patience and love. Being kind-hearted. Being humble. Don't lose your cool.

Carmen (pseudonym), a teacher in one of the senior classrooms, described herself as someone who had always wanted to help. When her mother introduced her to Immortelle, Carmen recalled a family friend that she grew up with who had Down Syndrome, and whom she had always seen as just a "normal person". So she decided to try the job. She worked at the school for about a year and then took the opportunity to go to Canada to do a two-year certificate program as a Developmental Services worker. After completing the program, she returned to Immortelle:

> *Carmen.* Being involved in it, I grew to love it even more. The children make me laugh with the unusual things that they think of doing. I would never think of them doing these things. That's what makes me have a huge passion of it. I'm happy in this field. There was a moment when I left the field, just because I really needed more money, and I was upset every single day.

Reynaldo echoed Carmen's sense of having fun with the students. Reynaldo held a bachelor's degree in behavioral sciences and still had a goal of returning to school to do a master's in counseling psychology. After graduation, he began as an OJT (on the job trainee) with the government, and was sent to work as an aide to a boy with autism who was in an inclusive program in a government primary school. He also assisted two girls who were visually impaired. His supervisor then sent him to Immortelle summer camp to learn about multiple disabilities. He enjoyed it and soon applied for a position as a teacher at the school. Despite finding the students' behavioral issues the most challenging aspect of the job, Reynaldo described the great enjoyment he experienced in the work:

> *Reynaldo.* I tell people, forget Learie Joseph, the comedian! Yes, he's funny. But I get so much laughter from the children. The things they say and do. Sometimes they're so literal. And they make you laugh at yourself too. For example, we were doing a chocolate exchange and I instructed a student: "Give John a chocolate and shake hands". He went up to John, handed John the chocolate, and then shook his own hand. That was so funny!
>
> It's rewarding to know that a child will learn a concept that they didn't know before, or was able to carry out a task whether it be life skills or academically, and to know that I helped them accomplish it. Something that they could take through the rest of their lives. That's the reward.

The theme of intrinsic rewards was echoed by Patricia (pseudonym), one of the senior teachers:

> *Patricia.* The reward for me is seeing them move on from one area. Their accomplishments. That is really rewarding for me. And they know when they accomplish something. We let them know. We applaud them. We make a big deal about it and the look on their face alone is priceless. That is rewarding.

Joanna, the teacher in the junior classroom, explained that she came to Immortelle "by accident", in the late 1980s. She was working in a business that was going through a difficult time, so she accepted the opportunity to help at another small private school for children with special needs. Although her initial introduction to some aspects of the work was challenging, she quickly "fell in love" with the work and accepted a position at Something Special and, ultimately, Immortelle:

> *Joanna.* The very first time I saw a child get a seizure, I started to cry. The teacher looked at me and said, "Just come out of the room because you're not helping!" I'm saying to her, "Do something!" She said, "You can't really do anything. You just have to make sure he doesn't hurt himself". I'm there just crying. Afterwards, I was so embarrassed.
>
> But I fell in love with the profession. It's the children. Their love. They might take this simple little pen cover and it means the world to them. Whereas we would not want it and throw it away. They are very contented. They are very, very loving. Regarding salaries, at the end of the day we do need money to survive. But I told the people at the job I left, it's not all about money. Hence I'm here.

Joy, another teacher who had been at Immortelle as long as Joanna, was one of three who worked with the adult students who had been at Immortelle for decades. Joy joined Immortelle in 1988 and worked at first in the independent living skills program that had moved from the Duke Street building to its own building, but then had to return because of lack of funding for support of both settings. Joy's own son had mild learning needs, which had caused her a great deal of worry until she began working with children with severe needs. She commented on the lessons she learned from this experience:

> *Joy.* It started as a kind of rude awakening. Because we had some very low functioning students. We had one who banged her head. She would bang her head on the desk. You'd pull away the desk and her knees would come up banging her head. And we had a student who would go into seizures if you turned on the tap. Or if a motor bike or a truck passes by—seizures! So then, to be honest, I started counting my blessings. I began to appreciate my own situation with my son. I said to myself, "Okay, this is not bad. Cheer up and move on." So I stopped my crying and fuming and fussing.

Val had been at Immortelle for 27 years. Like several of her colleagues, she started as a volunteer, with no experience with special needs. Right away she found that she really enjoyed the work. When Charlene went on maternity leave, Val filled in and soon became an essential member of the team. By the time I met her, Val was established as the person who delivered sensory integration and physical therapy activities in an intensive one-on-one setting. She told me how she came to develop that focus:

> *Val.* I started to learn from Crystal, an Occupational Therapist from Toronto. She would come for about 6 weeks at a time and I would work along with her. I would pick up ideas from her. If this is working, why can't I try it? I'm always up to something different, something challenging to do. Eventually Jacqui decided we would do full time therapy. Then we moved on from Occupational Therapy to Sensory and I said, "Jacqui! I can't do sensory, I don't know what it is." She says, "Just dealing with the senses. Okay, you're in charge of it!" So I just came up with different things. We'd been trying to set it up for years. What we used to do was have Sensory Day once a year because it's a bit costly. The whole school would take part in it. We'd organize different stations, hearing, smell, taste, touch, sight. Then the idea grew and the room came about. Then there was a student who went to Canada to have surgery and Jacqui sent me along to

accompany him because his mother is visually impaired. So I went along and observed what they were doing in the OT department and in the school, and when I returned I started doing the same things with him.

Val was emphatic in her view that working with children with disabilities required dedication and genuine caring. Like most of her colleagues, she emphasized the intangible rewards.

> *Val.* You need dedicated staff! You have to love what you do. It gives me satisfaction when I see the work move from point A to point B. You can't pay enough for that! It's really fun when you see a child do all these new things. Isaiah wasn't walking and Sarah wasn't either. Lorenzo came dragging. Never used to move around. He moved from dragging to walking to running.
>
> Yes, I'd like a better salary! The salaries are too low! But when I started 12 years back, I knew what I was getting and I accepted it. So when you're hired you know you're working for X. You have a choice. Yes I want to, or no I don't want to. I always say—you have the job, you do it!

Teacher Commitment in the Face of Daily Challenges

Val's comment above points to the fact that salaries were a central feature of discontent for teachers. Other difficulties included transportation, concerns about curriculum modifications and availability of updated materials, and, for some teachers, an expressed desire for more autonomy in making program decisions. While it was evident that all the teachers were fond of the children and of the actual work, for some, their dissatisfactions showed in a pattern of absenteeism and tardiness.

In Trinidad/Tobago, teachers' salaries were set by the government, but there were two complicating issues. First, the qualifications required for the designation "teacher" included a bachelor's degree in education. Second, the government did not pay eligible teachers at the private special schools the full amount of the salaries they were entitled to. The latter policy was based on the argument that the private schools should pay a share of the salaries. Teachers at these schools would usually earn less than teachers employed in the public schools. Consequently, teachers with the B.Ed., would often not choose to work in a private school since they may be paid less than in a public school. Hence, the most qualified teachers at Immortelle were those with bachelor's degrees, but not in education.

More likely, they would hold a degree in fields such as psychology or behavioral sciences.

Within a relatively thriving economy, these teachers' salaries were disappointingly low, especially for those who had gone to great efforts to earn a degree, only to find that jobs were hard to come by. Reynaldo explained that the position he had held as an "on the job trainee" (OJT) with the Ministry of Education paid a salary much less than a graduate with a B. Ed., would earn in a teaching position. However, since his degree in behavioral sciences did not qualify him as a teacher, he accepted the OJT position for a two-year period, as an opportunity to gain "skills and training" and "experience to put on your resume". After a summer camp placement at Immortelle, however, he applied for a teaching position and was hired, leaving his OJT position, although his salary increased by only $400 monthly.

Reynaldo liked the work at Immortelle but commented that, in addition to salary, one of the limitations of teaching in a private school was the lack of upward mobility. As he put it, "There are just two higher positions—the Principal and Vice-Principal". Consequently, it seemed likely that someone with his qualifications would constantly be on the lookout for opportunities to advance in their careers.

Carmen, a younger teacher, still single and living with her family, told me that, with a two-year diploma in developmental services, she still had to supplement her salary by working privately with a child with ADHD. She explained that while she could "make do" with her salary, this was not so for others, especially those who already had a university degree and had families to support.

In a previous chapter, I reported Jacqui's explanations about the difficulties of government bureaucracy and inefficiency regarding the payment of subventions. Noting her information that the subventions provided 80% of the school's funding, it seemed obvious that there would be occasions when a delay in payments would mean a delay in teachers' salaries. While the teachers did not know the details of the school's funding, they did know that the government subventions were often late. Indeed, at one point in my research, when Immortelle's checks were eight months late, there were several other private special schools experiencing the same delay and the outcry was published in the newspaper. This knowledge, however, did not necessarily quell teachers' dissatisfaction, since they had their own bills to pay. Jacqui, meanwhile, was frantically racing from phone call to phone call and visit to visit, trying to get the check released from the grasp of whoever's desk it was sitting on in the Ministry of Education.

As argued by several teachers, low salaries and government inefficiency should not diminish teachers' motivation and level of commitment. In this view, there was still a job to be done:

> *Val.* It's a matter of self-discipline. That you need to organize yourself. It is your job so you are the one who must take responsibility for that. So set your alarm clock for 5:00 a.m., if you need to. You can't want to lie down in your bed till 7:00 a.m., and hope to get transport to come up to St. Ann's.

The latter comment reflected a reality of life in Trinidad/Tobago: early rising was a traditional social norm made more essential by the difficulties of transportation and intense traffic, both coming into and getting through Port of Spain. This affected teacher attrition also, as evidenced by the resignation of one teacher during the period of the research, who moved to a position with the Catholic Board of Education to be closer to her home. For me, traveling from the Eastern suburbs, although I was driving myself and did not have to be concerned with negotiating the changes of taxis to get to St. Ann's, I seldom arrived in time to observe the early morning classes.

Curriculum and Instruction at Immortelle

Besides the inadequacy of salaries and the logistical challenges of transportation, issues related to the basics of instruction for students with significant disabilities were evident in four aspects of the work required of these teachers. First, there was the challenge of appropriate grouping of students to enable coherent small groups as well as one-to-one instruction. Second, and closely tied to the first, was the need for additional classroom assistants. Third, there was the on-going need to revise and implement appropriate curriculum for different ages and needs, which led to the fourth issue—maintaining a continuous stock of age—appropriate and challenging materials.

The rich body of information I gleaned from interviews was substantially complemented by my observations throughout the school. I observed at least once, but usually twice, in every classroom, and up to four or five times in selected classrooms. I made decisions about which classrooms to focus on based on two main concerns: first, my developing interest in certain students whose parents had agreed to participate in the study and, second, my desire to understand the strengths and challenges of curriculum and instruction in a school driven by dedication to a cause but challenged by limited resources.

The main challenges with the younger, more physically dependent children were related to the need for more hands and for teachers and/or assistants with well-practiced skills in managing challenging behaviors. At this level, the self-help focus with lots of attention to communication and socialization was very appropriate and the learning of elementary academic skills was something that all parents saw as important. The difficulty, however, lay in the inadequate numbers of staff to meet the students' instructional needs. For the older students, while behavior management was also crucial, especially in the case of some students on the autism spectrum, it seemed that the main challenge was the continuing need for an adaptive curriculum targeting real-life skills and using age-appropriate activities and materials. This was most evident in the two groups of adult students: those in the "senior classrooms", between the ages of about 16 and 25; and the older adults, between the ages of about 25 and 50, many of whom had been in the school since the very beginning of Immortelle and/or Something Special.

To illustrate both the strengths and challenges of curriculum and instruction across these levels, I will focus on three very different programs: the preschool program, one of the senior classrooms, and the work program, which housed the bag making and "cookie project".

Grouping students: Need, competence, and adequate hands. The challenge of appropriate grouping of students in any kind of educational program constitutes one of education's greatest challenges. Even for typically developing students, there is much argument regarding whether children should be tracked according to academic achievement or whether heterogenous grouping is more helpful to all. Many argue that heterogenous grouping ensures that there are bound to be failures, while current best practice recommends differentiating instruction within a mixed group, to meet different levels. The latter approach, undoubtedly, requires not only very skilled teachers but a small enough teacher-student ratio to allow for true differentiation. In typical public educational settings in Trinidad/Tobago teacher-student ratios are approximately 1:30, making such differentiation impossible.

In the Immortelle classrooms, with an overall student-teacher ratio of 6:1, teachers did their best to individualize and differentiate their instruction. But all expressed frustration with the difficulties of this approach when there simply were not enough hands to assist, or where there were individual students who needed specialized one-on-one attention. This was most obviously the case in the preschool classes, where individual children were not yet personally independent or really needed specialized behavioral interventions. According to Val, who had the advantage of working one-on-one in the therapy or sensory rooms with the younger children, if there could be one teacher assigned to a child who needed this much attention, differentiated instruction with the others would be feasible but would still require careful planning:

> *Val.* There must be one-on-one for a child whose program is really basic—focused on toileting, self-feeding, or identifying different parts of the body. Then another teacher could have 4 children and work with them at 4 different levels. So, for example, I would set work for the 4 of them: One might be colouring; one might be sorting; one doing something else, maybe writing. So I'm doing individual with one and then I switch. I give this one something to do that I know he can do independently. That way, I work with the 4 of them at different levels at differing times and they all get the individual attention. But you have to plan it!

In the Preschool Classroom: A Tale of Two Sarahs

I have previously introduced Sarah, a six-year-old in the preschool B classroom who needed intensive, though not necessarily total one-to-one instruction. Sarah seemed ubiquitous throughout the ground level of the school. I soon found that I could see her anywhere—in her own classroom, in Monica's classroom, heading down the hallway toward the gated, main entrance to the school, or sitting on the floor at the entrance. Most of the time, some adult would appear to quickly scoop her up and take her back to her classroom.

Sharmain, Sarah's grandmother, whom I cited in the previous chapter, described her as "spoiled" and determined to have her own way. Certainly, Sarah's behavior presented huge challenges. Her seemingly short attention span and resistance to direction made her exceedingly difficult to manage within the context of the "preschool B" classroom, where two teachers and possibly an additional volunteer struggled to provide engaging and adequately structured activities for Sarah, Isaiah, and four other children who also had significant disabilities. When the class was short-handed, Sarah would sometimes be taken into the "preschool A" classroom to be monitored by Monica's assistant, Danielle, with whom Sarah was a bit more cooperative. A third setting was the sensory room with Val, and it was here that the power of skilled one-on-one instruction was dramatically displayed. The contrast between the first and third of these situations left me incredulous. Below are the notes I took on Sarah in those two settings.

Sarah in her "preschool B" classroom. The preschool B classroom served six children ages approximately 4–10, all of whom had significant developmental needs and whose curriculum focused on self-help skills and a variety of tasks targeting eye-hand coordination as well as basic cognitive and communication skills. The room was large and laid out with several stations. There were child-size tables and chairs where the children sit to eat, a reading circle with a large mat, and several small desks with little chairs. There were also two triangle-shaped seats with fitted tabletops, intended to provide secure seating for children who need the physical support or who need to be constrained while seated. On most days, the room was staffed by a lead teacher, Colette, an assistant, Gillian, and a volunteer.

Val's earlier description of the needs of this room was clearly illustrated by the way the children were grouped. They seemed to fall into three basic "groups"—one group of four and then Sarah and Isaiah, each of whom really formed his/her own group. My observation notes described an active and differentiated nursery classroom where all the children were engaged. Sarah, however, stood out as the child determined to set her own agenda!

> *Beth's field notes.* Sarah is sitting in an enclosed chair with a laptop on the table, hands in her mouth, totally absorbed in the images on the laptop screen.
>
> Gillian sits behind Isaiah, putting a soft foam ball into his hand to squeeze. He smiles. Most of the time he keeps slapping the table with both hands.
>
> Collette sits with 3 boys in front of her, Ahmad, Jerome and Jemmy (pseudonyms). Collette has a box of colored sponges for a tactile stimulation activity in which the children take turns putting glue on small buttons, which they then try to stick on to a ball. The balls will become birds which the children will then put into a paper pouch—the birds' nest. Colette asks the group, "What color do you want? Now we're going to add our eyes and ears". Jerome immediately points at his eyes then moves the buttons around and puts one on his eye. Jemmy is very excited, flapping his arms as Collette lays out the buttons. Ahmad puts his fingers in his ears.

Sarah continues totally focused on the laptop for about 10 minutes, but when someone enters the room, she pushes the table away and crawls toward the door. The entering adult tells Sarah to return to her seat but, ignoring this instruction, Sarah walks over to the shelves by the wall, lies down on the floor, and rolls under a curtain on the wall that separates the room from the spacious back patio where a group of older students are on their break. For a few minutes, no-one is looking at her and she keeps rolling and peeking through the slats in the wall. Danielle enters the room, looks at Sarah then goes over and pulls her out from the curtain. She tells her "Go sit in your chair. I'm coming". Sarah does. Danielle gives her a book with large pictures and she nods, then looks through it, turning the pages for about 5 minutes, then gets up when Danielle leaves the room.

Meanwhile, Collette's activity with the 3 boys is progressing nicely, and she says, "We have Jerome's bird," and so on, for each attempt the children make. Gillian is working with Isaiah hand-over-hand on a large puzzle and some other tactile materials. Then she tells him "Lets' go get a book." She takes him and the 3 other boys to the reading corner and starts reading them a story. She reads and asks "where" and "what" questions, helping the children to point, hand-over-hand.

Now it's Sarah's turn to work individually with Colette on the bird nest activity. She is clearly not interested in this task and keeps looking over at the reading group. Soon Collette walks Sarah over to the reading corner where she sits for about two minutes then gets up and walks over to the table where the laptop is. Gillian goes and takes it away. Sarah goes back to her seat and pulls the table in, opening her book. She looks at it, turning it around several times before she gets it the right way up.

After about five minutes of looking at the book, Sarah pushes her table away and gets up and walks around. A volunteer takes her to sit back down. Sarah resumes looking at the book, points to pages, and verbalizes to herself, "Aah, aah…" for about two minutes.

Suddenly, Sarah does a somersault out of her enclosed chair/table. Collette takes her by the hand and leads her to Danielle in the pre-school A classroom next door. A few minutes later, Danielle brings Sarah back to the room and says. "Come in and sit down, Sarah". For about 5 minutes, she sits and watches as Danielle reads her a story. She responds, pointing to the book and turning pages, looking at the book, and reaching for Danielle's face and hair. Soon she gets distracted by Colette's group, who are now in a circle, singing "Old MacDonald". She crawls away from Danielle, who walks away and puts the book on a shelf. Sarah turns back to follow Danielle and reaches for her, puts her arm around Danielle's waist and looks up at her. Danielle leaves the room with her, holding her hand.

Sarah in the sensory room. The second place I observed Sarah was in the "sensory room", where Val worked with individual students or small groups. The room was carpeted and cozy, filled with stimulating materials, toys, and corners where children could play or work independently. Along one wall was an instructional area, marked off by different colored carpeting, where Val would work one-on-one with individual children (Fig. 6.2).

Beth's field notes. As I enter the room, Val and Sarah are sitting on the floor facing each other and are already working. I sit on the floor a few feet to their left. On the floor between them are seven cut-out letters arranged to spell Sarah's last name, RAMDIAL. Sarah's task is to match another set of those same letters to the ones that spell her name.

Val points to the R and asks Sarah to find the other R and place it below. Sarah begins by quickly picking up a couple of incorrect letters. Val persists, asking her to find the R. After about two minutes, Sarah starts picking up each letter and matching it correctly. It turns out she has certain knowledge of all but the D and A, which she misplaces. Val makes her repeat the task 3 times, calmly repeating her instructions despite Sarah initially flapping her arms and putting her head down.

Next, they work on spelling out her first name, SARAH, also in cut-out letters, and she is able to work on this without matching them to a model.

Fig. 6.2 Sarah Ramdial working diligently with teacher Val Nelson

Sarah readily picks up the correct letters but hesitates over the left-right sequencing. Val then puts her through a similar task with a set of bright orange paper numerals, which she is to arrange in the order of 1–5. As with the letters, Sarah selects the numerals correctly but needs prompting to follow the left-right sequence.

At times, Sarah stalls, seeming to refuse to continue. Val says, "Ok I'll wait", and, within seconds, Sarah attends again. At one point she gets up from her spot with Val and goes across the room and starts playing with a large blue ball. Val tells her quietly that she has a choice; she can stay over there if she wants but she's not allowed to play with anything, or else she can come back and sit with her. Sarah comes back and sits with her and resumes the task. After completing the next set of instructions, Val compliments her on her good work and tells her she can go and play with the blue ball now, if she wishes. Sarah does just that.

The moral of the tale of two Sarahs lies in central axioms of specialized instruction: consistency, structure, and individualized support. When Sarah enjoyed a personal relationship with an adult such as Danielle, she was more cooperative, but her work with Val demonstrated how much she could really accomplish one-on-one with a skilled interventionist.

What would it take for a school like Immortelle to provide this kind of intervention on a sustained basis? As Jacqui made so clear in her explanation of the financial needs of the school, "It all comes down to funding."

In the Senior Classroom: Adapting Curriculum and Creating Community

The curriculum for the two senior classes was essentially focused on simple arithmetic, literacy skills, socialization, and communication. Each class served six to eight students, between the ages of 14 and 22, but displaying a wide range of developmental levels in cognition and communication. I focused on the "Senior A" class, in which Charlene was the lead teacher and was assisted by Carmen (Fig. 6.3).

All the Senior A students were personally independent, socially cooperative, and capable of some amount of elementary academic work. Three of the boys displayed behavioral and communicative features typical of autism; one girl had the most noticeable overall developmental delay; and two boys displayed no behavioral difficulties, but their cognitive capabilities differed greatly: Michael, aged about 18, whose mother described him as having ASKOOG syndrome, displayed a higher level of academic skills and com-

Fig. 6.3 Teachers and senior students. Left-right/clockwise: Charlene Gittens, Jacqui Leotaud, Raquel Leotaud, Reynaldo Allen, Lyndon Collier, Oshea Callender, Shane Sutherland

municative competence than the rest of his peers. LC, a sociable and charming 19-year old, showed no signs of disability in his independence and ability to engage socially, except that he spoke in a rapid somewhat garbled manner that made him difficult to understand at times. Indicative of his social intelligence, LC traveled to school on his own in a taxi from a small town on the north coast, probably an hour away. Yet, up until that time, he could not identify colors, letters, or numbers.

Carmen felt that the curriculum for this group of students was reasonably on-target and appropriate. The focus at that time included "learning about healthy foods, living vs. non-living matter, the environment, the weather", and so on. Carmen's concerns with the curriculum were the need for more "age-appropriate" activities and materials such as modified scrabble, laminated flash cards that the students could take home to practice with, and more practical furniture, such as desks in which each student could learn to organize his/her materials and develop a sense of responsibility for their belongings. Carmen's recommendations for improvement focused on having more certified teachers as well as more volunteers in the classroom.

A senior classroom exemplar: Respect and reciprocity. Charlene, the lead teacher in the senior classroom, agreed with Carmen that more age-appropriate materials would be helpful and felt that it was crucial for teachers to be constantly "self-reflective", adjusting instruction to the interest and capabilities of the students. My observations in this classroom revealed a well-structured program based on elementary academic and social knowledge, with materials and tasks varied to the level of each student. Work sheets with simple sums and writing tasks were set out daily for each student and were alternated with lessons and conversations about the natural and social environment. Embedded in table games and casual conversation was a strong focus on appropriate social behavior, courtesy, and turn-taking. Below are my notes from one of about six observations in this room.

> *Beth's field notes.* The desks are in an L shape, each touching the next. Dimitri, John and Camla are seated at the short end of the L and Sydney, Lyle, Kendall and Casta are on the long end, closer to the door and the teacher's desk, where I am sitting. Charlene is sitting in front of Lyle, working with him on a paper-pencil task of adding by two's. She tells me that he is presently transitioning from the Junior class to this class and this task is an assessment of his number skills. The other students are all doing a writing task. Casta has a paper with two eggs and is coloring them.
>
> LC, walks in, passes me, and heads for a desk by the window. Charlene says to him, "Oh! LC? Somebody is sitting at my desk and it's not me, so what do you say?" LC turns to me with an embarrassed expression and says "Sorry! Good morning!"

At that moment, Carmen enters the room and Charlene says, "When you hear your name, go with Carmen". She calls Shakina, LC, and Casta, who leave the room with Carmen. They are going to the kitchen to get today's freshly baked cookies.

Charlene says to the whole group: "Ok, let's play a game". Now Charlene distributes cards and a matching picture board to each student while Lyle and Sydney finish their writing tasks. She encourages Lyle, who is still work-ing on his number task, saying, "Good job!" She takes the paper from him and hands it to me for review. She asks Sydney to hurry up and finish but he keeps on with his task, which is writing the names above a page full of small drawings (rabbit, flower, and so on). Charlene says, "I'm ready to start". Sydney keeps writing. Kendall seems excited and is clapping his hands.

Charlene starts the game. Her manner is very upbeat, with lots of smiles and encouraging comments. Sydney suddenly puts down his pencil and looks up as Charlene holds up each card, asking the students to call out if they have the matching picture on their board. Everyone seems very keen on the game, especially Sydney and Camla. Sydney is seated next to Kendall, who does not look at the board but keeps clapping and looking excited.

Sydney, seeming intent on helping Kendall, leans over and fixes Kendall's cards on his board, putting each card back on the proper spot. Kendall raises his hand to cover the board and Sydney says, "Put your hand down". But Kendall keeps messing the cards up. He has a slightly annoyed look on his face and seems to be messing them up deliberately. He does not appreciate Sydney's interference!

Soon, Dimitri has a card that Charlene has called. He says, "House! Praise the Lord".

[Observer comment: This echoes the way he introduced his name to me, as "Dimitri, praise the Lord"]

Camla wins the first round. She and Sydney have had the most wins up to that time. Charlene starts a second round but then Camla and another student leave to get lunches for the class. Lyle, who has been sitting quietly, starts to engage in the game, but has a few moments of hand-flapping, fin-gers in front of his eyes.

As the game continues, Sydney, about two seats away from Lyle, watches Lyle's board and shouts "He has it!" The competition for the win is now between Sydney and Lyle and eventually Charlene announces that Lyle has won and he put his hands in the air exclaiming, "Yah! Yeh!" Sydney looks downcast, rubs his eyes and looks away.

[Observer Comment: I sympathize with Sydney, wondering if he realized that he had been helping Lyle win!]

Camla enters with a handful of containers with students' lunches that they have warmed in the microwave in the kitchen. As students receive their lunch containers, they wait, not opening them. The only exception is Kendall, who starts to try to open his container. Sydney says to him, "Not yet!" and takes away his container. Camla leaves to get the rest of the lunches and soon she and Timothy return and everyone has their lunch. All sit waiting quietly as Charlene explains that Carmen gone to get them some cookies. Since it's taking a while, Charlene starts a conversation about how cookies are made. She leads this for a couple of minutes. Then she asks if they should go ahead and start without Carmen. Several students exclaim, "Yes!" "Ah beggin yah!" "Please!" "Ah hungry!" All this is in a good-natured tone, accepting that they must wait until everyone has their lunch and the teacher gives the word.

Charlene then asks them to say the grace, which turns out to be a chant in which all join, "Our father (twice), thank you for your blessings (twice), amen."

The students proceed to eat their lunches, chatting as they eat: LC talks about going swimming tomorrow; Casta nods, laughing and pointing out the window in recognition of the plan to go swimming. Shekina says she's not coming tomorrow, she has dialysis. Casta calls to me, pointing to her food to show that she's about to start eating. Camla says she went to Jouvert, which is the opening parade of the carnival. Sydney is talking to LC. Camla, sitting behind Sydney, teases him by tickling his neck; he frowns and says, "Camla, ah not talking to you. Ah talking to LC". But he's hiding a small smile.

The emotional feeling of this room was one of a family. Functioning at very different levels, some students had the more challenging responsibilities, such as going to collect or warm lunches. All seemed to recognize each other's needs and capabilities, the more competent ones attempting either to help or correct the others. As one would expect in a peer group, these offers of "help" were not always appreciated by the recipients. The teacher functioned in the role of a teacher/mother, gently but firmly enforcing the social rules that were a central part of the curriculum.

As a special educator, my only concern was with the limited evidence of practical applications of the academic knowledge being taught. I felt that the paper-pencil tasks needed to be greatly supplemented by real-life activities such as purchasing items using real money, reading headlines in the daily newspapers, or watching the news on TV and engaging in conversation about the stories heard. Of course, the latter suggestion could only occur if the school were able to afford a TV in classrooms such as these! This was not the case. There was, however, a pastry shop just a few blocks from the school and I wondered if these older students could not go there in a group of two or three to purchase a small snack. Once more, however, any suggestions regarding community-based activities would require the addition of the one thing most needed in the school—more staff.

Older Adults: "Where Do We Go from Here"?

The challenges of curriculum adaptation became exponentially more intense in program development for the older adults in the school. As Jacqui's story illustrated, she had made several different decisions over the years on adaptations for this group, with the goal of their developing a measure of independence and productivity. Currently, the focus for this group was on making, bagging, and selling cookies, a project that Jacqui hoped would prove a source of income for the students.

Life skills for adults. The teachers of this group described the changes that had been made over the years just as Jacqui had done, but seemed nostalgic for the program that they had been fond of. Their descriptions reflected their concerns about how to make the new "work-focused" program successful for these adults:

> *Joy and Arlene.* We started the life skills program because they needed to be able to help themselves. To be independent even in the household, if not going out into the world of work. So we started making sandwiches, mixing juice, or pouring a drink into the glass. Folding clothes, washing their socks, their underwear—that sort of thing. So we moved the bigger ones away from the main school at Duke Street with the junior students and we started in Kitchener Street. And then there was a problem with the building, I think, and we moved to Gordon Street, but finally we had to move back to Duke Street and our program was based in the annex. During that time, we were making ground seasoning. They were learning to type. They were making bags. They were making sachets. I loved it. I love doing household stuff too, so it was very enjoyable and then when we saw the progress of the students we got more motivated! It was a lot of fun! It still is.

One challenge identified by this group of teachers was the need to have an adequately varied program so that the students would not become bored with the repetition. Jacqui agreed with this and explained that she felt that the self-help and household skills program had become too repetitive. Continuing to search for new ways to create programs in which the students would be productive, making a success of the cookie project was currently her main goal. At the time of my observations, the morning program for this group consisted of two main activities—making bags for sales of the cookies and then going into the kitchen to do the actual baking of the cookies. In the afternoons, the plan was to engage the students in using an iPad for communication and for entertainment. At the time of my research, the latter goal was experiencing a delay, there not being a staff person capable of doing it adequately.

The cookie project. These teachers emphasized that they supported the idea of the cookie project, but had three main concerns. First, they did not want it to take over the entire program, fearing once more that the students would tire of the repetition. Second, there was the issue of how competent the students would become in the cookie making and, finally, there were the practical difficulties of marketing, which proved to be more challenging than expected, despite a careful marketing plan. Although the cookie dough could be frozen, it did have a shelf life and, at the time of this research, sales were so slow that there was a real concern regarding the surplus of frozen cookie dough building up in the school's refrigerators. The teachers in this program felt that the focus on work was too limiting and planned to discuss with Jacqui the idea of broadening the adult program to include more focus on socialization, communication, personal needs, and a broader range of creative activities (Fig. 6.4).

My observation of the cookie making supported the concern about students' competence in accomplishing various phases of the process and the need for intensive hand-over-hand support for most students in all the tasks. Another challenge was how to meet the needs of students with a wide range of skill levels. Most notably, there was one student whose level of cognitive and fine motor competence was unique in the group. Below are my notes on the process:

Beth's field notes. Two teachers are assisting five students in the cookie-making process. The teachers have set out the flour, sugar and butter with notes marking the amount of each ingredient. Following a factory production model, each student has a specific task to do, and some complete their tasks with full hand-over-hand support. For most students their tasks are fully supported, such as measuring the flour, adding sugar, or pouring the batter into the mixer. The more complex tasks are done either by a teacher or by one of the students, Mariana, whose level of competence in the entire process is way beyond her peers. While the teacher blends the butter, Mariana breaks the eggs and then pours the ingredients into the mixer. Once it is mixed, she scoops the batter into the baking dish independently and moves on to start washing some bowls, while the teachers assist the other students in wiping the counters and tidying up.

Fig. 6.4 Senior students, Samantha Lawrence and Aisha Inniss, selling cookies for the tuck-shop

The issue of the range of students' skills was certainly of great importance. This applied also to the plan to introduce use of the IPad. This was of great interest to some of the adult students but of little use to those whose limited eye-hand coordination made it difficult to "slide" across the screen. On the other hand, the teachers felt that some of the "higher functioning" students who had been learning to type on the computer and use email to communicate with each other should continue to develop those skills.

Among the older adults at Immortelle was a group of students, fondly designated "the Ruby group", whose severe multiple disabilities made it impossible for them to participate in the cookie project or other activities of their age peers. Most had been at Immortelle for decades and were dependent on the school for the only source of social activity outside of their homes. Their program consisted of sensory and motor activities designed to keep them as mobile and as active as possible. For the most part, the teachers of this group felt frustrated by a growing sense that the students were beyond further development, but the teachers cared about them and could not stand the thought of them not having a program of activities to go to. Moreover, they felt that the parent support system was weakening because the parents were themselves aging. As one teacher said, "So these students have to keep coming. If they're not stimulated they'll waste away."

This did not mean that there were no efforts to promote their development. Indeed, on one occasion, I noted a teacher working quite successfully with one member of this group on self-feeding, rather than taking the easier route and simply feeding her. Similarly, a volunteer who worked a couple of days with the group expressed enthusiasm for the work and felt that with new and more interesting materials, the students would be more responsive.

These challenges reflected the disturbing absence in Trinidad and Tobago of facilities for adults with significant disabilities. When considering the range of children, adolescents, and adults with vastly differing abilities enrolled at Immortelle, it was evident that the school was really stretched too thin. At the time of this research, Jacqui's next goal was to obtain a property that would house its own work center for adults with significant disabilities.

"The Bigger You Get, the Harder It Is"

In an earlier chapter, I quoted Jacqui's frustration as she described the challenges of moving from a small, family-like school employing about 6 staff serving 20–25 students, to a large business serving up to 75 students and employing up to 25 staff with varying levels of professional preparation and skill. My observations revealed these challenges first-hand and it seemed to me that the central issue was not teacher qualifications per se, but rather financial resources to engage the most skilled and committed teachers, and to reward them adequately both through salaries and through the continuous provision of updated resources and professional development.

Teachers' concerns about salary and resources were echoed by other professionals and community members who served the school in official or unofficial supportive roles. Helen Humphrey, who had been the originator of *Something Special*, the school with whom Immortelle merged, had remained a keen supporter of all things Immortelle. With her granddaughter, Becky, still enrolled, and Helen's continuing involvement in assisting the school with Carnival and other social activities, she was a welcome and much loved figure at the school. At the time of this research, Helen expressed concerns about teacher morale:

> *Helen.* It's not easy running a school like this. It takes a lot of money. And the teachers need more money. But it's not easy to get the money to pay them. Sometimes when the government subvention doesn't come through, Jacqui has to knock here, borrow there. But it's not easy on the teachers either. They have to spend a lot of money on transport. So by the time they get their salary, which is small, it's really very little. And it's not easy work. You have to have the patience of Job!

In a similar vein, Jane Bernstein, who contributed her expertise in psychological evaluation, agreed vehemently on the need for more economic resources, as well as for well-trained teachers:

> *Jane.* First of all—and most critical—we need a consistent funding source. Jacqui should not be scrambling for every dollar. Although government allocates money, it is inconsistently disbursed and requires constant prompting from school administrators—wasting time, resources and effort.
>
> Another big challenge for school administrators is the unevenness in the training and experience of potential teachers. This is particularly an issue when the student population being served is subject to discrimination and bias in the society—largely due to a pervasive lack of understanding, empathy and appreciation for their potential despite their limitations. Finding and developing good teachers of students with special needs is a huge undertaking!

Jane also observed, however, that many Immortelle teachers were very skilled, yet modest to a fault. Viewing this in a cultural perspective, she told an interesting story in which she related this point to her perceptions of local communication practices between adults and children. Referring to a lecture she had heard regarding "horizontal" (within age group) cultural organization among African cultures, Jane commented:

> *Jane.* I didn't fully understand what the lecturer was talking about, yet that's what I see in Trinidad. Trinis are very social but they don't seem to talk through the age cohorts. They're very family oriented but they don't tend to engage in real conversation with small children. In many situations, it's

noticeable that the 'problem' with Trini kids is you can't get them to talk; in the same situations, the 'problem' with American kids is you can't get them to shut up!

Also, I found that very different cultural expectations around expressing one's opinions played out in working with Trini supervisors of the American interns. The very knowledgeable and experienced Trinis tended to stand back and let the often naïve and inexperienced—but opinionated—American students go ahead! I didn't initially realise to what extent the teachers weren't taking on the necessary authority. Jacqui had to teach me about that. For example, two students from the US came into the staffing and reported with great pride that they had taught the students they were working with to sign 3 or 4 words. The teacher responded with: "I don't get this. These kids have been signing all the time." So we sat with the American students and said, "What is the first thing you do in a cross cultural situation? You ask what they can do!" Then we went to the Trini supervisors privately and said, "What are you doing? Tell them they're out of line! Tell them the children know those signs already—maybe you can build on this." But they don't easily tell these young Americans to just shut up!

Laura Palmer, who brought her doctoral counseling psychology students from Seton Hall University to do internships every summer, had great praise for the outcomes she saw among students at Immortelle and emphasized the benefits her doctoral students had gained from their internships at Immortelle's therapeutic summer camp. Emphasizing the importance of multicultural experience for her students, she explained:

Laura. I wanted international training opportunities for my doctoral students. And so it becomes an experiential learning, service learning project for them. The way Jane and Jacqui and I have set this up is it's a service-learning project and a training the trainer model. We're all multi-cultural beings, all of us. So to understand a person or a family or a community in context, you have to understand where they live and their identities. We all have multiple identities. So that is a cornerstone of our program.

My students love it! We try to do as much as we can before we come. They talk with people who have come before. We meet with people who are Trinidadian. I take them to eat in East Orange New Jersey, where there's a great Trini restaurant. So, we do what we can to prepare, because it's not just Trini culture—it's working with multiple disabilities, some they've never seen. And then the density of this population; when they meet the group the first day, they're overwhelmed! On the first day all they can see is what the children can't do. By day two, all they start to see is what they *can* do.

It's so much new experience. A new country, a new dialect. Some of my people have not worked with children with this range of disabilities. They say that it's one of the most impactful experiences of their entire professional development.

Speaking of the strengths, needs, and future of the school, Laura said:

Laura. I think the greatest strength is that, under Jacqui's leadership they have really developed the school to be as responsive as possible to a wide range of students. I've seen over ten years tremendous growth in the students. They are learning. These teachers are amazing for what they bring forward with the resources that they have. You know, they can't fly these teachers all over the world to do all kinds of fancy training. But the children are learning. They are reading, they are thinking, they are functioning.

I know Jacqui has some goals, aspirations to do a vocational center. I'm also seeing a need for independent transitional living. You have so many of these families that are getting old, with adult children who are 30, 40, 50 years old. Sometimes there are no other siblings. So what's going to happen to folks like these when their parents pass? Not everybody has an extended family that can take them in.

What are the disadvantages? Resources! Just that, not enough, not enough resources, not enough supplies!

I close this chapter with a powerful statement by Charlene, whose long-term view of the school captured its key strengths and challenges.

Charlene. The strength of the school is the level of caring that exists amongst the staff. Internally, yes, there are some little obstacles. You feel it. Sometimes, the atmosphere might not be as harmonious as it should be, because it's a large group and you feel a disconnection. You know, it's a large body and there are people with a different focus—you can feel disjointed.

But a positive thing about the growth of this school is that, nationally, the school is recognized for offering service to a specific population. Many people recommend our school. And some people would come and say, "Well, social services recommended the school" or "This lady recommended the school", and that kind of thing. That's good to hear! It makes you feel good to be part of something that is really flourishing and meeting a need in society.

CHAPTER 7

Building a Community of Advocates: Seeking Unity in Diversity

In these next two chapters, I step away from Immortelle to capture the views of a range of community members who, for different reasons, hold a deeply entrenched stake in the lives of people with disabilities in Trinidad and Tobago. I invited these people to participate based on three criteria: first, my own personal knowledge of their role in disability affairs over many years. Second, in a "snowball" manner in response to comments such as "So, do you know (so-and-so)? You really should talk to her!" Third, using what qualitative researchers refer to as "theoretical sampling", that is, decisions based on explanations emerging from the interviews, observations, and participation in public or private events focused on disability issues.

I refer to the 34 individuals who participated in this aspect of the research as "community partners". While some were directly related to Immortelle in an explicit partnership, many were not. All in all, the locally based group included seven community advocates or activists who were either family members or persons with disabilities; five medical or therapeutic service providers; two higher education administrators; one government administrator; and eight directors, teachers, or volunteers at private or public special schools. I also interviewed 11 individuals who were international visitors, which included a representative from the US consulate, two US professionals engaged in voluntary consulting with Immortelle, five occupational therapy students from the US, and three

© The Author(s) 2020
B. Harry, *Childhood Disability, Advocacy, and Inclusion in the Caribbean*, Palgrave Studies in Disability and International Development, https://doi.org/10.1007/978-3-030-23858-2_7

speech and language therapy students from Canada doing their internships at Immortelle.

These interviews revealed a landscape of disability services inspired by powerful individual motivations but undermined by an absence of support systems and by competition for scarce resources. Despite obvious improvements that had occurred over the years in provisions for individuals with disabilities, failed or poorly implemented policies reflected a deep-rooted resistance to systems change. However, while participants across the study echoed a resounding call for "systems", several stakeholders argued that the problem was not a total absence of systems, but rather a need to change embedded systems that were never really designed for equity. Specifically, they pointed to a public school system totally unprepared for adaptation to students with disabilities; medical services that responded well to urgent care but not to the chronic needs of individuals with disabilities; low priority on the value of therapeutic and preventive services; and a public agenda that continued to associate disability with charity.

Moreover, the hierarchical structure of the society and the absence of systematic procedures for implementation of policies supported a traditional reliance on social networking and what one participant described as "intuitive and relational" interaction systems. Against this landscape, the well-intentioned efforts of the public and corporate sectors stood out as sometimes complementary, but often uncoordinated spurts of goodwill.

In analyzing the interviews with these community stakeholders, I identified five dominant themes that overlapped to some extent and, overall, reinforced and complemented each other. Moreover, these themes carried strong echoes of the perspectives of parents and teachers:

1. Individual agency and competition for limited resources drives advocacy and activism.
2. We need systems!
3. Medical and therapeutic needs are minimally addressed.
4. The public school system is totally inadequate for needs of students with disabilities, therefore private services continue to be essential.
5. Disabilities are not on the public agenda; non-governmental organizations (NGOs) supported by corporate entities attempt to fill the gaps.

I will address the first two of these themes in this chapter and the last three in Chap. 8.

INDIVIDUAL AGENCY AND COMPETITION FOR SCARCE RESOURCES

As discussed in Chap. 6, parents have been the drivers of advocacy movements across the world. In the US, the parent movement, supported by a culture of litigation, has been credited with spearheading the major changes on behalf of persons with disabilities (Kirk, 1984). Moreover, Colin Ong-Dean (2009), in a study of parent advocacy in the US, highlighted the fact that it is usually "well-resourced" parents who can initiate these movements. For example, in the US, the ARC (previously the Association for Retarded Children) and United Cerebral Palsy were initiated between 1949 and 1950 by middle- to upper-income parents of children who had these conditions. As noted by Turnbull, Turnbull, Erwin, Soodak, and Shogren (2015), a similar process occurred in 1964 with the formation of the Learning Disabilities Association (previously the Association for Children with Learning Disabilities). In a vastly contrasting nation, India, the process was very similar. Reena Sen and her colleagues (Sen, Goldbart, & Kaul, 2008) described the history of the Indian Institute for Cerebral Palsy (IICP), which was initiated by just two parents in 1972 under the name of the West Bengal Spastics Society and was ultimately established as the IICP in 1974. Having started with services to just two children, the Institute currently provides a broad range of services both locally and nationally.

The purpose of these advocacy movements is usually twofold: to raise awareness of the needs of individuals with disabilities and, more urgently, to provide much-needed services such as education, health, and residential care. Mobilizing the support of professionals, religious leaders, and, ultimately, governments is an essential next step for such organizations.

At the time of this study, it was evident that individual motivation and agency continued to be the driving power behind disability advocacy in TT. Indeed, several of the country's leading advocates and service providers were either self-advocates or had family members with disabilities, although several came to this work through their professional concerns about disability issues. This chapter focuses on what I learned from the activists, doctors, therapists, academics, private and public school administrators, and a key civil servant, who provided invaluable insights into the conundrums of advocacy in the face of limited resources.

Challenges of Collaboration, Competition, and "Rights"

Community participants identified a lack of coherence and collaboration as a key issue in advocacy. In the face of limited resources, it was difficult for groups to commit to collaborating across their various agendas. Jane Holmes Bernstein, the neuropsychologist cited in the previous chapter, identified two key problems—a lack of public sector responsiveness to the efforts of professional and civic groups, and an absence of a "culture of collaboration". She exclaimed: "In fact, the NGOs get in their own way because everybody is guarding their own turn."

This was a common theme across the community groups, who described the efforts as "fragmented", "scattered", "not unified", and relying too much on the hard work of just a few individuals. Dr. David Bratt, Immortelle board member and a pediatrician with a focus on disabilities, highlighted the fragmentation in this way:

> *David.* They're too scattered. There are many different groups but they don't want to come together to make one strong group. Everybody knows somebody who will do something for them in the Ministry. Then they think they'll get *this* place for *their* children in *that* area. Instead of saying we need a national centre of some sort and everybody comes together to make it happen, they block each other. It's like, the pie is only so large and I have a little of it and I feel I could get a little more so I block somebody else.

Dr. Beverly Beckles of the National Centre for Persons with Disabilities (NCPD) agreed:

> *Beverly.* In addition to no money, we are not unified, not one voice, not pooling resources and trying to see how we could help each other. In a small country of 1.5 million there are so many groups out there talking about serving the sector. For example, there maybe 10 groups serving the deaf! This also creates problems for corporations who are bombarded with requests by so many groups.

Another way of looking at the issue of advocacy focused on the absence of a strong sense of individual "rights" in Trinidad/Tobago. Penny Camps, a speech and language therapist of some 30 years' experience, who currently provided services in a government clinic in Tobago, felt that parents could gain much more if they really believed they had the right to services:

Penny. The parent who thinks they and their family are worthy of it are the ones who will be persistent. Persistence is the biggest piece. So the parents who get the services are, apart from the ones who can pay for it, the ones who, at some fundamental level, don't buy into the myths that exist around special needs—that somehow something is wrong with them, that it's their fault, or that this is what God wants for their life. The parents who have not bought into that say, "No! My child is as deserving as any other child!" Those are the ones that get through.

Parent Power: A Cautionary Tale

Penny's point that even parents who could not "pay for it" could get things done was borne out in a powerful interview I had with Crystal Jones, a parent advocate for Cerebral Palsy (CP). I discovered that there were two CP associations, one called the Cerebral Palsy Society, which seemed to focus mainly on providing training and seeking services, and the Cerebral Palsy Association initiated by Crystal, which focused on gaining financial or job assistance for parents and on developing self-help opportunities.

My introduction to Crystal came from Sister Bertil at the Lady Hochoy Home. Describing Crystal as having done "a very good job", Sister also cautioned that Crystal's success would be vulnerable to political winds. In her words, "What she got is not long term. It will change with the government!"

I interviewed Crystal in an office in the Ministry of Labor. She began by explaining that this was not her office, but just a space she was being allowed to use occasionally for her advocacy efforts. Crystal's story of her son's brain damage at birth, his challenging life, and his death at age 20 was painful but awe-inspiring:

Crystal. My first child was diagnosed with CP at the age of 3 months. I was 17 years old when I went to the hospital to deliver him and because of my age the nurses were saying, "Young child making baby! You should be in school!" and all of that. With that, they were not responding when I was telling them I was ready to deliver. They were saying "You don't know what you're talking about, the child is not ready to come yet". At minutes to five in the morning I kept calling the nurses and they were not responding. Two were resting their heads on the desk. When I screamed out, they realised the child was in my passageway. They delivered the child and said it was a normal delivery and sent me home. When he was 3 months we realised he was not keeping up his head.

He never went to school. The schools that were in existence, like the Lady Hochoy home and Princess Elizabeth, only accepted children who could at least help themselves or were potty trained; so the children who were in pampers needed the parents to be there to assist them. In my son's case he couldn't do anything for himself so he was not accepted into the school. But they offered therapy—patterning—so I'd take him for patterning and then go home. He was 1 year at the time—1995. At age seven, because of the therapy that he was getting, he started to roll and lift his head while lying down on his tummy. But then they said he couldn't come anymore because of his size and age, and the limited number of volunteers to help with therapy. The parents had to be the volunteers.

It was really devastating when he was taken off therapy. After that, his situation deteriorated a lot with no more therapy and no more advice as to what to do. Nobody advised me that he could get speech therapy to learn to speak. He was my first child and because he couldn't respond I didn't know I could speak with him and teach him to speak. It wasn't until I had other children and they started to speak that he started to learn words. My daughter started to treat him like he is the baby and started to teach him his name. She'd say, "T-i-b-a", and he started to say it too. I was in shock! When my daughter first started to say mummy, I didn't know that he was learning the word "mummy" too. One day when he and I were alone in the house, I heard "Mummy", and I'm thinking, "It can't be him. I must be hearing things!" Then I realised it was him! I was so shocked I started to cry!

So I left the nursing assistant job that I was doing and I stayed home to be with him. Many times we tried to get Tiba in a day-care centre but they said, "If he gets a seizure we will not leave all the other children here to run to the hospital. This is not a place where we could deal with special children!" Up to this day there is no institution or day-care centre that a mother of a child with severe/moderate CP could leave their child and go to work.

This mother's determination and conviction drove her to publicly challenge the Minister of Health and demand that something be done for families who could not get gainful employment because of the needs of their children with cerebral palsy. After initial success in getting such government assistance through the URP (Unemployment Relief Program), Crystal went on to establish a business effort that would move parents beyond dependence on government assistance. I will quote this inspiring story at length:

Crystal. I didn't know then that I could get a grant for my son. There was public assistance but I never used to receive it. So one day I went with my son to the welfare office and waited. There was another parent with a disabled child next to me sitting there crying. She was going through the same frustration and nobody was paying attention. The whole day we're sitting there with the children and I reached a stage where I couldn't take it anymore. I started to scream at the top of my voice. They thought I was going mad. I said, "It has to have somebody here to help these parents! You're not understanding the situation that we are going through. Nobody wants to depend on the government! I want to work!"

Next thing I know, they came home to my house! They brought me a box of groceries. They brought clothes. But, for me, it wasn't about that. I wanted an avenue for me to be independent with my children but I just needed some assistance.

So I went to the Minister—that's like 5 years ago. I said "Sir, this is the situation. A lot of parents are facing it. I am unable to work. I have a child with CP and I'm looking for assistance to see if we could have a day-care—anything where parents could leave their children and go to work." He sat there listening to my plight. I'm pouring out my heart! He dismissed me. He said, "I hear you. I will look into it". I said, "If you don't acknowledge within the next two weeks, I'm going to protest in front of your building with other parents."

So I got about 14 other parents and we went in front of the building with placards. I carried my son in his wheel chair. I called all the media and told them to come out and see what other parents are facing. It wasn't a lot of parents but the media did come and they highlighted it. The Minister saw us protesting and he left and went up to the parliament building. But he didn't know the media were there! When the Prime Minister saw us she told the Minister he had to go back down and deal with us. So they called me and said, "Ms. Jones come up and let's have a meeting". I left my son with the other parents and I went over to meet him. This is him in the meeting: He's sitting around a table with all his executives watching me as a simple parent. He says, "Who the hell are you coming in front of my building to tell me about parents and all the people are outside watching! What the hell is wrong with you?" Well, I gave him a piece of my mind: "Your building? You are here to work for *us*, to work for the people! We have a problem and you have to address it!"

Finally, he apologized. He walked outside, talked to one executive. In the end the resolution was that they started a program where parents would be paid to stay home and see about their children! All the parents who can't get out to work are getting $1800 to stay home and see about their children. That was the resolution and it's not just one person getting help, it's hundreds.

At the time of this research in 2015, Crystal was heading "the CP program", provided by the Unemployment Relief Program (URP) housed in the Ministry of Labour. She explained that parents could access this relief by providing medical proof of the child's Cerebral Palsy, but the funding was limited to the neediest cases, such as parents who not only could not take a job but had to carry their child to therapy appointments, thus needing transportation costs. Crystal's efforts did not stop there, however, as she explained:

> *Crystal.* Then we took it to another level. We registered a business called "For My Child Services Limited". Everybody sacrificed and pooled $900 out of the $1800 they received from URP, and we bought tools to start our own business for each region. So the parents in Arima chose to do catering because a lot of them are cooks and they do their own preservatives. The parents in Port of Spain chose to do joinery—tables, medicine cabinets. The parents in Penal (further down South) have a lot of land space so they decided to do short crops, and grow-boxes and so on.

Reminiscent of Jacqui's complaint that "the bigger you get, the more problems you have", Crystal explained that taking her advocacy "to another level" brought unanticipated challenges. For example, the business was required to have a registered office, which the group could not afford. Consequently, they were seeking guidance with administrative and legal issues, and were hoping to gain assistance with a business plan from the phone company, Digicel.

I refer to Crystal's story as a "cautionary tale" to emphasize both the wonders and the pitfalls of her tremendous advocacy. Starting off totally on her own, with the support of only 14 parents experiencing similar needs, and trusting only her own conviction of her right to a better life for her family, she accomplished not only access to government assistance but the establishment of a true self-help project for families like hers. But the longevity of her accomplishments was limited by two caveats: first, the requirement that a business must have an office points to the missing piece—the need for either public or private resources as well as organizational know-how. The second caveat, and perhaps more daunting for Crystal's efforts was that, as Sister Antoinette had pointed out: "It will change with the government". Two years later, this prophecy was proven true as funding for the project was no longer available.

PARENT-DRIVEN ADVOCACY ORGANIZATIONS

The theme of individual parent agency in advocacy was powerfully demonstrated by the work of three groups who participated in this research—two focusing on Down Syndrome and one on Autism. As mentioned in a previous chapter, during the early years of Immortelle's existence, a group of parents deeply connected to the school had initiated the National Association for Down Syndrome (NADS). At the time of this research, the activities of that group had waned and been largely replaced by the Down Syndrome Family Network (DSFN). Also in the foreground of parent advocacy was the Autistic Society of Trinidad and Tobago (ASTT). The leaders of these associations shared their accounts of these efforts.

Creating the National Association for Down Syndrome (NADS) in the 1980s

Chief among the movers and shakers of NADS were Lydia and Tony Pierre, Helen and John Humphrey, and Martin and Lana de Gannes. Together, these families mobilized others to create a vibrant organization that led the way in public advocacy for Down Syndrome, while also providing therapeutic and social activities for children and their families. All this took place in a property leased to NADS by the government through Helen and John's political connections. Lydia, Tony, and Lana told the story this way:

> *Lydia.* How did we start? At that time Tony and I were doing a lot of work with parents. A doctor at Mt. Hope Hospital would bring us in to meet with parents whose children were born there. She was fantastic! She would talk with the parents and then bring us in to talk with them. It was great because you felt you were touching people when they needed it. Tommy by that time was very active very lively and so on, so we were able to take him, and they were able to see him and see that it's not the end of the world.
>
> And then Helen Humphrey came to visit us with her daughter and granddaughter, Becky. She needed an operation for a heart problem and they had done some fund-raisers. From talking with them we moved towards thinking of forming the National Association for Down Syndrome— "NADS"—using whatever funds were left from their fund raiser. Two other key families were Martin and Lana de Gannes and Eric and Arlene Williams. We used to meet regularly and we would arrange camps in the summer for the children. That's how it started.

We started getting the word out through television and different media. Then I was sent by the group with a couple of other members to visit the Down Syndrome Association in New York. It had a big name and there was a lot of talk about it. But when we went we discovered that it was a lot of simple people doing things that we could do. We said, "But this isn't so hard!" And that was the impetus to start NADS.

NADS just grew exponentially! We put so much energy into it. And it had an impact on policy. For example, it led to the disability grant for parents that we have now. I think we opened their eyes—that disability is acceptable and disabled people have rights. I think that is what we did. We were so in the government's face!

Then the Government gave us a house for the Association! John Humphrey, who was a Minister of government, was in the group, which gave us a kind of a status from the get go. So Helen Humphrey maneuvered it so we got the building. We developed a beautiful program there, providing all kinds of services to a small group of children who came every day. We had facilitators. There was a person who was in charge of the program—a speech therapist. But it took over our lives!

Martin de Gannes was so involved—he was a real soldier! And Martin Jones. But we were struggling and they eventually pulled out. People have their lives. It's a full time job! We had a Board and elections, so it was open to whoever wanted to be in any office. But the trouble was that when new people were voted in the work didn't continue. It breaks my heart that that centre is dead now.

Tony. I think people got a little tired. It came to a point where we were the only ones—just Lydia and myself. So by that time we needed to pull out. It was mashing us up. And things just went further and further and further down.

Lana de Gannes echoed Tony and Lydia's account:

Lana. I think we did more than our part to try to bring Down Syndrome to the fore, and to let people be aware. After a while Martin handed over the presidency of NADS to others and unfortunately they did not carry it on. You have to be consistent. You can't just talk about it. We did and we carried it forward. I don't have the energy to go back in that now. Somebody else needs to take up the mantle and continue, and walk the walk and not just talk the talk.

So what you're seeing now is another group of people with children who have Down Syndrome. They have formed another network and I remember telling Martin the other day that this reminds me of us—twenty, thirty years ago. Seems like rehashing the same thing all over again.

The Down Syndrome Family Network (DSFN): What Happens When the Fund-Raising Party Is Over?

Coming some three decades after the formation of NADS, Lana's comment referred to the Down Syndrome Family Network (DSFN), which was initiated in 2012. Glen Niles, chairman and founder of DSFN, spoke in an urgent voice that reflected the changes in attitudes toward intellectual disabilities over the years. Like the Pierre, de Gannes, and Humphrey families, Glen became a leading voice in advocacy in response to his own experience with his son, Tyrese, who had Down Syndrome. However, DSFN's focus reflected a significant change in focus over four decades—an urgent call for full inclusion. In this sense, Glen's voice represented a relatively unique voice among the participants in this study.

When I began my interview with Glen by telling him that I was studying the processes that had allowed the Immortelle Children's Centre to thrive, he pulled no punches:

> *Glen.* How has Immortelle thrived? If people were thriving they would leave and go to an inclusive facility. We are so far behind re inclusion. I want special children to not be so special!

Glen described his early years as a parent as having been unduly influenced by negative stereotypes and advice that dissuaded him from trying to get Tyrese included in the regular education system. When Tyrese was about seven years old, Glen had the opportunity to attend the National Down Syndrome Congress in Boston, an experience that revolutionized his approach to raising his son. In his words:

> *Glen.* I was blown away! Seeing so many people with Down Syndrome! Everyone dressed in different ways, nobody holding their hand, parents giving them their hotel room key—full independence! I saw people with Down Syndrome discussing political elections! That experience changed my whole perspective! When I came back we changed our whole approach to him. Soon he was doing his own laundry, making sandwiches, cutting the lawn. He's 19 now and he's been working for 2 years at Aeropost.
>
> This is a human rights issue! Advocacy should not be just a matter of looking for funding. Look, corporate TT is part of society so they go with the flavor of the month, but how effective has this approach been for persons with disabilities? How have they benefitted? What happens when the fund raising party is over? Children go back to the same situation!

With total commitment to the goal of full inclusion, Glen argued vigorously that if parents truly believed in their children's rights, advocacy efforts would be much more successful. He described the challenge as including two key aspects: first, education for independence must start in the home and, second, the entire society needs to get rid of its "preconceived limits on persons with Down Syndrome". This belief, he felt, should be demonstrated through legislation to specifically support persons with disabilities, and through persistent advocacy that would accept nothing short of meaningful opportunities for full inclusion. Without full commitment to that goal, advocacy and private sector efforts that accept the status quo simply serve to reinforce it. The argument that "we would still need special schools" held no water for Glen.

Glen's intense voluntary efforts in DSFN earned him a unique honor in 2018—a Commonwealth Point of Light award from Queen Elizabeth of England, for exceptional voluntary service.

The Autistic Society of Trinidad and Tobago (ASTT): We've Come a Long Way!

Teresina Seunarine was the founder and current president of TASTT. She described the prevalence of autism in TT as being possibly more than 10,000, but the ASTT was aware of and working with some 600 families, focusing on parent training. Teresina's own story revealed the combination of personal drive, energy, and social resources needed to accomplish a thriving movement pursuing goals of public awareness, education, and services. Her son, Kester, has autism and was about 34 years of age at the time of our interview. When Kester was about 10, Teresina agreed to go public about his situation through an interview with a newspaper reporter. She described some changes between that time and the present:

> *Teresina.* It was many years ago—maybe 1991/1992, when a reporter interviewed me and our family. We live in a village, and there was a terrible backlash. People were calling and asking me why—saying that we should not have disclosed this. So that was a big issue in the early 90s.
>
> But we have come a long way. Now everybody looks out for my son. If they see him walking alone they wonder who's with him. But we do get stories from families that there's still a big stigma attached to having a child with a disability and especially one that people don't understand. Many parents don't want to take their child out in public. They're difficult to travel

with in public transport and there are parents who cannot face that kind of embarrassment, so they keep them at home. So there are still a lot of hurdles to surmount. The public awareness is happening, but very slowly. It's been 25 years and I've seen a difference.

At the time of this study, the Autistic Society was working toward developing a "life-span approach" and had applied to the Housing Development Corporation to reserve five units in an upcoming residential project for the Autistic Society. Teresina explained that, like Immortelle, much of the Autistic Society's support for the previous seven years had come from the Republic Bank's *Power to Make a Difference Fund*, but the financial support via this program would end in 2017. Most of those funds went toward therapies and bringing experts from overseas to conduct training with local providers and advocates. However, the society reached out in several directions and was constantly trying new initiatives to seek funding. In Teresina's words:

> We have to be constantly writing proposals. We could not survive without donations!

Passing and Continuing Phases of Advocacy

The fact that DSFN had, effectively, replaced NADS in advocacy for Down Syndrome points to the challenge of longevity of organizations that rely on the motivation of a few individuals without systematic support from the public sector. I gained a long-term view of various phases of advocacy from two people who had been deeply involved in the work of the Lady Hochoy Home for over 30 years Sister Bertil, who was currently the Director of the Home and Lucille Tom Quong, a long-time parent advocate whose son, (since deceased) had attended the Hochoy day school for most of his life. These ladies reminded me of several attempts at disability advocacy during my time in Trinidad, such as CAMROD, the Caribbean Association for Mental Retardation and Other Developmental Disabilities, which included all the Caribbean islands and focused on conferences and training programs. Despite interest from several foreign groups, it seemed that lack of proper accounting had undermined the efforts of that group.

Nevertheless, advocacy continues, perhaps, as Lana de Gannes suggested, each subsequent phase seeming to "rehash" the same issues addressed by previous efforts, yet simultaneously reflecting the nuances of its time. For example, the inspiration Glen Niles gained from his participation in the U.S. Down Syndrome Congress cannot be underestimated. Similarly, other groups with a focus on inclusion have become more visible since the time of this research, such as the Autism Parents Association of Trinidad and Tobago (APATT) and the online support group, Autism Spirit.

TRYING TO PULL IT ALL TOGETHER: THE CONSORTIUM OF DISABILITIES ORGANIZATIONS (CODO)

The limited scale of my research project allowed me introductions only to the few organizations I have referred to so far. I gained a much broader view through interviews with the then leaders of the Consortium of Disabilities Organizations (CODO), an umbrella organization that represented a much-needed effort to counter the tendency to fragmentation already described. Representing over 40 advocacy groups, the Consortium functioned as a mechanism for building a cohesive coalition that could effectively advocate for persons with the full range of disabilities.

My interviews with Bhawani Persad and Sharda Ramlakhan, the former and then current Directors of CODO, provided me with two unique perspectives: first, an in-depth understanding of the power of individual agency arising from personal needs, and second, an inspiring perspective on the possibilities for coordinated efforts. Both Bhawani and Sharda also offered powerful accounts of the importance of self-advocacy.

Advocacy for Persons with Visual Impairments

Bhawani Persad was born with a visual impairment and received his primary education at the Trinidad/Tobago School for the Blind, which was a residential school. His account of his schooling also provided information on the situation across the Caribbean at that time:

> *Bhawani.* We were taught academics, but we were also taught to do household chores and to live in harmony with others around us in a residential capacity. We didn't have to pay anything to go to school. We had children from all races and socio-economic backgrounds, and, in my day, from up and down the Caribbean. I don't know what the arrangements were government to government which allowed these children to come here for an education, but in the Caribbean, except for Jamaica and Trinidad & Tobago, there were no special schools set up for blind and visually impaired children.

It was in the late 70s early 80s that we saw pockets of services set up as units in various parts of the Caribbean.

Bhawani outlined some key changes over the years. One such change was that individuals with visual impairments were probably the first group to be gradually integrated in public schools in TT, starting in 1967, when one student was accepted into St. Joseph's Convent for girls and one to Trinity College for boys. Other schools gradually came on board in the 1970s. Bhawani pointed to the establishment of the Special Education Unit in 1981 as the beginning of a "paradigm shift towards more integration". Schools that previously had been totally residential began to loosen the restrictions, allowing children to spend more time at home with their families. On graduating from the School for the Blind, Bhawani pursued his interests in broadcasting, public relations, and business. Starting by becoming involved in several voluntary efforts, including participating in an advocacy group called the Congress of the Blind and hosting a program that highlighted blind musicians, Bhawani eventually earned his own weekly radio program and gradually became a well-known voice for blind issues throughout the Caribbean. Among many advocacy roles he has played, Bhawani is noted for being a foundation member of both PAVI (Persons Associated with Visual Impairments) and the Trinidad & Tobago Chapter of Disabled Peoples International, Secretary for the Caribbean Council for the Blind, and an advocate for blind cricket in the Caribbean, which resulted in the launching of the West Indies Cricket Council for the Blind in 2005. At the time of this study, Bhawani, not interested in retirement, continued to host a program on an internet radio station owned and operated by blind persons as well as some other colleagues from the disabled community.

Advocacy for Persons with Physical Disabilities

Sharda told a very different personal story, yet, at its core, highlighted the same issues of individual drive to overcome huge social barriers and the same intense concern for improved cohesion for disability advocacy.

Self-advocacy. Describing herself as having been born "just an average person with average abilities", Sharda explained that she had developed muscular dystrophy at the age of 27. At the time she was living in London, England, where a "very inclusive" system provided her with tremendous support.

Sharda. Muscular dystrophy is a very gradual thing. When I first started getting symptoms I went to the doctor. It's also such a rare thing that the doctor did not readily recognize it and diagnose it. Diagnosis came about 18 months after I started recognizing the symptoms. In that 18 month period I went from walking with high heel shoes to walking with braces.

I didn't notice how the environment in London was able to accommodate me because it was an inclusive environment. Using ramps and slopes and sidewalks and public transport was not an issue. It was a very open, inclusive society.

When I got diagnosed I realized that I had to come back home because my family was home in Trinidad. Up until then I'd had no interactions with persons with disabilities. I was not brought up in an inclusive environment in Trinidad and Tobago. There had never been a child in my school with a disability. Never really interacted with anyone in a wheelchair or anyone who was blind. The average citizen in Trinidad just does not have that exposure and I was one of them.

When I came back to Trinidad I found it very difficult to get a job. I had not completed my ACCA—Chartered Accountancy—and in fact I still haven't finished it, but my last job had been as a managerial accountant at the BBC, so I thought getting a job in TT would not be an issue. At that time I was walking with calipers and you could see a distinct limp. I applied for a job at one of the big five accounting firms. I submitted a CV and within 20 minutes they called me. When I went to the interview a couple weeks later, the woman at reception, on seeing me, thought I was there to beg! She didn't think I fit the corporate profile. I soon realized that, no matter what I did, I would not be able to get a job at one of the big five. That was a lesson for me on the mindset and attitudinal barriers that we needed to overcome. It was a patronizing attitude.

But I did manage to get a job at the Board of Inland Revenue doing tax audits. For a number of years that was a very rewarding job. I was able to very quickly reach as high as I could because it was a contract position and they would not allow you to climb the public service ladder.

When I was working there I wrote a letter asking them for a parking spot on disability grounds. They never responded to the letter. When I spoke to the facilities manager, he said, "I'll see what we can do". So I bold-facedly started to park in a spot reserved for someone else. There was no disability parking and my health was deteriorating. The sidewalks were bad and there is no accessible route into the building. The only way for me to get into the building was for me to drive into the building and reverse my car into a spot that was close to the lift. In the meantime people were telling me, you know this is a contract position and if you really push them they will find grounds not to renew your contract. But they never told me anything about parking. They just turned a blind eye. They knew my case was genuine.

So, from the very little that I knew, I knew it wasn't good in Trinidad. But when I came back I hadn't realized it was this bad! That made me want to do something about it.

Advocacy on behalf of the group. In 2004–2005, Sharda started doing volunteer work with a group called *Combined Disabilities* and, in 2007, she joined CODO, working on regularizing procedures and financing. During that time, the membership in CODO increased from an initial 12 disability organizations to over 40 groups. The organization visualized several innovative projects to raise awareness of disability issues, some more successful than others in gaining the needed financial support. One disappointment was a carefully planned proposal for a traveling center that would provide "experiential learning", which, despite support from the UN and initial interest from the government, did not gain funding. A very successful effort, however, was a music festival that started as a small parang competition in 2011 and, by 2015, had grown to a big event at which each member of the organization was invited to perform. With grant funding from United Way, and later from First Citizens Bank, this effort pointed to the welcoming attitude of the public toward individuals with disabilities:

> *Sharda*. It was a tremendous success. Everyone loved it. Children ended up on the front page of the newspaper and I was just so proud to see all the joy that it brought. They started clamoring for more and that developed into what is now the music festival, which has the Arts and Disabilities conference where we focus on a particular topic. Last year we focused on teachers. We brought out all the teachers in the special schools. And we had an art auction of pieces created by persons with disabilities. We had the music classes where we engaged the universities (UTT), their music faculty and their music students to go out and teach music to our children in various schools. And in 2013 we did a music camp in Tobago.

CODO was also working on improving accessibility in TT, and was participating in developing codes for the National Building Standards of TT—an equivalent of the US American's with Disabilities ACT (ADA). The TT efforts, so far, were at the level of establishing policy, not yet reaching the level of legislation: with a committee that included representatives from relevant services and stakeholders, such as fire, occupational health and safety, and the Autistic Society, CODO had received an encouraging response from the Bureau of Standards and was working toward a strategy for implementation that would weave the standards into the mainstream system through buy-in from the town and country department.

Despite many challenges, Bhawani and Sharda remained optimistic about the potential of CODO to promote unity in advocacy for the disabled. Our interview closed on a note of tentative hopefulness from Sharda, with a passionate call for leadership by disabled people themselves to be actively sought and encouraged:

> *Sharda.* Never before has the community been this united. But it's a very fragile union. I think people with disabilities need to recognize that although we have our own identities we have more in common than we have apart. Also, people need to accept that there are organizations that are disability-led and those that are service providers, and there is a huge difference between the mandate of the two. For persons to really actualize a rights-based approach, persons with disabilities must be able to live self-determined lives. I don't see that. This is where ableism comes in. As a result, persons with disabilities remain naive, sheltered, and with an attitude of, "I would take whatever you dish out!"

Dr. Beverly Beckles of the National Center for Persons with Disabilities (NCPD) stated her concern this way:

> *Beverly.* There is still confusion in the minds of people who are members, who ought to continue with their own identity while also joining in one voice. There should be no competition between a member and the group's voice. All should feel comfortable and not threatened.

CODO's efforts were certainly gaining recognition. In 2015, I was fortunate to be invited to a meeting at the US consulate, to hear a presentation by a legal expert from the US who had been one of the leaders in the development of the Americans with Disabilities Act (ADA) in 1990. The meeting was attended by approximately 30 people in the TT disabilities community. The tone of the meeting was upbeat, with the expressed intention of sharing information and insights with the local community regarding the kinds of processes that it took for the US to come to the institutionalization of the ADA.

Shortly after this event, I interviewed a representative of the US consulate in Trinidad/Tobago, who referred to that meeting and pointed out that fragmentation within the disabilities community is common world-wide, but is exacerbated in societies where there are not enough resources to go around. The representative described his agency's involvement as including a grants program that supported certain interventions, a training for the sign language program at UWI, regular meetings with advocates through CODO, and lobbying the government to ratify the UN Convention on Persons with Disabilities. He explained:

> *US Representative.* We've seen through the US experience what happened over the last 25 years since the passage of the American's with Disabilities Act and how when you start making accommodations for persons with disabilities their profile in the community rises. Once their profile rises their sense of empowerment rises and once their sense of empowerment rises they participate at a much more robust level. Now people look back at their objections to the American's with Disability Act and wonder what they were thinking. That's why, if the government were to take some positive steps, even if they're symbolic, it would mean a lot. The big issue for the recent visit is ratification of the UN Convention. We got a lot of very encouraging signs of commitment from people at varying levels of the government. But look—the US government hasn't ratified yet!

Improvements Over the Years

There were, indeed, many signs that optimism for positive change was warranted. The very fact that there was now a system for private special schools to become eligible for government support for teachers, children's meals, and utilities, was an improvement such as I had only dreamed of when I initiated the Immortelle Centre in the 1980s. All the research participants acknowledged that the situation was better than it had been. Yet, all expressed deep disappointment at the limitations that kept people with disabilities on the margins of the society.

I gained an enthusiastic and balanced perspective from Sister Bertil, the Director of the Lady Hochoy Home. Describing an early intervention program that had not been in existence in my time, she said that this early support for children and their families had resulted in less of a demand for residential placement. Also, private special schools were increasingly providing options for children needing day services. Showing me her residential "waiting list" (which was just a list of whoever came and requested admission), Sister explained:

Sister Bertil. Back in 1978, there were 32 names on this one page. Now, in 2015, we have only 2 names on the page! As a result of the early intervention program, and our teaching the parents how to manage, and the CP Association, we're not getting requests for residence. We do still get requests from hospitals where children have been abandoned. What we have in the home now is several adults. One of our older adults is going to be 60. But among the younger children I have 7 or 8 girls under 18 and about 10 boys. We have 82 residents in all now. Years ago we had 150. It shows that the parents are managing better and once they can manage they tend to not give up.

Another good thing is that, with our early intervention program, we have got some of the private schools to take our children into their kindergartens. The government ones are supposed to take them, but they still don't. We work with parents and if we get them very early, we teach discipline, don't spoil them, and once the child can pass a milestone with toilet training you could get them into school. We would liaise with the kindergarten to take this child even for a day or half day. So that helps the parents a lot. Our class size in the day school now has dropped to about 8, where it used to be 15–18. The vocational centre for those over age 18 is where we have bigger numbers.

The theme of positive improvements was supported by Wendy Gomez and Allyson Hamel-Smith, a speech therapist and psychologist who had been in practice since the first opening of Immortelle. Allyson was the most positive:

Allyson. So there have been improvements, a lot of these are related to the work of NGOs: Teachers, Parents, Principals, clinicians from many disciplines, who have worked hard to create services. Examples are the Dyslexia Association, Eshe's Learning Centre, The Immortelle, The Cotton Tree Foundation, the National Centre for Persons with Disabilities (NCPD), the Adult Literacy Tutors Association (ALTA), and many others. Many started 20–25 years ago and continue today. It is my impression that the many different initiatives have had a positive impact.

For example, I was in a school 2 weeks ago to discuss the case of a restless, 'naughty' 8 year old with significant reading problems. The teacher didn't get it; she understood his problems only in terms of a "bad family environment", but the principal had a very positive approach to helping this child. Twenty five years ago I could not have had a conversation like that with a principal. There's more of a sense that children with invisible disabilities should be getting the services they need and that it's unfair that they do not.

Successive governments have been spending significant portions of our budget on education. When the young psychologists in my office quarrel about poor services, I say, "You have no idea where we're coming from!" That does not mean that things are where they need to be, there is an enormous amount of work still to be done. An important area is legislation for special needs persons, and mandated budgetary provisions for persons with disabilities.

Wendy Gomez was a bit more tentative:

Wendy. In my 35 years I have seen a big difference. But it's not enough! Not with the funds we have in T&T! So it is frustrating!

WE NEED SYSTEMS!

The combination of individual motivation and a "lot of goodwill" in the country should make for positive results. However, the theme, "we need systems", which came through so strongly in interviews with current parents, was echoed consistently by the community participants. They argued that reliance on individual agency, surrounded by no matter how much "goodwill", undermines longevity if there are no procedures in place for continuation of leadership. Further, reliance on individual networking without institutional procedures undermines the effective implementation of any policy.

Charles Mouttet, a prominent banker, member of the Immortelle Board, and himself a parent of a child with a disability, was emphatic on this issue:

Charles. I cannot say I've seen any sustained and concerted effort to institutionalize or create strong, self-supporting institutions for the disabled communities in TT. That's what's so disheartening because with the amount of currency that flows through this country there's absolutely no excuse for the lack of support and services!

There were several thoughtful analyses of the lack of a "sustained effort" toward addressing disability issues. Some were economic, some political, some bureaucratic, and there was one that I would describe as philosophical.

It's Economic! The Paradox of Plenty[1]

Charles Mouttet's analysis focused on the economic issues he saw facing TT. Relating TT's economy to other similar, resource-rich developing nations, he referred to the notion of the "paradox of plenty":

Charles. In the conversation about the future of emerging economies that are commodity rich there's a concept called "the paradox of plenty". Having so much through our energy resources, but not having the institutional infrastructure to deal with those riches, allows for corruption, misuse, and abuse of public funds, without the ability to direct those funds into programs, into building institutions to support the community.

So, currently, we have this diminished flow of cash, but what's happening is that in Trinidad we lead a subsidized life, from several perspectives! One is that government transfers and subsidies form a significant part of the budget; that is, transfers of funds from central government to state enterprises to help them run. It's a form of subsidy. For instance, a subsidy is where the consumer does not pay the market price of the gasoline. We've got to watch what we're doing by having all these subsidies and transfers. That's why our budget was 63 billion dollars—it's madness! I don't recall the exact number but a large percentage of it is recurrent expenditure.

I suppose the subsidizing approach was a way to distribute the wealth coming from the energy sector to the wider population and it was a fair way to do it because everybody could benefit more or less. But now it's just a question of affordability and it allows us to lead that subsidized life—to buy BMWs and Mercedes Benz and 50-inch TVs and go to Miami whenever we want. When it's a long weekend you can't get a parking spot in the airport. This place sweet you know! If you can get out when you want, you're insulated!

[1] **Paradox of plenty**
The **resource curse** (also known as the **paradox of plenty**) refers to the paradox that countries and regions with an abundance of natural resources, specifically, point-source non-renewable resources like minerals and fuels, tend to have less economic growth and worse development outcomes than countries with fewer natural resources. This is hypothesized to happen for many different reasons, including a decline in the competitiveness of other economic sectors (caused by appreciation of the real exchange rate as resource revenues enter an economy), volatility of revenues from the natural resource sector due to exposure to global commodity market swings, government mismanagement of resources, or weak, ineffectual, unstable, or corrupt institutions (possibly due to the easily diverted actual or anticipated revenue stream from extractive activities). http://dictionary.sensagent.com/paradox%20of%20plenty/en-en/#anchorWiki.

This concept of the "paradox of plenty" has been applied to TT by Ernst and Young (2015), a global accounting firm who published a commentary on the nation's economy. Their critique pointed not only to the subsidies referred to by Charles, but also to numerous government assistance programs:

> Our real challenge has been about using energy wealth as a means of diversification and to build a sustainable competitive advantage… It is against the foregoing bench-marks that the performance of the country should be judged and, in this regard, there is much to be desired. The most worrisome trend is the continuation of the perennial state of dependency: dependency of the nation on its energy resources and, perhaps more disconcertingly, the dependency of our citizens on Government transfers and subsidies. Transfers and subsidies include, but are not limited to the petroleum subsidy, spending on the CEPEP and URP programmes, unemployment assistance, the increased disability and public assistance grants, the increased senior citizen pension, the newly announced "baby grant", free education up to tertiary level, the school book grants, the school feeding programme and the grant of 75,000 laptops to secondary school students. (Ernst & Young, 2015, p. 2)

This statement, however, raises challenging questions about some of the very support systems that many participants in this study felt were essential for persons with disabilities. Do we not need the very "disability and public assistance grants" referred to here? Where does a society draw the line between "dependence" and publicly funded support for those who need it? Charles Mouttet offered his view of this question:

> *Charles.* Government does need to provide a base-line of education for people with disabilities. Then charitable sources can build on that. That's different from creating a society of dependency, which is what has happened over successive governments. Yes, they've been able to get unemployment down to 4 percent, but really it's a system where people get paid for less productive work, which has repercussions on the labor pool because many people are not motivated to work hard.

It's Lack of Planning! We Do This All the Time!

The second reason offered for the lack of a "sustained effort" pointed to poor planning. Charles Mouttet highlighted what several participants identified as an endemic lack of detailed planning for government projects:

Charles. We do this all the time! Look at the Couva children's hospital. I don't know when it will open because I don't know when they will put in the equipment. It was the same with the Eric Williams medical complex—it was top-notch. But for a long time it was, 'you can't get this and you can't get that' because when you go the machines are broken down and need to be fixed. Even in the private medical institutions the service is no better. It's not thoroughly thought through. There is no plan.

A case in point: The National Enrichment Centre for Persons with Disabilities. Charles' reference to "the Couva children's hospital" echoed a story that was mentioned across the interviews with advocates and medical and therapeutic service providers. Frequently referred to by stakeholders as "the Couva centre" or "the Carlsen Field centre", the National Enrichment Centre for Persons with Disabilities was opened by the Prime Minister in 2015, and was to provide assessment and related therapeutic services for individuals with disabilities.

I received numerous versions of this recurring theme, all of which focused on a plan that apparently had not gone beyond the construction of a building, and with that, had failed to implement important logistical features for persons with disabilities. Sister Bertil of the Lady Hochoy Home provided me with an overview of this recurring theme:

Sister Bertil. The Ministry of the People and Social Development has a Disability Affairs Unit. That's a plus that has happened over the years. They've built this building in Carlsen Field, right on the Highway—the turn-off just after Chaguanas. It's easily accessible once you come off the highway.

Now they say they're waiting for input from the stakeholders, which I find is nonsense. A steering committee came together to advise on the building. It included directors from Goodwill, NCPD, and CODO. The first floor is supposed to be therapeutic centres and upstairs are the offices. But, just recently, Sharda Ramlakhan was showing a reporter on her TV program how difficult it is to move from one place to the next using a wheel chair. The kitchen is brand new but it hasn't got enough space for wheel chairs. The wheel chairs could probably move around but there's not enough space to wash the dishes. This is although we had given the Ministry copies of the international standards!

I had heard that the center came about in response to the protest led by parent advocate Crystal Jones at the Ministry of Health. Crystal confirmed this report:

Crystal. Yes! This is how it was created. That therapy centre in Carlsen Field was built recently because of our protest! The Minister had a meeting and asked what we need. We said we needed the disability centre. But it's still not open, because they still need equipment. We had a meeting recently with the operations of the centre and we asked, "Who will be managing the centre? What workers are required?" All of that. They spent over 12 million dollars to build it and not one piece of furniture is there yet! The centre was built with no ramp. So who are you building this centre for with no ramp? When the assessment was done they said the elevator isn't wheelchair suitable—you can't turn the chair. So who was being catered for? So now it must go back to parliament to get additional funding.

Everyone I talked to knew about the Couva Centre. Penny Camps put the matter simply: "The Couva Centre? At the end of the day that's an example of what is seriously lacking. No follow through!"

The foregoing statements were made in interviews that I conducted in 2015. Two years later, the policy statement of the Ministry of Social Development (Government of the Republic of Trinidad and Tobago, National Policy on Persons with Disabilities, 2017) stated the following:

Construction of a facility for the establishment of a National Development Centre for Persons with Disabilities was completed, to provide a range of therapeutic and rehabilitation services. It is expected that the Centre will be operationalized by the end of 2017. (p. 11)

In July of 2018, the center had still not opened and the T&T Cerebral Palsy Society staged a protest at the site of the building, calling on the government to open the center. The president of the Society, Philip Metivier, told the media, "They're playing politics with disabled people. Three years ago they said the Centre would be finished. Now they keep stalling, saying there were infrastructural problems." (Loop News, 2018).

It's Political: "Too Much Politics!"

But why this lack of planning? As in the foregoing quotation, several interviewees pointed a finger at "politics" as the key reason for the lack of coordination and follow-through in services and provisions for individuals with disabilities. They argued that policy decisions were frequently made for political purposes, whether to gain in upcoming elections or to negate the work of previous political administrations. This, they argued, led to a severe lack of planning at the front end, when decisions were made simply to impress the public that something was being done. It also led to a lack of continuity on the back end, when a project that had been started no longer served current political purposes. Like the Couva Centre, there were numerous examples of this kind of process in medical services, educational services, professional preparation for teachers and therapists, and special social projects.

Teacher preparation and teaching positions: "There was no plan in place". Disruptive policy shifts were particularly evident in education, where abrupt changes affected not only children with disabilities, but also the process of preparing and providing trained special education teachers. My interview with Dr. Elna Carrington-Blaides at the University of the West Indies (UWI) Trinidad campus was instructive regarding the challenges of teacher preparation. Elna was the person who had developed and instituted the Bachelor of Education program at the University of Trinidad and Tobago (UTT) some years before.

Elna told me that she had come to UWI in 2011 in response to an advertised position for a lecturer in inclusive and special education. She was tasked with developing a master's degree in special education, which, it turned out, would attract most of its students from among graduates of the UTT bachelors' program, since UWI itself did not offer a bachelor's in special education. Elna focused on developing the master's program and pointed out several challenges.

A key challenge was the absence of legislation regarding special education. Since Elna's degrees in education were from US universities—the City University of New York and Southern University in Louisiana—she was trying to introduce the US framework for special education services in the training program at UWI. As she explained, however, this was difficult because of the lack of any local system for special education: "Because we don't have the laws or even the policies to guide us. We're still talking about the Education Act of 1967. That's a real problem!"

Another challenge Elna identified was the continuing uncertainty regarding what jobs would be available in the Ministry of Education for graduating teachers. She described the disillusionment facing newly graduated teachers when they found that they were not going to be placed in situations where they could use the skills they had gained:

> *Elna.* It's unfortunate that special education is so closely tied to politics. It's like education in general gets roughed up, but special education gets the

worst end of the stick. Every time elections were coming up a lot of those teachers that we trained from UTT did not get put in the setting that they were trained to be in. Now the Minister gets up one morning about 2 weeks ago and says he's pulling 109 of the teachers out of the schools and sending them to Student Support Services. We don't know what that means because he hasn't rolled it out. We hope they're going to be used as consultants to ensure that our special children get the services they need in the regular classroom.

It's not a bad idea, but what happens to the classes that you're pulling them from? You're going to pull the teachers and send them to Student Support Services and then have them sitting there for 2/3 weeks before anything happens. And you'll frustrate the living daylights out of some of them, leave some kids unattended and mess up the whole system.

There was no plan in place. They're just doing things that might appease voters but there's no desire to improve the system, to serve the students or be beneficial to the school system. We depend on policies that come out of the Ministry of Education. We had gotten to the stage where we had an inclusive education policy document. But now the latest document from the Ministry of Educations says, "Special Education policy", with no mention of inclusive education.

Occupational Therapy: "Then the government changed and everything froze". My interview with Lesley Garcia, Secretary of the Trinidad/Tobago Occupational Therapists Association, revealed a very similar story of the negative impact of political changes.

> *Lesley.* A student of mine and I presented her paper on starting a Master's in occupational therapy, and UTT was interested in taking up the possibility. I met with them a couple times and worked out a skeletal curriculum and we worked with UTT for about a year. And then the government changed and everything froze!

Aligning national policy to the UN Convention. Dr. Beverly Beckles, CEO of the National Centre for Persons with Disabilities (NCPD), underscored the difficulty of unpredictable political agendas and pointed to the impact of this problem on the development of a national policy on disabilities:

> *Beverly.* In 2015 we ratified the UN convention and we thought we'd see something happening. But we are still trying to get government to review the national policy on persons with disabilities to be in alignment with the

convention. There was a national policy before, so aligning it to our document should be an easy task. So we've consulted, submitted comments, provided information but we're no further ahead.

It's a lot to do with the policy makers, as disability is not at the top of the agenda. We might do something at the service level but then in the middle we have a change of government. The last policy was ratified under the previous government and the new government came in in September of 2015, and now it's like having to start the process all over again, trying to lobby with the powers that be and sensitize them to the value and importance of moving forward.

There's such a level of frustration! If you're not committed you would give up but you look around and see why you can't give up. You see all the people who depend on you.

It's the Bureaucracy!

Professor Jane Bernstein attributed the lack of progress in education to a rigid bureaucracy. Referring to the situation that Elna had described regarding the government's failure to provide promised positions for new special education teacher graduates, Jane offered this emphatic interpretation, tying politics to a dysfunctional bureaucracy:

> *Jane.* UTT had a special education training program. They trained a cohort of students who are really interested in the field and then the Ministry just dropped the ball. Didn't give them placement. They trained them, they did practicum, did this and this and this. The government said they would give them jobs and—nothing! The bureaucratic failure here is a disaster, the problems are entrenched in the bureaucracy.

In keeping with this view, several community participants blamed the rigid bureaucracy for the continuing roadblocks to progress on disability issues. Dr. David Bratt reflected on the history of the Ministry of Education's support for private special schools and the repeated failures of implementation of official policies, such as the timely provision of subventions for teachers' salaries. His comments also point to the heavy reliance on individual agency and vision to get things done:

> *David.* Mrs. Manning, as Minister of Education, was very interested. As far as Special Education is concerned, she's the person that got things going. She was doing a good job but when her husband won the election she was

moved to another ministry. So we have had to deal with a number of Ministers of Education who didn't really understand the problem. On the late payments of subsidies to private schools, it seems the process, the system has broken down. Why it breaks down, nobody seems to know. All of this should be computerized. The cheque should go out automatically. What's the problem? People say you go to a ministry and you get this attitude that they don't want to help you. It's a small island. We're all living next to each other!

According to speech therapist Penny Camps:

Penny. The bureaucracy in Trinidad and Tobago has a lot to do with people passing the buck. Not wanting to take responsibility. So it's not going to stop here; I'm going to pass this on. Somebody else will do it.

It's Personal! "Change Happens When Needs Are in Your Face"

John Humphrey, who had held various ministerial posts in the government between 1986 and 2001, described the process of how things happen as a function of citizens' initiative and government response. Laying the responsibility for initiative on the citizens, John said:

John. I don't think you get from a government any initiatives to help in something like this. What you will get is the government supporting citizens who initiate. Because the government gets taxes and it's supposed to use those taxes in the interest of those who need help.

However, Penny Camps offered a more skeptical view of how citizen initiative interacted with social and political processes. Describing services as sometimes being driven by a cross-over between political and personal needs, she told the following story:

Penny. For example, someone high-up politically had a stroke. Two months prior to his having the stroke, I had called the Ministry to say there was a well-qualified speech therapist waiting for a job, so could we try and get her interviewed and a post created so she could start seeing adults, as there was no speech therapist for adults. I was told it was on the back burner, there are other more important things we must see about. Then the official has a stroke and suddenly it got moved to the front burner! Within 3 weeks the therapist was employed.

I think in small countries in the developing world things happen when needs are in your face. They're not planned for. Things get on the front burner because they are needed in the time of crisis.

Equally skeptical, but focusing on politicians' motivations, Charles Mouttet said:

Charles. For the most part, the politicians are motivated by the need to get re-elected. They will do things that they think are populist, rather than doing the things that are required for the good of the country, because it's harder to do those things. The theoretical ideal is that politicians want to do good. But the reality is they are not driven by altruism.

Contacts Are Essential!

In the face of an entrenched bureaucracy and unpredictable political influences, where it comes to creating new services or resources, what works in Trinidad and Tobago? How do new things get done? How does change occur?

Charles Mouttet's answer to this question echoed the words of Jacqui and many other participants in the study: change occurs by knowing how to get around the obstacles, but that kind of know-how depends more than anything on personal and social resources:

Charles. How did we get the St. Ann's property for Immortelle? It was because of Helen. Her husband, John, was in government at the time and we were able to get the lease. In the normal day-to-day operation in Trinidad, it is who you know. If you know somebody, or know somebody who knows somebody. If you want your passport and you don't want to line up at 5:00 in the morning, you need somebody who knows somebody.

Unfortunately, I did not know anybody in social work when I went to apply for Mathieu's disability grant, so I had to take Mathieu in so the committee could interview him to see if he was really disabled. So when we walked into the room, they looked up at us and said, "Oh. It's okay".

They don't make it easy. It's almost as if they're trying to disprove, or to deny you. When I went in there I saw that they deal with the infirm, the elderly. I felt terrible for some of the people there. I was struggling with Mathieu a little bit but I could have managed, but some of the others could not.

I just put it down to the Public Service. That's just how it works. There's no urgency, no concern. A school could be closing down, it doesn't matter. There's no commitment to service. The "public service" is a great misnomer!

Systems as intuitive and relational. Psychologist Allyson Hamel-Smith agreed that "contacts" were essential to getting around the politics, bureaucracy, and personal agendas that so often impeded the growth of new ideas or services. However, she offered a philosophical view of the process, describing the way things worked as a kind of system within a broader framework of "developmental milestones", which societies, like individuals, must traverse:

Allyson. The delivery of complex services starts with an intention to help. Then it must move to a hard commitment: "How do I execute this?"

I think that, in the absence of legislation and reliable public funding, there are systems that people use to solve problems and create services. These tend to be intuitive, informal, and relationship based. When teachers, parents, or clinicians need help for a child or family, they often call someone in their personal or professional network. You use goodwill and connections to get things done. So, in a developing country the pivotal issues are networking relationships and finding limited resources. These are the starting points, the early milestones in the process of building services. However, this is not a satisfactory long term approach, because it does not offer equity and it's not sustainable.

The next stage may be where one challenges the status quo and demands what is fair. Just as adolescents claim their rights and reject a paternalistic authority structure, the country needs to reject the belief that persons with disabilities can survive on the goodwill of a few persons, or occasional handouts from the state or private sector. More rational thinking and demands for formal services will happen when people know their rights and demand them.

And there *has* been partial state funding for private special schools over the past ten years or so. Also, there have been intermittent attempts to fund specific clinical services like speech therapy and psychoeducational evaluations. But, currently, due to the financial shift with declining oil prices, these are vulnerable. No clinical services appear to be funded and there is a very long waiting period for special school subsidies. This reinforces the need for legislation that mandates services for disabilities and positions the budgets for special schools firmly within the Ministry of Education budget as a core recurring item. While we will have to come to terms with the change in the country's financial situation, we do need to protect vulnerable groups.

Allyson's perspective on systems as "intuitive and relational" was supported by Jane Bernstein, the Harvard professor of psychology who worked closely with Immortelle. Giving an example of her own initial cultural misunderstanding regarding the need for personal networking, Jane recounted an episode where she assumed that she had to use the formal systems approach required in the US, but eventually realized her mistake. As the mentor for a student from Harvard who wanted to conduct a research project in Trinidad/Tobago, Jane set about seeking approval from UWI's Institutional Review Board (IRB). Rather than seeking assistance from Jacqui at Immortelle, Jane struggled through official channels that presented contradictory information and numerous obstacles, only to finally realize that a simple phone call from Jacqui was what was really needed:

> *Jane.* I ended up trying to do everything. I wanted to lighten the burden on Jacqui, who was doing us a favour to have the student come in. So I said, let's not bug her. What I did not understand and had to learn was that, if Jacqui had committed to being part of this project, then Jacqui understood that to mean that she would network, call in favours, and just generally do what you do in Trinidad to get things to happen. So I wasted a lot of time by trying not to burden her and not understanding that she didn't see it as a burden and expected to be doing A, B, C and D because she'd taken it on. It was an interesting cultural shift for me, learning that you must go and talk to Jacqui and tell her what the issues are and then she'll say I'll call so and so. Of course as soon as she called somebody … it happened!

In Allyson's words:

> *Allyson.* Overall, I think that, in a developing country the critical thing is relationships—networking relationships. That may be true anywhere but terribly important here.

REFERENCES

EYGM Ltd. (2015). Ernst and Young: Focus on T&T budget 2015. Executive summary, "The Paradox of Plenty" (p. 5). Retrieved from http://www.caribbeanelections.com/eDocs/budget/tt_budget/EY_tt_budget_analysis_2015.pdf

Government of the Republic of Trinidad and Tobago, Ministry of Social Development and Family Services. (2017, June). *National Policy on Persons with Disabilities*. Port of Spain, Trinidad.

Kirk, S. A. (1984). Introspection and prophecy. In B. Blatt & R. J. Morris (Eds.), *Perspectives in special education: Personal orientations* (pp. 24–55). Glenview, IL: Scott Foresman.

Loop News. (2018). *T&T Cerebral Palsy Society calls for new centre to be opened*. Retrieved from http://www.looptt.com/content/watch-cerebral-palsy-association-calls-new-centre-be-opened

Ong-Dean, C. (2009). *Distinguishing disability: Parents, privilege, and special education*. Chicago: University of Chicago Press.

Sen, R., Goldbart, J, & Kaul, S. (2008). Growth of an NGO: The Indian Institute of Cerebral Palsy from 1974–2006. *Journal of Policy and Practice in Intellectual Disabilities, 5*(2), 105–111

Turnbull, A., Turnbull, R., Erwin, E., Soodak, L., & Shogren, K. (2015). *Families, professionals, and exceptionality: Positive outcomes through partnerships and trust* (7th ed.). Boston: Pearson.

CHAPTER 8

Health and Education: Seeking an Explicit Place on the Agenda

The foregoing chapter highlighted the voices of just a few of the leading advocates and service providers working on behalf of persons with disabilities in Trinidad and Tobago. Against a backdrop of public systems that were not created with disability in mind, these voices stood out as evidence of the struggles of individuals and small groups attempting to fill in the gaps. At the center of these public systems were health and education. Surrounding this center were a multitude of related services, policies, and programs too numerous and complex to be detailed in this small study. Indeed, participants in the study included in their concerns everything from sports, entertainment, and advertising to transportation, communication systems, and the maintenance of public roads and spaces. The solution, they argued, was for disability to have its own explicit place on the public agenda.

An explicit place on the public agenda, however, was nowhere in sight. As Michael Reid, Director of the Disability Affairs Unit, explained, rather than enact "stand-alone" legislation, the government would be more likely to amend existing laws, such as the Road Traffic Act or the Equal Opportunities Act, to ensure that persons with disabilities would be included in these protections. On the one hand, this seems like a reasonable approach. On the other hand, participants in this study consistently emphasized a need to carve out an explicit place for disabilities on the

© The Author(s) 2020
B. Harry, *Childhood Disability, Advocacy, and Inclusion in the Caribbean*, Palgrave Studies in Disability and International Development, https://doi.org/10.1007/978-3-030-23858-2_8

public agenda. In Penny Camps' words, there was a need to "put disabilities and poverty in your face".

The consensus arising from the interviews was that disability services were not integral to education or health systems. Rather, they were add-ons to cumbersome bureaucracies that were never intended to be held accountable for the needs of persons with disabilities.

DISABILITY AS THE MAJOR PEDIATRIC PROBLEM IN THE COUNTRY

Health and related therapeutic services represent the earliest beginnings of children's and families' needs. Charles Mouttet put the matter bluntly:

> *Charles.* There are the health centres, but they're basic health. There's a lot of work to be done regarding disabilities but there's no commitment to deal with it. So if people who are wheelchair users make some noise and have a protest around the Prime Minister's office, they may chip out a few pavements to give them wheelchair access or something like that. They need a plan!

A Lack of Priority

Dr. David Bratt, speaking from decades of experience as a pediatrician, described the situation in greater detail:

> *David.* Together with violence against children, childhood disability is the major paediatric problem in the country.
>
> I would say I've been seeing about one new child with a disability per a week every year for the last 10 years. Everything from CP all the way to mild forms of dyslexia and attention deficit. At the more severe end is CP and children with syndrome—Angelman syndrome, Down, unusual ones like Aarskog, Rett and so on. Then unexplained causes of intellectual disability which I can't find—I'm able to suspect their diagnosis but most of the time they would have to be sent away to be diagnosed.
>
> The main thing I do is support the mothers to accept the condition and to get education for their kids. That's the main thing, because diagnostic services in Trinidad are hopeless. We badly need a diagnostic centre and a treatment centre or management centre where we can concentrate scarce resources. For example, since 2004, we were trying to get a cooperative child development centre established, and we approached several companies

and they all said this is very important, very much needed for the country. They said, "We're willing to give you seed money. But before we give you the money government has to buy in to make sure it continues." And that was the sticking point—we couldn't get government to buy in. The companies wanted the government to commit that it was part of their health plan. We never got that, so they refused to give us the money and I don't blame them. It's the same thing with foreign agencies. They say okay, we're willing to give you seed money but what is the government's philosophy on this? We want a commitment from your government saying, "Yes, this is part of our 10 year health plan." We're not getting that.

David attributed the low priority on disability issues to a general lack of awareness and concern, and placed responsibility squarely in the lap of the medical profession. He said that lack of attention to these issues was perpetuated by the type of preparation medical students received:

David. The medical profession in Trinidad and Tobago does not realize what can be done for people with disabilities—including children. The attitude generally is, shut your mouth, put the child in an institution and go about your life. Even within the ministries, the technical officers are not child-oriented in my opinion. In the Ministry of Health, they definitely are not. And I have met people in the Ministry of Education who have told me they do not believe that things like dyslexia, and attention deficit exist. They see these as social problems—not educational problems. It's about people who do not take care of their children and so on!

So the med students coming out don't know anything about disabilities. All of them should go to Immortelle and spend 3 months there. Because they think there's nothing that can be done. They know nothing about physical therapy, occupational therapy—nothing about the allied sciences. They don't understand the concept of team work—social worker, special Education teacher. So they feel there's nothing they can do.

So the attitude is: "What can you *really* do with a child with CP, Dr. Bratt?"

Dr. Natalie Dick, the only US Board-certified developmental behavioral pediatrician in the Caribbean region at the time of this study, spoke in the same vein. Natalie provided services in the Neonatal Intensive Care Unit at Mt. Hope Women's Hospital, in addition to twice-weekly, half-day service in the child development clinics, monthly consulting at the Scarborough Regional Hospital in Tobago, and a small private practice in San Fernando—South Trinidad. Having received postgraduate training in her sub-specialty in Maryland, USA, Natalie had been working in TT since 2006, shifting between the intensive demands of the neonatal ICU and the poorly understood diverse sub-specialty of developmental behavioral pediatrics.

Natalie identified two serious challenges in her work in the public sector: first, the absence of systematic follow-up of newborns at risk for developmental problems, particularly premature infants, and second, the unavailability in her hospital practice of appropriate evaluation tools needed for full understanding of children's development, behavior, and overall functioning. Linking these two areas of her work, Natalie explained that "in an ideal world", babies born prematurely would be closely monitored for developmental anomalies and engaged in early intervention programs upon their discharge from hospital. However, there was no systematic process for such follow-up:

> *Natalie.* Unfortunately, the referrals are not timely. Often, it might be recognized from the neonatal period that an infant would likely have developmental issues, but even when they are referred it takes about a year to get an appointment at the clinic. I try to do magic and attempt to fast track some of those when I see them in the unit. Or sometimes I try to get as many referrals as possible done before they leave the neonatal ICU, but that's impractical. So sometimes, by the time they get to the clinic things are already deteriorating, and the disability is quite well manifested.
>
> The smaller and more pre-term in size they are at birth and the more eventful their neonatal intensive care unit stay is, the higher their risk of having some sort of chronic developmental and/or health issue and that could manifest itself during their stay in the Neonatal Intensive Care Unit. Other neonates might have issues that manifest a little bit later, even early to mid-childhood. The challenge, especially in the public health setting is that the types of intervention that would be most appropriate and urgently needed in an early intervention type of model (starting within the first three years of life) are not available. So the family must pay a fee if they can afford it. And most are not able to afford fees privately.
>
> A significant difference between the private practice and the public sector, both here and Tobago, is that in the private sector I personally purchase my tools and I use them, trying to adhere more closely to what the international best practices are. In the public sector I have no professional tools with which to do any sort of evaluation! Why don't I have tools? And why is it taking as long as it is to get tools? I think part of it is how the public service functions, and I think part of it is lack of awareness. Because my specialty is not one that was followed before so there is a great lack of

awareness and a lot of attitudinal issues and even organizational resistance to change.

Natalie expanded on her concerns with an in-depth analysis of the low status of disabilities on the nation's medical agenda:

> *Natalie.* From a point of view of policy and planning, there isn't an understanding of the interconnectedness between disability and health. Disability issues are seen more as needing social services assistance or social welfare. There is a lack of understanding that there needs to be collaboration between the Ministries of Social Development, Health, and Education. I've seen this in successive health ministers—they don't quite understand how disability could be a health issue, and they're the ones that drive policy. Many of them are still stuck with the concept that dealing with disability is a charity issue, not a human rights issue.
>
> Even the concept of accurate diagnosis and data collection is woefully lacking. A lot of the disability related data in Trinidad & Tobago is based on self-report when there is the national census. So the enumerators might ask a question like, "Is there anybody in your home with a disability?" It would boil down to what the person's concept of a disability is. So they may say, "No, there's nobody with a disability here". So that negatively impacts the ability to plan. There have been small well-designed studies done from time to time in various parts of the county, but the funding was limited.
>
> In the Ministry of Health there's an emphasis on chronic non-communicable diseases as being worthy of population studies. Like diabetes, hypertension, life style diseases. They're chronic, they're not infectious diseases like tuberculosis or HIV or so. I have often made the point that disability is also chronic and non-communicable.

Assessment for Appropriate Intervention

It was obvious that the challenges of assessment were closely tied to the difficulties in providing medical and therapeutic services. Dr. Natalie Dick described her goal of establishing a pilot multidisciplinary unit within the public health service that would provide children with suspected or established disabilities with access to professionals who would conduct assessments and recommend the most appropriate interventions following international best practices. By providing these services for children and their families within one setting, Natalie hoped to lift the burden on parents who, in her words, "often have to go from one end of the country to another" to access services that are very fragmented and uncoordinated. She explained some of the "heavy logistical and financial challenges" facing parents who must travel from remote parts of the country to attend the clinic at Mt. Hope Hospital (Eric Williams Medical Sciences Complex):

> *Natalie.* We have some families who might be coming all the way from Toco (in East Trinidad) without their own car, trying to bring a child with cerebral palsy who requires a stroller. Mummy and Daddy both coming because they have to manage the child and the stroller and a bag and so on. If they take public transport it would be changing maybe three or four taxis or trying to manoeuvre all of this in a bus. There are some who would hire a taxi, but let's say transportation by bus or regular taxi may cost you ten to thirty dollars, if you hire a car, you pay two hundred dollars for the person to pick you up from your home and return you there. Then, depending on what your arrangement with the driver is, if they have to wait too long, the driver charges extra. So, many of the clients that come from Point Fortin (deep South) and from Guayaguayare (in the South East) take the four o'clock bus. Four in the morning! So there are people who get here from six, seven o'clock. And then they are sometimes distracted or in a hurry to leave because they must catch the bus back. If you live in those remote areas and you miss that bus, you don't have money to take other transport.

Natalie further explained that the fragmentation of medical and therapeutic services made this challenge all the worse for parents, many of whom must take time off or quit their jobs to access needed services. She illustrated this situation with the following poignant example:

> *Natalie.* There is a little girl, she's five now. She was born with spina bifida—a defect to her spinal cord. The family lives way past Princes town—deep South. She gets some of what she needs at San Fernando Hospital. Children with spina bifida sometimes have excess fluid on the brain, so she needed neurosurgery to insert a shunt to take some of the extra fluid out. San Fernando General Hospital doesn't have a neuro surgeon right now, so she had the surgery done in Mt. Hope. Also, as part of the challenges of spina bifida she has some abnormalities in the nerves that control her bladder so she gets urinary tract infections frequently. The Pediatric Urology clinic is also at Mt. Hope. She comes to my clinic to try to put everything together. In addition, she has lower limb deformities and has to go to Princess Elizabeth Centre to see the doctor and also the private orthotic devices provider. That's in Port of Spain. So it's back and forth! That's the kind of expense and inconvenience that I dream of reducing for parents.

We also try to assist the parent in penetrating the education system so it's recognized that although she can't walk and requires a wheel chair to navigate, she's as bright as a button! It will be a task convincing the authorities in the education system that, although she's very intelligent and will be able to handle academic tasks with ease, her personal hygienic needs would require a relative (likely her mother or grandmother) or even compassionate aide at school, to preserve her dignity.

The Multidisciplinary Unit: A Project and Its History

Natalie's vision for a multidisciplinary clinic was of a pilot project to start with, because the hospital did not have the capacity to be a full national service. This pilot, she explained, would be based on a team model, in contrast to the "old fashioned way, the paternalistic doctor, very insular, all-knowing, all wise, handing down wisdom and direction".

The themes of "too much politics" and "no planning" were illustrated perfectly in Natalie's detailed summary of the frustrations involved in attempting to establish the unit over a period of five years. In 2010, joining forces with Teresina Seunarine, the director of the Autistic Society, Natalie presented the concept of the unit to the Minister of Health, garnering enough interest to begin what turned out to be a protracted process of advocating that included in-depth preparation of the model. At one point, she was offered the use of a government facility in Tacarigua that had been abandoned, and as initial steps were taken to clear the property of grass that had grown "taller than the building", Natalie set about collaborating with colleagues from related disciplines to fill out the details of the material and human resources that would be needed. With helpful guidance from the North Central Regional Health Authority, in October of 2010 a budget was finally put forward on the Annual Services Agreement for the Ministry of Health, which should guarantee an annual allocation of funds to implement the service. Sadly, however, the theme of "too much politics" intervened:

Natalie. Then we had changes of administration after a national election. Different executives, different priorities. Lots of politics. Lots of letters had been written; lots of presentations had been made. They're supposedly on file somewhere. I don't know what they do with all the papers they get. But when a more recent Board was installed and a new accountant came in with a fresh pair of eyes, different people said they didn't have a clue. So, she was phoning around—nobody knew anything. So she was getting ready to take her pen and say, "re-allocate this money", but she got on to the Medical Chief of Staff who said he wasn't too sure, but he thought Dr. Dick might know! Now if they had just taken the time, all the information would have been on file!

So they gave her my number. It was a Friday afternoon. This was around 2013. The phone rang, she identified herself and asked the questions. I started to talk. She asked me to meet her. I went home and gathered all my documents, put them in a pink trolley bag (the only thing that would hold all my documents; I didn't want to miss anything)! I carried every bit of information that I had. She asked me to answer every question. Everything she asked for—I asked if she wanted a document to back up. I was able to provide a few documents that had already gotten stamps of approval. So they realized the project had gotten to a certain point and there were some things I didn't have to re-do.

At the time of Natalie's sharing this account, the needed professional materials were finally being ordered, but continuing issues included no space having been allocated, no existing posts for the relevant professionals, and an "extremely unattractive financial compensation package", which would not provide any incentive for medical practitioners currently in private practice. Natalie's best hope was for a few qualified professionals to agree to work in the public health sector maybe half a day per week. This, she hoped, would "get a team going, collect data, and talk and push. Then you have something you can say is working and can be expanded!"

Therapies: There's a Misconception That Time Is Not of the Essence

Drs. Natalie Dick and David Bratt both lamented the lack of therapeutic services publicly available to children. Natalie explained that while physiotherapy was provided in the general hospitals, the extremely high caseloads resulted in low priority on the out-patient services that are needed by children with disabilities. Consequently, these children would get physiotherapy "on average once a month to every three months for about 15 minutes". Meanwhile, occupational therapy and speech/language therapy were not publicly available at all in Trinidad, although there were two of the latter therapists working in the public health service in Tobago.

Penny Camps was the speech therapist referred to by Dr. Natalie Dick as being employed in Tobago. Both Penny and Wendy Gomez, the therapist who had participated in the initial formation of the Immortelle Center, echoed Natalie's concerns, explaining that gaining recognition for their field had been an uphill battle. The Speech Language

Association of Trinidad and Tobago had been established in 2009, and in 2015 there were 20 speech and language therapists in the country, but only two were hired by the government. Penny and Wendy said this had been the case ever since their time as professionals in the country. Penny explained how the services in Tobago had come about, pointing to the hard work of Dr. Helene Marecau-Crooks, who, as the head of psychiatry in 2008, spearheaded the creation of a primary care therapy unit in the community, which ended the practice of children having to receive services in the adult psychiatric unit of the hospital. However, the situation for many children was still dire:

> *Penny.* In Tobago there are still children who must travel an hour and a half to get to me. If the 2 year old child is coming for a half hour session and they have to travel by bus or taxi, that can't work. You can't do therapy that way!

Emphasizing the "cross-over" between deficits in attention control and communication skills, Penny pointed out that these combined difficulties frequently led to problems in children's socialization, behavior, and "overall sense of well-being". She explained that the provision of two speech/language therapists in Tobago still fell far short of the need. Further, like Natalie Dick, Penny also pointed to the inequitable difference between public and private services:

> *Penny.* To access the speech therapist at Scarborough General Hospital you must be referred to the paediatric department by a doctor. That department has a huge waiting list, so children are given appointments for a long, long time. Then they go through tests and assessments and evaluations by the paediatrician, and then they may be referred eventually to the speech therapist. Now that can take a 2–3 year period! Then when they get to the speech therapist there is a waiting list. It is very, very cumbersome.
>
> But in private practice a child can be referred to a speech therapist by a parent, a teacher, a colleague, or a psychologist. They request an evaluation and the speech and language therapist can refer the child to the other types of intervention that may be necessary, whether that's hearing evaluations, vision, or psycho-educational assessment or occupational therapy, or whatever it is. You refer them, but you're also getting on with the intervention, which is the whole point of early intervention.

As with speech/language therapy, the availability of occupational therapy services was totally inadequate. Lesley Garcia, an occupational therapist who had returned from the US in 2003 with her master's degree and had initiated the Trinidad and Tobago Occupational Therapy Association (TTOT), underscored the view that a lack of systems and poor planning had resulted in facilities being built but never adequately equipped or staffed. Speaking of the circumstances she found when she returned to Trinidad/Tobago after completing her studies, she said:

> *Lesley.* Apparently in Mt. Hope Hospital equipment had been ordered, a room had been set up, and there was a sign "OT" on the door - and an empty room! So I came back to this sort of dormant stage of the profession. There were certain doctors who had an interest. Once they saw what OT, in addition to physiotherapy resulted in, my practice took off. But then I realized that I would have a comfortable practice and only those who could afford it would come to me and I would still be the only therapist 10/20 years down the road. I wasn't interested in that kind of professional environment, so I continued to work on setting up the association and working toward establishing a master's degree programme in OT.

Lesley also described her participation in the origins of the private therapy organization, CKFTO, which had been initiated by Laura Escayg, whose son, Isaiah, was a student at Immortelle. She pointed out that, since the government subventions for occupational therapy amounted to no more than $1000 per year per child, private efforts such as Immortelle, LIFE Centre, and CKFTO had no choice but to rely heavily on the same pool of charitable funding.

Penny Camps' concluding comments emphatically reinforced the theme of low priority on the needs of children with disabilities:

> *Penny.* There is the misconception that in the case of developmental disabilities, time is not of the essence. This attitude allows some providers to pass the buck. But those of us who are involved with daily intervention know that it is urgent. You can transform somebody's life by giving their families and the other service providers the information and the expertise that they need, and by intervening yourself.

PUBLIC EDUCATION: FREE FOR ALL, EXCEPT CHILDREN WITH SIGNIFICANT DISABILITIES

The public education system in Trinidad and Tobago is free of charge to all children, but this does not mean that all children can be included in the public system. Schooling is essentially structured around academic competition.

The primary and secondary systems include schools that are totally supported by the government as well as some that had historically been initiated and supported by church groups but which now also receive subsidies from the government. Despite the democratization of this system and expressed goals of equitable access for all, the vestiges of academic elitism are still evident in a hierarchy of valued schools, based on which parents seek placement for their children in the most desirable schools. While there are places for all children in this combination of public and partially private schools, the over-riding question for every family is what level of school each child will gain entry to at the secondary level, and, therefore, what quality of primary school is most likely to prepare the child for success.

In earlier chapters, parents' reports of their search for a school reflected a common theme—"trying normal school". This frequently used phrase indicated the divide between schools that are expected to serve "normally developing" children and those that serve children with developmental anomalies. Since the public schools were never intended for the latter group of students, and since there continued to be no legal requirement that these children should be served by the public system, two parallel sets of schools have existed since the middle of the twentieth century. The School for the Deaf, the School for the Blind, the Princess Elizabeth School for students with physical disabilities, and the Lady Hochoy schools for those with intellectual disabilities continued to be the main service providers for students with those visible disabilities. These services, initially started by advocacy groups, continued to be run by individual boards assisted by government subsidies.

Meanwhile, privately run schools such as Immortelle, Eshe's Learning Center, and many others initially struggled to provide services based on charitable funds and fees paid by parents. However, as described in Jacqui Leotaud's story in Chap. 6, when the government initiated the system of subsidies to private special schools that met eligibility criteria, many of these schools, like Immortelle, established themselves as NGO's and formed the Private Special Schools Association of Trinidad and Tobago (PSSATT). Government subsidies helped tremendously by contributing to teachers' salaries and a range of costs. Nevertheless, parents of children attending these schools still must pay a considerable portion of the fees. This situation clearly sets children with disabilities apart as a group who are not fully eligible for a free, publicly provided education. Moreover, the existing provisions for places in the special schools are inadequate for the numbers in need of such placements. As speech therapist Penny Camps explained:

Penny. We have free education for children in Trinidad. But that's not so for children with disabilities. It's totally inadequate. Our schools are not outfitted at all to facilitate anybody with disabilities.

I have not been able to refer any child to either of the two special education schools in Tobago over the last year because they're full. I'm talking about children who would be on the (autism) spectrum or have speech and language disabilities. The two special education schools cannot absorb all the children that require specialized instruction. In any general education classroom in TT there are several children who would be perhaps have a mild form of disability, but the teacher, with no special education training, is faced with a class of 30 children. And even if they had the training it would be overwhelming because the classes are too big. So the kids exist, but the supports aren't there. The Division of Education has a student support service division or department, but they are very under resourced and they're not in every school. Here in Tobago, for example, one special education teacher would serve 3 or 4 schools. I feel that with some planning that model may be the way to go, but we do not have special ed teachers in public schools in TT. This is driving everybody crazy. It's frustrating the children, the teachers, and the parents. And it's leading to behavioural problems.

Teacher Preparation

As described in my earlier discussion of the theme of "too much politics", the issue of teacher preparation was complicated. It was not that there was a total absence of high-quality teacher preparation for special education. The issue, as Dr. Elna Carrington-Blaides of UWI explained, was the absence of a consistent political agenda to maintain and further the good work that had already been done. At the time of this research, the two main teacher preparation programs in the country were at UWI and UTT. Other, smaller bachelor's degree programs also existed, such as the one at the University of the Southern Caribbean, which offered primary education and early childhood education, but not special education. In addition to public teacher training programs, advocacy groups would engage in "filling the gaps" by offering their own workshops, focused on specific disabilities. For example, the TT Autistic Society were actively working towards creating their own certification program.

My focus was on the programs at UWI and UTT. While I did not gain first-hand information from UTT, I learned about that program through Elna, who had developed and directed UWI's masters in special education, and had been the original developer of the B.S. degree at UTT.

Elna's critique of the negative impact of political agendas supported the argument that "too much politics" undermined the development of systematic planning in education. Further, she found that, at UWI, the field of special education was not regarded as a "real area", the focus being on curriculum and educational administration and leadership.

After 4 years at UWI, Elna's plan of attracting graduates from the UTT's B.Ed., program into UWI's master's program had worked quite well, but she was concerned about the absence of any preparation for special education in UWI's bachelor's program. In keeping with a recent Ministry of Education mandate, Elna was working toward developing a solid introductory special education course at the bachelor's level. Meanwhile, she was very enthusiastic about the continuing good quality of the UTT bachelor's degree, which had a strong practical component. Despite all the challenges, Elna maintained high hopes for making a difference and lamented that many professionals who study abroad do not return to TT.

Overall, reports of teacher preparation for special education indicated that, while the available training was solid, the question of whether graduates would find jobs for their skills was entirely up to the government's unpredictable decision-making. Unfortunately, training for general education teachers did not seem to prepare them to respond to the needs of children with the "invisible" disabilities who filled many seats in the public primary schools.

"Invisible Children" in the Public Schools

The children who face real but less obvious learning challenges were of great concern to educators, therapists, and psychologists. These professionals spoke with one voice on the issues facing children with such "hidden" or "invisible" disabilities, specifying three key concerns: the absence of publicly funded supportive educational and therapeutic services, the pressure of a single-gate examination system required for placement in secondary school, and the bureaucratic and financial obstacles to accessing "concessions" that would facilitate students' achievement on the exams.

Dr. Esla Lynch, founder and director of Eshee's Learning Centre, expressed great disappointment at the slow progress in the education system in TT given the nation's resources.

Echoing the theme of lack of planning and follow through, by which well-intentioned ideas imported from high-resource countries were only partially implemented, Esla explained that children with "hidden disabilities" are allowed to sit the SEA (Secondary Entrance Assessment) examination two years later, prior to their fifteenth birthday. However, despite a white paper commissioned by the Ministry of Education in 1994, which recommended that children being allowed to delay the exam should receive a diagnostic assessment followed by remedial interventions on a resource room model, the assessments and interventions were never implemented. Ironically, children in private special schools benefitted from the delay because those schools did focus on remediation, but children in the public schools gained no benefit from this presumed "accommodation".

Another issue was that, while special concessions, such as a scribe or a reader, were available for students when writing national exams, a psycho-educational assessment was required for students to qualify for these concessions. Once more, as observed by several community stakeholders, the issue was private versus public services. In other words, an assessment - how soon and at what cost?

> *Esla*. To obtain a free assessment, a parent who applies to have one done by Student Support Services or The Child Guidance Clinic can wait for several years. So, if this assessment is a pre-requisite to concessions, is it intended to be only available to "haves" in the society? What about those who cannot afford $6,000.00 or $8,000.00? Should the children of the poor and the struggling working class not also benefit? Imagine also, a parent gets an assessment to qualify for concessions for their child who is about to write the SEA but, on entering and throughout secondary school, no one ever looks at the report. It is simply filed. An investment of $6,000.00 to $8,000.00 for one day!
>
> And what of the child whose learning needs are obviously tied to medical issues, such as a stroke in infancy, birth issues, hospitalization for long periods? Shouldn't an alternative to the psycho-education evaluation qualify the child for services/concessions/subventions, and so on? Can the doctor's or the therapist's report not be used? There is no flexibility or understanding of the kind of assessment needed by the child! This becomes an additional hardship for parents.
>
> The government copied a foreign system that is able to provide services to its citizens, and even though our system is not able to do likewise it could seek options for adapting those models to our context. For example, the

White paper on education that we produced in 1994 proposed the training of public school principals and teachers in diagnostic and instructional procedures for children with learning difficulties.

Esla's concerns about concessions for exams were reiterated by several community participants. Wendy Gomez highlighted how this issue affected students with speech/language difficulties:

> *Wendy.* For 25 years I applied for concessions for kids who I thought needed extra time on the SEA. Suddenly, last year they decided they won't accept just a speech and language assessment for the concession. This year the kids I applied for were told they must have a psychoeducational assessment. I'm fighting for a Speech-Language Assessment to be the determining factor for concessions for those students with challenges which are affecting them academically. That psychoeducational assessment can cost $6,000 to $8,000. I don't agree with the fees that are charged!

Wendy explained that, although the situation had improved with the ministry starting to pay for certain assessments, there still tended to be lack of recognition of some disorders, as a result of which children do poorly in school and many progress from an early language delay to a specific language impairment. She praised the improvements over the years and the many wonderful case workers she had worked with but she lamented the inability of the system to cope with the high numbers of children needing services. She exclaimed: "It's not enough. Not with the funds we have in Trinidad and Tobago!"

As was often the case in this study, reports of helpful interventions reflected the role of individual rather than systemic efforts. An excellent example of this came from Phillis Griffith, the administrator of the private special school, New Beginnings, who reported that her school had been linking with a support group called *"Parenting TT"*, who offered psychoeducational assessments for $3,000. This group would supplement the difference in cost based on their access to other funding. Reports produced by this group, she said, proved more timely and more comprehensible than the usual privately provided reports, and parents were able to work out a payment plan to cover their share of the cost.

Psychologist Allyson Hamel-Smith, who had provided private services since the time of the original Immortelle Centre, reiterated all the points made by her colleagues. She concluded, "Remember that awful rule— 'those who have, get!' It applies to the school system!"

THE PRIVATE-PUBLIC EDUCATION SPECTRUM: TWO
EXEMPLARS

My intention in this research was to use the Immortelle Center as an exemplar or case study of what it takes to develop and sustain private educational services for school-aged children with significant disabilities in a developing country such as Trinidad/Tobago. As I outlined in earlier chapters, educational services were available to students with four discrete disabilities—intellectual impairment, physical handicap, deaf/hard of hearing, and blind/visual impairment. These schools had for decades been operated by voluntary associations for each of the specific disabilities and, as early as the 1960s, had begun receiving subsidies from the government.

In addition to these government-assisted schools, there was an array of private and, in one case, a public school, which sought to fill the gaps in the general education system. The private schools received government subsidies if they were formed as non-profits, and if they met criteria specified by the government. I will here give a brief outline of the spectrum of such schools and will then focus on two—the LIFE Centre, which bore a striking resemblance to Immortelle, and the Wharton-Patrick School, which was quite an anomaly in that it was the only fully publicly funded school offering specialized instruction to children with disabilities.

The Private Special Schools Association of Trinidad and Tobago (PSSATT)

At the time of this study in 2015, there were approximately 12 private special schools holding membership in the PSSATT, all of which met the government's criteria for eligibility for subsidies. In addition, all held non-profit status as non-governmental organizations (NGOs).

Of those serving children from the age of five upward, at least five had been in existence for 25 years or more: Servol, Immortelle, LIFE Center, Eshee's Learning Centre, and New Beginnings. The latter three programs served up to about 25 students each: LIFE Centre focused on students on the autism spectrum, while Eshee's and New Beginnings catered for students with academic or attentional learning difficulties rather than developmental disabilities. Eshee's was founded and directed by Dr. Esla Lynch, cited above, who was the (unpaid) consultant who helped hold Immortelle together for the initial years after my departure from TT in 1986. New Beginnings had been started in 1975 by a group of parents and psychologists and began as the Association for Developmental Education, but later took the name New Beginnings to reflect the school's commitment to serving children who had struggled unsuccessfully in the regular public schools. Servol, a pioneer in offering a range of education options for children and adults who did not fit the mainstream education system, had for some 40 years offered a wide range of services, including preschool, primary education, and adult vocational training programs, all of which often included students with mild disabilities.

Additionally, two leading programs that provided vocational preparation for young adults with disabilities were Goodwill and the National Center for Persons with Disabilities (NCPD). NCPD, instituted in 1964, was the largest and longest standing program focusing totally on preparing adults with disabilities for employment in a range of trades, such as woodwork, printing, and garment construction, as well as structured programs certified by the Ministry of Education's National Examination Council. A unique feature of NCPD was its international status, gained in 2013, with accreditation by the United Nations and registration as a civil society organization to the Organization of American States (OAS).

All of the schools participating in PSATT relied on government subventions. Thus, all were at the mercy of the timely or untimely payment of these subventions. Based on her 34 years of experience in running Eshee's Learning Centre, Esla Lynch's view of the social implications of this process echoed the theme of "contacts are essential" that ran throughout the study:

> *Esla.* Subventions to Private Special Schools: Wonderful! Great! But late payments to schools creates real hardships. Some schools, because they are NGO's or because they are funded by two government ministries, or they have strong social capital, that is—parents who are affluent and/or who have affluent contacts—have an easier time at fund raising or getting resources. On a scale of 1 to 10 some schools score 8 to 10 in this area, some 5 to 6, while others would be overjoyed if they ever reached a 3 because they function at a 1 to 2. The schools with financially challenged parents and educated administrators, but little or no social capital, experience lots of difficulty to survive. Who you are, who you know, who knows you, and who knows those you know, result in significant gains, monetary, as well as things and services.

Phillis Griffith, of New Beginnings, supported both of Esla's points: first, the reliance on "who you know and who knows you" for access to financial support and, second, the extreme hardship imposed by late government subventions. Phillis explained that, in the case of New Beginnings, there had been a time when the bank would allow the school an advance, in anticipation of the late subventions from the Ministry of Education. These allowances, however, were no longer provided because the bank did not trust that the ministry subventions would necessarily come through. Thus, in December of 2018, Phillis reported the worst-case scenario caused by this situation: not having received their subvention for the entire September–December term, this school had to close for lack of funds:

> *Phillis.* We closed the school last Friday because of no money to pay staff! The ministry is saying they don't think we'll get funding before Christmas. But we've just been told that the PS [Permanent Secretary] and the CEO are aware of the situation so maybe things will move now.

The Life Centre: A Private Special School for Children on the Autism Spectrum

The LIFE Centre, despite serving less than one-third as many children as Immortelle, bore great similarities to Immortelle in several ways. First, both schools served students with severe disabilities, and had been started by parents during an era when there was no financial assistance from the government for private special schools. Second, both were now members of the Private Special Schools Association, receiving substantial, though often very delayed subventions, from the Ministry of Education. Third, both continued to be run by a parent with huge motivation and persistence, complemented by considerable social status. Fourth, both were able to buffet the inadequacies and inconsistencies of the public system by being the beneficiaries of financial assistance from the private sector.

The director of LIFE Centre, Rose Anna Trestrail, was deeply connected to disability issues through her own experience as a parent. Rose Anna had joined a group of other parents in the LIFE Centre in response to the needs of her first child, Rebecca, who had Rett Syndrome and was 23 years old at the time of this research. Until the age of nine, Rebecca had been thought to have autism, a diagnosis given at the Mailman Centre in Miami, which occasioned great pain for Rose Anna, because of the unfounded beliefs of that era, which placed blame for the condition on what psychologist Bruno Bettleheim (1967) referred to as the "refrigerator mother". Like numerous mothers who have written about this painful theory, Rose Anna experienced deep conflict upon receiving the diagnosis:

> *Rose Anna.* That afternoon I went into the largest bookstore in Miami. I could find only one book on autism and it was called "*The Empty Castle*", by Bruno Bettelheim. That book said it was the parent's fault. This child has been neglected. And I thought, "when did I do this?" I planned, I waited, I adored! When did I unknowingly reject her? Was there something I did unconsciously that caused this child to be like this? I took it as truth since this thing was printed. I think that was the lowest point in my life.

In 2001, however, Rebecca received a diagnosis of Rett Syndrome, for which a blood marker had recently been identified. By then, Rose Anna was pregnant with her fourth child, Gareth. Ironically, Gareth was later diagnosed with autism, which Rose Anna linked directly to his immediate deterioration the day after receiving the five-in-one vaccination at 15 months.

When I met Rose Anna in 2015, she had been involved with the LIFE Centre for almost 20 years. The school had gone through many iterations, including efforts to be inclusive of normally developing children as well as those with disabilities, and, like Immortelle, had been housed in several different locations over time. Currently, the school operated in a rented property in Diego Martin and served about 20 children between the ages of 6 and 21, all diagnosed with, or thought to be on the autism spectrum. The staff of five members included a program coordinator and a business manager.

Rose Anna explained that the school initially had served only students who could pay fees, but gained "charitable status" from the Ministry of Finance in 2001 and then could include children regardless of family income. Her accounting of how the school came to this point illustrated both the themes of "individual agency" and "contacts are essential" that ran through all the interviews with community stakeholders:

> *Rose Anna.* One of the students in the original Life Centre—her Granny was a lawyer and she had gotten the charitable status from the Ministry of Finance, and that was a big help. We were able to use that to open up to other children who couldn't afford and get funding for their fees. What was also available at that time was a Deed of Covenant, by which a company can deduct a donation from their taxes. We also do fundraising—plant sales,

cupcake sales, all sorts of things to make money. My cousin Catherine and myself sometimes had to take the money out of personal finances to pay rent and teacher's salaries, because we were really struggling. So we're constantly just begging and begging.

Like the other private special schools, LIFE had experienced severe delays in receipt of government subventions. According to Giselle, the school's manager, they had received a variety of unlikely explanations from ministry personnel:

> *Giselle.* I was told by the Minister of Education that the reason we are so low on the priority list is that the government has a duty to serve public institutions first, because the public put them in power so he is mandated to serve them first.
>
> Then we were told our delay this term was because they did not receive the information from any of the other Private Special Schools. They do it in batches, they won't just send Life Centre by itself.
>
> Last time, when I didn't get it on time, he apologised to me and said it wasn't because the NGOs didn't submit the forms, but because their department did not send the paper work in fast enough, so the money allocated went to another ministry. He said that is how it is rotated.

These delays, regardless of reasons, were potentially devastating for the Centre. Fortunately, like Immortelle, this school had kept its doors open through support from the corporate sector and individual philanthropists. Sounding very much like Jacqui Leotaud at Immortelle, Rose Anna and Gisele expressed great exasperation, and referred to the private sector as the school's "saviour":

> *Rose Anna.* You have no idea how many times I would look at the cheque book and say, "We have to close next month", and then a cheque would come in. We got to that brink at least 3 times. The private sector has really been our saviour to make up the difference. For example, one of the big oil companies might have a donation and they choose us out of the blue. We've had help from BHP, National Gas, Atlantic LNG, Royal and Scotia banks, women's groups, private individuals. And, of course, United Way has been a great help.

Giselle's previous background working in banking provided her with the necessary skills, confidence, and contacts that proved invaluable in raising funds for the school. While she admired the strategic public commitments made by large companies to show that they are "giving back" to society, she expressed amazement at the generosity of private donors who would give up to "a hundred thousand dollars".

Like Jacqui at Immortelle, Rose Anna's vision was increasingly focused on developing services for adults and, at the time of this research, was working with the Autism Society on a proposal for a program to be called "Life Span", which would include socialization, therapy, and vocational opportunities. Also, like Immortelle, LIFE Centre had been treated generously by Republic Bank's *Power to Make a Difference Foundation*. After years of struggling to keep the rented property "up to code" to meet the Ministry of Education's requirements, and having once lost that funding because of a move from one property to another that had to be certified, the school was about to receive a donation of four million dollars to buy a building. In keeping with the theme of "contacts are essential" that runs throughout this study, Rose Anna summarized the process this way:

> *Rose Anna.* So different institutions are helping. They see the need and it is really the good grace of private institutions. But, I'll tell you, it's really who you know or who you know who knows somebody. Somebody who is willing to say, "Help this person!"

Wharton-Patrick: A Public Special School

The Wharton-Patrick Special School (WPS) was unique in being the only publicly funded "special" school that served children who might "fall through the cracks" of the "visible"/"invisible" wall between disability and normalcy. These students, seen as too challenging for the "normal" school, were also too "normal" for the special schools. Receiving support from both the ministries of health and education, the school did not charge fees and all teachers were paid by the Ministry of Education. At the time of this research the school was serving 33 children who represented what professionals referred to as "invisible" disabilities—children who were failing in the public school primarily because of serious emotional/behavioral challenges.

The school was originally established in 1958 as the School for the Mentally Handicapped and was housed at St. Ann's Hospital, which was and continues to be the public hospital specifically serving individuals with mental illness. Initially, its purpose was to provide schooling for the children housed in the boys' and girls' wards in the hospital. Around 1990, in response to growing sensitivity to the stigma attached to mental illness, the school was moved out of the hospital to its current location in St. Ann's and renamed the Wharton-Patrick Center, having as one of its patrons Dr. Nesta Patrick, a much loved pioneer in services to children with mental illness and developmental disabilities.

Margaret Bruce, the school's principal, gave me an overview of the school's history and current programming. With teaching and special education credentials from both Mico Teachers College in Jamaica and the University of Sheffield in the UK, Margaret had been a teacher at Wharton-Patrick since 1998 and had been the principal since 2008. She explained that the school's unique programming was based on a commitment to inclusive services for children with behavioral disorders. Over the years, the school had practiced both inclusion of typically developing children from public schools into Wharton-Patrick, and placement of its students into public schools. In addition, school personnel had collaborated with the Ministry of Education's then Special Education Unit, and later its Support Services Division, to provide professional development for teachers in certain public schools that offered "support units" for students with disabilities. As described by Margaret, and in an article by Trinidadian scholar and previous principal of the school, Dennis Conrad and his colleagues (Conrad, Paul, Bruce, Charles, & Felix, 2010), these efforts had some successes but were challenged by shortage of staff and persistent discomfort of the host schools regarding children with disruptive or antisocial behaviors.

In addition to a strong social skills focus, the school emphasized opportunities for academic advancement by following the regular school curriculum with adaptations, as appropriate. While the goal of the school was to return as many children as possible to the regular school system, it was more typical for graduates, at age 17, to seek placement at adult rehabilitation programs such as SERVOL, Goodwill, or the National Center for Persons with Disabilities (NCPD).

Despite its publicly funded status, Wharton-Patrick shared one common feature faced by the private special schools—on-going issues with financial and logistical support. At the top of Margaret's wish list was the need for "timely maintenance" of everything from roofing and toilet repairs to computers. She explained that the lack of building upkeep could result in possible loss of status for government funding or even the need to close for a period because the toilets were not functioning. Related to this was limited accessibility in the building for persons using a wheelchair because of the absence of an elevator. Also on Margaret's list was a need for more staff to maintain a ratio of six children to one teacher, who, optimally, should be supported by one or two classroom aides, although this was most often not possible.

Like most other community members involved in this study, Margaret felt that the failure in attention to the school's needs reflected the low value placed upon persons with disabilities:

> *Margaret.* Maybe people feel that persons with disabilities have little to give—or do not have anything of value to offer. I think that we pay attention to those persons and things that we value. When I asked for the lift they told me that it's only for one child, and I said, "No, it is for a community!"

Supplementing the Public System Through NGO's and Volunteerism

The issue of private versus public service provision came up in all the interviews with special education professionals. This was often most directly related to the children with the "invisible" disabilities, such as speech/language or academic learning needs. While most of the service providers in the study offered private services, they were conscious of the lack of public services and had a sense of obligation to contribute in the public sphere. Some offered some amount of pro bono work to "homework clubs", organizations usually run by churches or community groups, where children could come after school until the end of their parents' workday. Wendy Gomez described one such effort, housed at a church and run entirely by volunteers.

> *Wendy.* There's a homework club in a parish in the West. It started with the Social Justice Committee when crime first started to escalate. So, for many years now every Saturday all these kids come from various locations in the West. The teachers are overwhelmed with all the disorders—lots of learning challenges. These kids have varying issues—they may be 1 of 12 children, or no father in the home. A few have had life changing accidents. So over the last 5 years I've assessed the speech and language of many enrolled in the program. From 10:00 to 12:30 every Saturday the kids come in and they bring their school bags and they are helped with their homework. The ones who are to be confirmed go to confirmation classes. The program gets a certain amount of money from the parish and they raise the rest.

Another prominent effort of this sort was Cotton Tree, a multi-service NGO that Allyson Hamel-Smith described as follows:

> *Allyson.* Cotton Tree is a community organization started as an NGO 20 years ago by an attorney named Desmond Allum, who was a criminal attorney and had been a Minister of Parliament for the area. He understood that a lot of people were in jail who shouldn't be, and he knew they had problems with literacy and poverty. A lot of people started with him. I was one of them and we opened the pre-school, an after school-program, and a summer camp. The pre-school is free. We started it and then government took over paying the salaries. We got into doing screenings to try to identify both talents and difficulties in children's early years. The screening is part of the Service Learning Program that started at Immortelle and was extended to Cotton Tree. It also provides psychoeducational evaluations to primary age children in our Homework club, which is an after school programme. These are in great demand since they are so expensive privately.

The overlap among private efforts was evident in Allyson's reference to Immortelle. The screening program at Cotton Tree was initiated by two US professionals, Jane Bernstein, the psychologist from Boston Children's Hospital who participated in providing assessments at Immortelle, and Laura Palmer, the professor from Seton Hall University in New Jersey. These professionals engaged in the Cotton Tree effort in several ways, including supervising students in UWI's Clinical Psychology program, who were placed at Cotton Tree for internships or service learning. Jane and Laura would also bring their doctoral interns from the US to Immortelle and Cotton Tree to do developmental screenings and neuropsychology evaluations of children with potential, not-so-evident difficulties. As documented in a paper published by Jane and her colleagues from Immortelle and Cotton Tree, a sensitivity to cultural nuances was central to their approach to psychoeducational assessment, emphasizing an understanding of children's social/emotional contexts (Bernstein, Hamel-Smith, Leotaud, Lynch, & Palmer, 2013).

The Vision: Separate Schools or Inclusion in Public Schools?

The theme of inclusive versus parallel education systems introduced at the beginning of this book and discussed with Immortelle parents continued to be a central consideration with community providers and advocates. All were sharply aware of the country's commitment to the United Nations'

Convention on the Rights of Disabled Persons (CRPD) and to the centrality of inclusive services among the Sustainable Development Goals (SDGs). All expressed agreement with the intention of these goals. Yet, given the limited adaptability of the public school system for students with disabilities, most participants expressed grave reservations about the possibilities for inclusive education. The entire debate was marked by a contrast between a universal principle and the reality of the local context.

"Realistically, We Don't Have the Resources"

Elna Carrington-Blaides, the UWI professor in charge of the master's program in special education, explained two key points about the possibility of inclusion: first, that the only special education supports available for students in public schools was through the Student Support Services of the Ministry of Education and that this was very limited. Second, such services as did exist were focused only on students with "mild" disabilities, not those with significant developmental delays or physical or sensory impairments. Citing the dangers of interpreting inclusion in terms of simply the placement of bodies, she explained:

> *Elna.* We have real issues with the concept of inclusion because there are various interpretations of it. The prevailing interpretation of inclusion in the school is very narrow. Most people tend to see inclusion on a very physical level. Just put the child in the school and we're practicing inclusion. We have Student Support Services through the Ministry of Education, but I've found that there isn't an emphasis on special education. And if you don't understand where special needs education fits, then you don't understand inclusion.
>
> The students with mild disabilities, with dyslexia or reading issues, tend to get some services but you're not going to find a student who has cerebral palsy and who is a little bit different, 'included'. The teachers still have that fear if they see a child who looks different. I would like to see CP, blind kids, as far as possible, in regular classes. If necessary, we would have some self-contained classes within the regular schools where they could still socialize. What I would like really, is that mandate. But I know realistically we don't have the resources. So the special schools are going to have to continue.

"There Needs to be a Range of Education Provisions"

Teresina Seunarine of the TT Autistic Society, speaking mainly from the perspective of a parent and advocate for children with autism, focused on the specialized needs of this population of students and emphasized that one size could not fit all:

> *Teresina.* For autism there needs to be a range of provisions offered and they can gradually get into the school system. There are some children who may need the one on one, or even home schooling for a period, but they can be included and it should be gradual and they should be comfortable, because school is a very social place and that is so hard for children with autism. An autism-friendly environment has to be gradual, not forced. But the more normalizing their experiences, the better for a child with autism. We stress that with our parents: Bring them out into the community. Let them meet as many people as possible. They may not become close but eventually you want them to have at least 1 or 2 friends. You want them to be a good room-mate (if they go to a group home), so they need to learn socially acceptable behaviors, coping skills for when they're annoyed, functional life skills. That should be the focus and not the academics so much.

Like Teresina, Michael Reid, who was at that time an administrator at the Ministry of Social Development, did not see full inclusion of students with disabilities in the educational mainstream as feasible at that point in time. However, his doubts were directly related to the fact that he did not see the "range of educational provisions" indicated by Teresina as feasible within the public education system:

> *Michael.* Yes, we want integration and inclusion but there are some children who will need special attention, which, in a typical school with a curriculum to fulfill, would not be feasible. So there will always be that need for private special schools. Because they need specially trained people, the fees are sometimes very high. Then, some children will have to remain in school longer than their typical peers. It's a long-term expense.
>
> As government we need to look at that. We have a policy of education for all from the nursery to tertiary but there is still a group of people who must pay for their children to go to school. That is something that must be addressed. Government may need to pay the fees for the schools or pay a reasonable amount so that there isn't that burden on the parents. Then we could really say that we have free education from nursery to tertiary!

Despite Michael's strong support for public funding, his statement that schools "have a curriculum to fulfill", underscores the deep commitment of the education system to a standardized academic curriculum. Secondly, the government's support of free tertiary education reveals the high priority placed on advanced education for an intellectual elite as contrasted with the low value on citizens who occupy the opposite end of the intellectual spectrum. I will return to this theme in the final chapter.

"At this Point, We Don't Have an Alternative!"

Laura Palmer, Professor of Counseling Psychology at Seton Hall University and a consultant to Immortelle, was emphatic on the impossibility of inclusion within the current education system:

> *Laura.* Well, at this point, we don't have an alternative! It would be disastrous—it *is* disastrous for the children in most of the school settings. The teachers just don't have the resources, training, adequate special education support staff, assessment and monitoring mechanisms that would allow for students with special education needs to receive appropriate educational services in an inclusive setting. Immortelle is an environment that allows children to learn to their capacity and not feel like they're so terribly different and limited compared to other peers.

Similarly, Phillis Griffith, from her experience at New Beginnings, expressed doubt that inclusion would work because of the model of education valued by the society and a lack of understanding that children who "look like regular children" may have social/emotional or learning difficulties that make it impossible for them to succeed in a "strictly academic curriculum". In contrast to the differentiated curriculum implemented at New Beginnings, Phillis described the typical attitude of teachers in the mainstream system as being "Well, we have to finish the curriculum", rather than being open to modifying the educational expectations for children whose learning processes differ even from their siblings. Rather, she said, families tend to take the attitude that, "Why not you? What's wrong with you?"

Advocates for the deaf and blind also expressed concerns about the challenges of effective inclusion. Bhawani Persad, whose views were cited earlier in the chapter on advocacy, expressed the opinion that, although "integration is the way to go, there are students who still need that special care and attention". Dr. Ben Braithwaite, a lecturer in UWI's Department of Modern Languages and Linguistics, who works and does research with the deaf community, underscored the unique perspective of deaf people who view themselves as "proud deaf people" representing a cultural/linguistic minority. Distinguishing between "inclusion" as an appropriate social goal, and "mainstreaming" in a non-signing school system, he felt that without a community of signing peers, deaf students experience isolation in a regular public school.

FILLING THE GAP: THE ROLE OF THE CORPORATE SECTOR

As noted throughout this book, most of the private educational services for individuals with disabilities relied heavily on assistance from the corporate sector. Many schools received funding from businesses both large and small, and generous donations from individuals too numerous to mention.

Most substantial was funding from charitable foundations. Predominant among these were the Digicel Trinidad and Tobago Foundation, which was increasingly engaged in supporting disability issues, providing private schools with materials, scholarships, and even workshops by therapists brought in specifically for the purpose of professional development. Also providing considerable support was Republic Bank's *The Power to Make a Difference* (PMAD) fund. This foundation was a philanthropic initiative started in 2004, operating in five-year cycles. For example, PMAD contributions to Immortelle consisted of $700,000 toward renovations of the school in St. Ann's in 2003, and $1 million toward the seniors' wing in 2012.

As reported in its website, the PMAD supported community efforts in sport, culture, disability, health, education, and poverty alleviation. In its second phase from 2008–2013, the initiative had "sought to give voice to the differently abled community and to bring greater awareness and access to medical options", and had invested an unprecedented "TT$100 million" in these causes. Recipients of this support included the Autistic Society of Trinidad/Tobago, the Dyslexia Association of Trinidad/Tobago, Immortelle Children's Centre, the National Centre for Persons with Disabilities, Adult Literacy Tutors Association, Persons Associated with Visual Impairment, and Cotton Tree Homework Club, as well as similar organizations in the neighboring Caribbean nations of Grenada, Guyana, Barbados, and Suriname. The third phase, 2013–2018, developed a focus on "improving literacy levels and building skills and capacities in our societies" (https://republictt.com/pmad/power-make-difference-history).

The Charity Model

Charles Mouttet, Chairman of the Immortelle Centre board, had worked at Republic Bank of Trinidad/Tobago for 37 years and was currently the bank's general manager of foreign exchange. He described his work at the bank as having been "heavily involved with charities", such as various trusts whose income was dedicated to specific charities. Charles was also involved in *The Power to Make a Difference* fund, and when I asked him why Republic Bank had developed the PMAD, his reply was an honest combination of pragmatism and altruism:

> *Charles.* Well, I guess it stems from the fact that we believe that we are a part of the community in which we operate, and there is also a profit motive. We are a business but we know that if we give back to the community and enable members of the community to better themselves, that better community is going to come right back to us. They're going to bank with us, make deposits, open businesses, get loans. So while there is some altruism, we also must sell it this way to our shareholders as this is their money we're giving away! There's also some degree of public relations as the banks often suffer from a bad name for whatever reason, so we'll also get some PR out of it. But when this program was developed, I do believe it came from the heart. That the people running the bank wanted to do something positive. We wanted to make a difference.

Having been a parent of a child with multiple disabilities, Charles was particularly sensitive to this cause and believed that separate schooling for such children was essential but should be the responsibility of the government. He expressed great disappointment in the lack of continuity and reliability in government support for schooling for children with disabilities:

> *Charles.* I believe everybody has a responsibility to do what they can. We can't sit back and rely on the Republic Banks or the Neal and Massy's or the government to do everything for us. Everybody has to chip in. What is disheartening is the lack of structure on the government side, so whatever we do on the corporate side is going to have a lesser effect than if there was a structure in place. We keep putting plasters, but we're not treating with underlying issues. That's a real problem. We do what we can but it is never going to be enough.
>
> Look at the school subsidies from government—it's almost two terms late! So that has cost Immortelle thousands of dollars in overdraft interest. I

was able to arrange an overdraft. But when you have an overdraft at
$500,000, or $700,000, which David and I have had to personally guarantee, you can't operate like that!

A statement by Teresina Seunarine of the Autistic Society of Trinidad/
Tobago exemplified how deeply reliant her organization was on what she
described as corporate social responsibility. Once more, this report illustrated the theme of individual agency combined with the role of the charity model in "filling the gaps":

> *Teresina.* I think it's happening slowly. Republic Bank is leading the way.
> And we've gotten help from some of the other banks. They're getting more
> into corporate social responsibility. They realize that the government is not
> doing enough. So for the last 7 years, Republic Bank's *Power to Make a
> Difference* program has been funding us mainly for therapies and bringing in
> overseas people for training. We write proposals and some companies might
> give us a deed of Covenant, a certain commitment—maybe $2,000 a year.
> Also, individuals or women's groups help us.
>
> Right now we're writing United Way. They helped us to put up a build-
> ing that is formed around 4 shipping containers. So it's in a U shape and
> inside is 40 feet by 40 feet and it's covered. United Way helped us to cover
> it. Then the Rotary Clubs helped us with the flooring, outdoor furniture
> and play equipment. We have an acre of land that was given to us by the
> Trestrail family. And we got donations from Lara Foundation at the time we
> were doing the building. We got from Coosals, all sorts of donations, and
> Peakes with the air-conditioning for each container.

However, as Charles Mouttet pointed out, the charity model can only
go so far. Inevitably, there will be groups that fail in accessing sources of
support. Wendy Gomez, the original Immortelle speech therapist, served
for a time on Republic Bank's PMAD board and explained some of the
challenges in making decisions about funding. Faced with many worth-
while proposals, the board would focus on efforts that they believed would
"have positive repercussions down the way".

Penny Camps, the speech and language therapist in Tobago, however,
pointed to the limitations of charitable support that relied on proof of visible outcomes. From her perspective as a community activist who had
spearheaded a local community-based effort called Yaweh, Penny discussed the difficulties of gaining support for less prominent efforts that
were less material and more process oriented:

Penny. There's interest in contributing to NGOs and organizations that are disability oriented. But they don't support enough organizations that are doing what I would term psychosocial work in communities, or interventions for the health and well-being of communities, because it's not visible enough. They are more likely to support organizations where the disabilities are very obvious. It would be interesting to find out how long, in the minds of the corporate world, an organization needs to have been established for it to become credible and worthy of their support. They are wary, and probably for good reason, about supporting an organization that is unknown.

No matter what criteria and careful thought might go into making decisions about funding, Charles Mouttet acknowledged a painful truth about the inequities built into reliance on charitable support:

Charles. Private efforts depend very much who you know. So if you're unlucky to be born in a family with very limited resources, and you're disabled, you don't have a chance. We ought not to live like that. Every citizen ought to have access to all the facilities that are available.

This cry against the inequities of structural discrimination was echoed by Francis Escayg, whose son, Isaiah, a student at Immortelle, was the inspiration for Francis and Laura's efforts to establish, first, the therapy organization, CKFTO, and later, the media company *Cause an Effect.* Presenting a critical view, he expressed a deep concern for what he saw as a superficial patching of society's wounds rather than a genuine caring for people with disabilities and attention to the essence of true giving:

Francis, Isaiah's father. Corporate social responsibility in Trinidad and Tobago is a joke! It's generally about bragging rights. They think if they take care of their employees and have a sports day where employees can dress up and feel special, then have the event splashed across the media, that's their corporate social responsibility. They should understand that we need to drill deeper. To see that the problems that exist in our communities and societies will affect everyone.

I have this vision of a better place. A more collaborative society where corporations partner with our organization to achieve these results and these goals. A place where we won't always have to wait on government subventions. I don't like that people have to think of us as charity. We are doing important work. We have to become a business. We have to be bold. We have to take it, create it, brand it.

As a board member at Immortelle, Francis expressed gratitude for the charitable support the school had received, but longed to see the society move beyond short-term, tangible products of the charity model to a deeply entrenched societal commitment to large-scale change:

> *Francis.* The boards of most NGOs are made up of influential persons and/ or persons with access to influential friends. That stratification makes it all about who you know. But I walk with my energy and my vision and I think that's important!
>
> Who you know can accelerate and increase funding. But that's still one side of the coin. If you provide a service e.g. therapy, and you want to offer it to persons who can't afford it and you want to get funding, that is something corporations understand. But a movement that is big and existential in nature—that requires sustained effort and investment over long periods, is often not as appealing to funders. They don't see immediate results and can't justify it on their books to their shareholders. Which is why my board at *Cause an Effect* is my wife, myself and one other person. My wife and I bring our creative skill sets in film, music and publishing to create content. If we are to change things, we have to tell a truth about our humanity and our society, and we have to tell it from our perspective.
>
> We don't need anybody with a big name on our board just for the sake of being able to say I have this person on my Board so I need to get support from your organization. I want to break that mould, that's old school! It feeds into the charity model. It's not supposed to continue that way. If I need to figure out how I'm going to put gas in my car until I find the right corporate partner I will do that. I am not compromising my vision or my dream of a fair and just society where everyone wins, just to say, "Yes! We got through with some money!"

THE ECONOMIC RECESSION OF 2016–2018

As I was completing this book, two years had passed since the start of my research, during which time the economic situation of Trinidad and Tobago had taken a turn for the worse, following a dramatic drop in oil prices in 2015. Obviously, this situation would take its toll on the fragile infrastructure for citizens with disabilities.

I interviewed Dr. Beverly Beckles of the NCPD in January of 2018, when the seriousness of the economic recession had become undisputed. Beverly described severe government cutbacks, including a reduction of 23% in the government's subvention to NCPD. With almost a quarter of its funding precipitously withdrawn, NCPD was faced with the challenge of maintaining quality services to its 150 individuals with disabilities. Yet, Beverly resisted the idea of cutting staff as an option because of the challenging mixture of disabilities among the clients and because she wished to continue to "value and cherish the committed, dedicated people" who work with the organization.

Beverly's hope, at the time that we spoke, was to respond creatively but thoughtfully to increased requests from individuals offering to volunteer— a strategy that would have to be managed very carefully to ensure maintenance of program quality. She also felt that years of consistently cultivated relationships with the business sector would continue to yield positive results in employment opportunities for graduates of NCPD.

The severe impact of the economic recession was further reflected in Beverly's description of the closing of several recently emerged tertiary institutions and cuts in registration at UTT and *COSTATT (College of Science, Technology and Applied Arts of Trinidad and Tobago)*. Also, in 2017, the government made critical reductions to funding of the free tertiary education system known as *GATE* (Government Assistance for Tuition Expenses).

Beverly pointed to the tremendous burden being borne by the NGOs. Speaking of the role of an organization such as NCPD, she said:

> *Beverly.* We just got approval from a Caribbean group out of Barbados on the UNCRPD to do a public awareness campaign. This needs to be a continuous, sustainable program, so we've combined it with social media to keep the disability message on the top burner. I'm hoping that it will spur policy makers on with our UNCRPD work. One problem is changes in the government ministries, where people come in and out; the issue is how to get government people who are committed!
>
> So it comes back to the NGO Sector to drive the agenda!

Charles Mouttet, however, consistently brought this argument back to the role of government in providing a safety net onto which NGOs could build:

> *Charles.* There needs to be a base-line provided by government. Then we must have a system that is well enough entrenched for it to work. Plus accountability! The main issue is, in Trinidad and Tobago, we have wonderful ideas, but are weak on execution.

REFERENCES

Bernstein, J., Hamel-Smith, A., Leotaud, J., Lynch, E., & Palmer, L. (2013). Limin' n' learnin': Implementing collaborative service-learning programmes in Trinidad and Tobago. *Caribbean Journal of Psychology, 5*(1), 93–107.

Bettleheim, B. (1967). *The empty fortress: Infantile autism and the birth of the self.* New York: The Free Press.

Conrad, D. A., Paul, N., Bruce, M., Charles, S., & Felix, K. (2010). Special schools in the search for social justice in Trinidad and Tobago: Perspectives from two marginalized contexts. *Caribbean Curriculum, 17*, 59–84.

CHAPTER 9

Trinidad and Tobago in a Liminal Space

My purpose in this study was to describe the experiences of those who have built and participated in the Immortelle Center over a period of some 40 years and to understand how this small history fits into the landscape of disability issues in Trinidad and Tobago. Based on a detailed analysis that I will describe in the Appendix, I present the following statement as a summary of the main message of this effort:

As a private "special school" in Trinidad and Tobago, Immortelle Centre's longevity reflects persistent individual agency based on personal motivation and high status social capital, assisted by government policies that are helpful but are impeded by their status as "add-ons" to the system and by bureaucratic implementation. Because of inconsistent and inadequate funding, the school faces continual personnel and financial sustainability issues.

Located in a liminal space between the developed and developing worlds, Trinidad and Tobago's official ideology of equality and diversity is challenged by a combination of traditional social, cultural, educational, and economic hierarchies which reinforce the low priority placed on disability issues. This is evident in a medical system that retains a view of disability as a chronic illness not in need of urgent or therapeutic attention, and an educational system based on academic competition and minimal responsiveness to learning needs that do not fit the traditional mold. With no legal mandate for the education of children with disabilities, many parents are left to seek or create their own solutions. Despite the nation's relative wealth, there are marked

© The Author(s) 2020   235
B. Harry, *Childhood Disability, Advocacy, and Inclusion in the Caribbean*, Palgrave Studies in Disability and International Development, https://doi.org/10.1007/978-3-030-23858-2_9

disparities in the accessibility and quality of private versus public services for individuals with disabilities. A culture of charity and volunteer advocacy strives to fill the gap, but the partial, selective, and time-limited nature of these efforts is not sustainable. A consistent cross-cutting theme throughout the interviews was the exclamation: "We need systems!"

Where does this statement lead us in envisioning a future for persons with disabilities in Trinidad and Tobago? The US Consulate representative whom I quoted in previous chapters expressed great optimism on this, exclaiming: "This is a country that is ready to move forward on disabilities". I believe that this is true. However, the key question is: move forward from what and to what? While we admire and may seek to emulate the strides made by, and on behalf of, persons with disabilities in the developed world, we need to consider the types of adaptations needed to make such a transfer feasible and effective. First, what, really, is the "developed" nature of this vibrant Caribbean culture, known for its creativity and joyful expression of life? How do the nations' most vulnerable citizens fit into this picture of development?

Is What's Good for the Goose Necessarily Good for the Gander?

I begin my discussion of the goose-gander dilemma with a personal anecdote. In 1976, when my daughter, Melanie, was just seven months old, I took her to Toronto for medical evaluation of her condition. Arriving in the Toronto airport with the most fragile of infants in my arms, I was overcome by a sense of relief at the superb organization of the airport, as I moved easily through immigration and customs without a hitch, enjoying the consistently courteous greetings of airport personnel. Stepping out of the customs area, my heart leaped as I saw my brother, Philip, waiting for me at the gate. Delighted to see him, I gasped, "It's so great to be here! Everything's so well organized! Everything works!" My brother, whose 10 years as a practicing physician in the equitable and supremely structured Canadian public health system had rendered him quite skeptical of its advantages, replied, "Yes! Organized! It's too damned organized!"

I believe that many people who grew up in the "developing" world will immediately grasp the meaning of that exchange. By comparison, say, to North America, our societies seem disorganized and unpredictable, subject more to individual vagaries than to dependable systems. At the same time, we believe that they also provide us with the joy of greater spontaneity, more personalized relationships, and the possibility of individual creative solutions to daily challenges.

Based on the information in this study and on my own familiarity with the culture, I see Trinidad/Tobago as existing in a liminal space between the developing and the developed world. Its social philosophy is modern and progressive, as seen in the national anthem's vision of inclusiveness, marked by ethnic and religious equity and harmony. The goal of finding an equal place for every citizen is reflected in the official recognition of a wide range of public holidays celebrating religious and historical events and by the government's provision of free education from primary through tertiary levels. As one participant commented, social connections to the US are evident in the fact that, on a Friday afternoon, the airport parking lot is jammed with Mercedes Benzes and BMW's left by weekend commuters to Miami. More importantly, outcomes of the investment in equality can be seen in how well the nation compares with developed countries, boasting a 99% literacy rate, an unemployment rate of 4%, with more than 98% of all primary age children attending school (UNICEF, 2015).

Despite this picture of development, two societal features provide a worrying contrast: first, the uneven distribution of wealth evident in the estimate that approximately 20% of the population lives below the poverty line (Borgen Project, 2017; Central Intelligence Agency, 2018). Second, with no explicit legislative mandate to provide for them, persons with disabilities stand on the lowest end of the ladder of educational and medical priorities. Essentially, there exists no safety net—no baseline provision for the education of children with disabilities.

Thus, while progressive policies and measurable data on education and the economy support a designation as a society with a high level of development, I believe that a more qualitative and nuanced understanding of the culture of Trinidad/Tobago points to the "other foot" still standing in the developing world. The question is: what would it take to "step up"? And in "stepping up", should the key word be *adoption* of "developed" principles or *adaptation* of such principles to the character and economic circumstances of the country?

In this closing chapter, I try to draw connections among the nuanced perspectives that reflect this dilemma. I hope to offer a grounded view that can, at once, acknowledge the strengths of that posture, while also pointing the way forward.

We Need Systems!

I came to the summary statement of this research project by comparing and interrelating the themes that stood out to me across my interviews with 70 individuals. Thus, the statement that opened this chapter is an amalgam of the following five cross-cutting themes:

> *From "something not right here" to "she's wonderful"*
> *Contacts are essential: Individual agency and social capital work hand in hand*
> *Inclusion is an ideal, but…*
> *Government helps, but…*
> *We need systems!*

Although all these themes were powerfully expressed, the cry "We need systems" seemed to capture their essence and to stand as an explanatory centerpiece for the entire picture. Identifying this theme as what grounded theorist Cathy Charmaz (2014) calls the "core category" of the research, I interpreted the call for "systems" as a possible way forward, while simultaneously taking into account the intuitive and personalized processes that characterize the culture of Trinidad and Tobago.

In bringing this book to a close, I will review these themes through the lens of a "liminal" space in which this developing/developed nation stands with regard to disabilities. Relating the findings to the broader landscape of international discourse on disabilities, I will follow up on my opening discussion in Chap. 1 regarding the challenge of determining an appropriate balance between indigenous and imported principles and systems of practice. This applies most evidently to three key issues: the meaning and value placed on the experience of "disability", the principle of inclusive schooling, and the relative places of advocacy, charity, and public responsibility in societal development.

From "Something Not Right Here" to "She's Wonderful!" Meanings of Disability

Parents' narratives proclaimed their journeys from the pain of "something not right here" to the joy of "she's wonderful!" Yet, this was often in the face of an evident lack of adequate systems of care in the medical and educational policies and practices that could have made parents' journeys easier.

This contrast illustrated the truth of both "medical model" and "social model" perspectives. The notion proposed by disability scholars Michael Oliver and Colin Barnes (1998) that disability is essentially a social construct and therefore should not be seen as a personal tragedy, would be quite incomprehensible to the parents in this study. Parents' initial experience with their children's disabilities were marked by shock and disappointment, even shame, sometimes exacerbated by distressing health challenges accompanying the child's condition.

Many social theorists have discussed the meaning of the concept of "normality", and the word "abnormal" has long been shunned by disability advocates. As Shaun Grech (2015) noted, "an understanding of 'not normal' necessitates a notion of 'normal'" (p. 58). In other words, it is against a set of medically defined and socially acknowledged expectations or norms that persons are identified as "having disabilities". As I argued earlier, and as has been supported by the United Nations' (2018) definition and an update by leading disability studies scholar Michael Oliver (2013), both the medical features and the social aspects of these expectations are valid. Based on my own research on the disproportionate and inappropriate designations of disability to children of color in the US (Harry & Klingner, 2014), I know that designations based on clinical judgments can be very subjective, reflecting the essential ambiguity of the meaning of "disability" in many school-based learning differences.

On the other hand, I also know that there are conditions that are clearly well outside of the normative pre-and postnatal development of children, and that these conditions often occasion great pain and suffering both for the children and their families. These norms for development are not fictional. They are based not only on advanced medical knowledge but also on traditional folk knowledge by which a mother who has just given birth quickly wants to know if her newborn has, for example, 10 fingers and 10 toes! Thus, although I share the intention of disability scholars who argue for a focus on social responses to evident impairments, I think that seeming to exclude the truth of biological conditions confuses rather than clarifies the issue, as in, for example, the statement by David Connor, Beth Ferri, and Subini Annamma (2016) that "all disability categories, whether physical, cognitive, or sensory, are also subjective…Dis/ability categories are *not* "given" or "real" *on their own*". (p. 10)

As I have stated before, the reality of both models of disability was evident in this study, in that parents' initial reactions were often intensified by unresponsive, even uncaring, medical attention, as in the tales of two

Daniels, both of whom had heart anomalies associated with Down Syndrome. Moreover, the difference between the quality of care provided through private medical practices and those accessible in the public system underscored deep inequities in the social system of the country. The attitudes of some medical professionals towards treatment for these children, and the frustrating search for appropriate schooling, convinced the parents that their children's lives were not valued. Most notably, however, the perception of congenital disability as a tragedy was by no means a permanent marker of parents' experience. On the contrary, regardless of the availability or unavailability of professional supports, parents made practical and philosophical adjustments to their daily lives, to their expectations for the child and for their families, and to their sense of purpose in life.

There is an additional point that is not readily noted in scholarship on disability studies, but that was consistent in this study—an overwhelming reliance on religious beliefs. This characteristic of the culture of Trinidad/Tobago was evident in that the interviews were marked by a deep faith in a loving God who provided spiritual and physical sustenance in times of trouble, and who had a purpose for their child's life. For the majority of families, this belief was also supported by a faith in extended family systems, on whom parents counted to resolve the fear of "What will happen to my child when I'm gone". On the other hand, advocates who worked with a broader swath of families expressed concern regarding the weakening of these systems and identified a need for the creation of residential settings for the aging population of persons with disabilities.

Contacts Are Essential: Individual Agency, Social Capital, Advocacy, and Charity

The inequities reflected in the absence of systems for care and education were most evident in this theme. The history of the Immortelle Children's Centre reveals that individual agency on the part of the Principal and a small group of committed individuals combined with social capital to constitute the core of the school's longevity. The concept of social capital is most often credited to sociologists Pierre Bourdieu (1986) and James Coleman (1988). Coleman's analysis includes three key components: obligations and expectations based on trusting relationships; information channels through social networks; and social norms that include effective sanctions. Depending on the social structures of any society, these processes may be further enhanced by other aspects of individuals' identities, such as race, ethnicity or socio-economic status. In this study, the intersections of these aspects of identity were all important to varying extents, and reflected centuries-old hierarchies that included race, socio-ethnic group, education, and socio-economic status.

Social capital and the intersections of identity. While it is beyond the scope of this study, or my academic expertise, to engage in a thorough consideration of the role of racial and ethnic identity in social status in Trinidad/Tobago, a basic understanding of these factors is essential. A key point is that, as in most Caribbean countries but perhaps most notably in Trinidad/Tobago, racial identification is not constructed as a binary concept, as it is in the US. This does not mean that race is unimportant in the society's hierarchies, but it does mean that a tremendous amount of racial mixing is acknowledged as normative, so much so that there are numerous words in the local parlance to indicate different "looks" produced by these mixtures. Of course, the fact that these "looks" are often the first aspect used to describe a person points to the continuing importance of perceived racial affiliation. However, in a somewhat different pattern from the mainly Black/White spectrum of racial mixing in several formerly British Caribbean colonies, Trinidad/Tobago's racial/ethnic landscape includes large Indian and African-origin groups as well as smaller but socially and economically prominent groups with origins in China, Syria/Lebanon, and Europe. Centuries of economic power held by the European group have supported its continued dominance, with the usual attendant social value that accrues to those in power. However, as in the rest of the Caribbean, since the time of Independence from the UK, political power has been grasped by African and Indian-origin groups, while a strong education system has produced a professional class that cuts across all ethnic/racial groups. Thus, social critiques developed in the US and UK such as critical race theory (Brown & Jackson, 2013), while still relevant to the Caribbean, must be tweaked to capture the nuances of this uniquely complicated social system.

So, the question arises, how are different identities valued in a society as multicultural as Trinidad and Tobago? This question resonates with the concept of "intersectionality", by which Kimberle Crenshaw (1996) and many others have emphasized the importance of taking account of the numerous intersections that combine to produce any individual's identity. By this lens, for example, we note the way gender might interact with race, or race with socioeconomic status, or both of these with religion. In other words, the value that a society places on an individual is seldom based totally on one characteristic. A key point is that the lens of intersectionality can reveal contrasting effects: on the positive side, for example, in Caribbean societies the boundaries of race and social status are highly flexible, so that the high value placed on European ethnic/racial identities can be significantly countered by the high value placed on education or socioeconomic status. On the other hand, when we add poverty to any portrait of identity, severe discrimination becomes likely, as studies by Shaun Grech (2015) and Nirmala Erevelles (2011) have shown.

The addition of a disability designation further intensifies the picture and it is likely that disability will become the most stigmatizing feature of the individual—what sociologist Erving Goffman (1963) described as the "master status". In considering the impact of the intersection of race and disability, David Connor et al. (2016) proposed DisCrit—a theoretical framework that combines perspectives of critical race theory and disability studies, whose aim is to counter the tendency to assume that one aspect is more influential than the other. Nevertheless, they note that in most discourses, there remains a prioritizing effect, which "seems to leave one identity marker foregrounded" while other markers "default into the background" (p. 11). This was illustrated in Kamal Lamichane's (2015) study of disability in several developing countries, which noted that families who would normally invest more in boys than in girls, would shift their priorities in the case of disability, investing more in the education of a non-disabled child, regardless of gender. In Shaun Grech's (2015) study of disability in Guatemala, the stigmatizing of women who became disabled while living in poverty led to their perception of themselves as being particularly devalued as "sexual or marriageable partners" (p. 81).

Thus, for example, in a society where traditional racial/ethnic/socioeconomic hierarchies continue to assign privilege, to be black, disabled, and poor will constitute barriers far more daunting than those faced by a child in a privileged family. In this study, this point was poignantly noted by Charles Mouttet, a banker and Immortelle board member, who noted that, despite the tremendous challenges presented by his son's disability, his own privilege made these challenges more manageable than those faced by families who lacked his social and financial resources.

The advantage of relative privilege was certainly true for me when I initiated the rudimentary Immortelle Centre in 1978. While my economic resources were modest, my husband had a secure, middle-to-high level job as an economist in a governmental agency. Moreover, my possession of a master's degree and previous position as a lecturer in the School of

Education at the University of the West Indies combined with my mixed race ("light skin") identity to increase my own social capital. My serendipitous meeting with physiotherapist Joan Knowles and speech therapist Wendy Gomez was truly fortuitous. Not only did they have the professional qualifications needed to strengthen the project, but their identities as Trinidadians from the "white" ethnic group with high social status and strong social connections lent considerable credibility to our efforts. This not only made us able to attract families who could pay fees, but also to secure scholarship donations from business groups such as the Rotary and Lions Clubs, for families who could not. I believe that this would have been much more difficult had we not had the combination of social, ethnic, and educational capital needed to persuade these community members that our effort was worthy of their charity.

Social capital and charity. Jacqui's narrative of the development of the school dramatically illustrates how social identity combined with economics to sustain the school after its early beginnings. When her wealthy "Uncle Lyn" asked her "what kind of rinky-dink school you running, Jacqui?"—she leaped at the hint and asked him to help. Uncle Lyn's regular donation continued after his death until his estate terminated. Moreover, when there was not enough money to pay staff, Jacqui could count on a not-to-be-paid-back "loan" from a wealthy donor closely connected to the school. When the government subventions were months late in coming, members of the school's board could put up enough money to back an overdraft for the school. An overdraft, which, nevertheless, undermined the school's budget by requiring interest payments to the bank!

Thus, the theme, "contacts are essential", embedded in the realities of social capital, ran through the study. We heard it in Rosanna Trestrail's story of the LIFE Centre and in the Gulston family's ability to access surgery for Daniel in New York through a Trinidadian doctor there. We heard it also in Jacqui's and Helen's accounts of how Immortelle came to be granted use of a property on state land. As psychologist Allyson Hamel-Smith maintained, personal relationships and social positioning represented a set of informal, "intuitive and relational systems" that took the place of officially sanctioned paths for getting things done.

Fortunately, this is not to say that "contacts" were the only avenue for advocacy and initiation of services. Indeed, the story of Crystal Jones demonstrated that intensive individual agency and advocacy could be accomplished with empty hands and a courageous spirit. Crystal pursued her goal with nothing but her own sense of desperation and a powerful conviction that her cause was God-given. Nevertheless, the sustainability of her efforts was constrained by the lack of systemic structures to support the organization, which remained at the mercy of a special dispensation from the government. As Sister Bertil predicted, the organization's longevity would depend on the next change of government.

Neither Crystal nor Jacqui wanted charity. Crystal's goal was a self-help project for parents, and Jacqui hated every time she had to ask an Immortelle supporter to fill a monetary gap. But, in the absence of legislation requiring schooling for children with disabilities, charity has been essential to this work.

This is not to negate the appropriateness of charity. As international scholars, Shaun Grech (2015) and Maya Kalyanpur (2015) have argued, charity has a natural and appropriate place in all societies and especially in cultures built on traditional hierarchies. In India, for example, it reflects commitment to a shared philosophy of interdependence and duty. At Immortelle, the need for charitable support has continued unabated over the 40 years of its existence. Charity comes in several forms: From individual donations such as those cited above; to unofficial arrangements made by the Principal to allow extremely needy families to send their children to school free of charge; to roti sales and golf tournaments; to donations of building materials from businesses; and to funding awards from Republic Bank's *Power to Make a Difference Fund* or other similar charities. The comments below by David Bratt and Charles Mouttet, two Immortelle board members presented the situation in stark reality:

> *David.* The other thing Immortelle needs is more money so they could give the teachers a better salary. I've been a Director for about 20 something years and our Board meetings basically constitute … "Well, we owing this bank 1 million, and we owing this one that, and—how we getting the money?" That is what we do. There is very little opportunity for long term or medium term planning about where we are going or what we want to do.
> *Charles.* My main job is to find money. But the problem is—it's fine to raise the money to build it. But how do you run it? Really, this is a job the government should be doing. Charity can only go so far. There needs to be a base-line provided by the government.

Volunteerism and non-governmental organizations: An unstable alliance. A step beyond the pure charity model can be seen in the development of non-governmental organizations (NGOs), which, as public/private partnerships, continue to build on and expand the charity model.

In this, we see the nation continuing to occupy the liminal space on a spectrum of "developing to developed", as evidenced by the absence of government provision of a baseline provision for citizens with disabilities.

Certainly, this model is an improvement over total reliance on citizens' and social groups' personal charity. However, in the developed world, there would be a stable and adequate safety net below which no-one should fall, which then could be supplemented by efforts by individuals, charitable organizations, and partially state-supported NGOs. As Shaun Grech (2015) asserted in his study of disability services in Guatemala, NGO's cannot replace that basic safety net: "Over the years, NGOs have become more palatable to the government but only as a cheap alternative, while permitting the State to further evade its responsibilities toward its people" (p. 243).

Grech's point is very relevant to Trinidad/Tobago. The Immortelle Children's Centre, and all 12 private special schools that constitute the Private Special Schools Association of Trinidad/Tobago (PSSATT), had NGO status, and most of the professionals in this research who were engaged in advocacy were either initiators of, or participants in, NGOs. While all were proud of the work being done by their organizations, the severe limitations of these structures were evident. In the words of Teresina, president of the Autistic Society of Trinidad/Tobago:

> *Teresina.* It would be good for different agencies of the Government to get more involved in public awareness of persons with disabilities. They've left it to the NGOs, but how much money do we have for public awareness? There is only so much a parent support group run mainly by parents of children and adults on the autism spectrum can do with limited resources.

It is notable that being an advocacy group did not ensure receipt of a government subvention. The Down Syndrome Family Network, for example, was an NGO with no subvention from the government, no paid staff, and total dependence on volunteers and on sponsorship from the public and private sectors.

Advocacy and litigation: Trajectories of advocacy. Parents' avenues to advocacy were similar to the paths initiated by parents and other dis-ability advocates in both developing and developed countries. In the US, however, the courts provided the bridge from advocacy to legislation. The Association for Retarded Children (now The ARC), established by parents in 1950 in Minneapolis, Minnesota, rapidly developed into a nationwide advocacy movement that culminated in the Pennsylvania Association for Retarded Citizens' successful class action suit against the Commonwealth of Pennsylvania in 1972. Subsequent court cases led ultimately to the passage of the *Education for All Handicapped Children Act* in 1975, which legislated a "free, appropriate public education" for all children with disabilities. Under this law and its subsequent revision as the *Individuals with Disabilities Education Act* in 1990, no child in the US can be turned away from a public school on the basis of any type of disability.

Perhaps the use of litigation is one area in which, culturally, Trinidad/Tobago's "other foot" remains in the developing world. Based on my personal knowledge of the culture, I would speculate that the relative absence of litigation may reflect a continuing preference for a greater value on collectivity rather than individualism, also on a personalistic, rather than legalistic approach to managing conflict. However, the absence of a culture of litigation makes it difficult for an advocacy movement to succeed in getting government "policies" to move toward legislation. Consequently, it seems to me that advocacy in Trinidad/Tobago tends to get "stuck" at a relatively preliminary level, leaving the movement to rely largely on societal goodwill. Goodwill, in turn, continues to rely on a combination of individual efforts, social capital and charity.

"Inclusion Is an Ideal, but ...:" Ironies and Paradoxes in the Global Context

A third pervasive theme in the study was the challenge of creating inclusive schooling. As noted in the opening chapter of the book, the international movement on behalf of persons with disabilities has exerted tremendous influence worldwide. With inclusive education as a primary goal specified in the CRPD (2006), the UN Department of Economic and Social Affairs reported in 2019 that 177 countries, including Trinidad/Tobago, had ratified the Convention. The report defines ratification as meaning that a state has "signaled the intention to undertake legal rights and obligations contained in the Convention" (United Nations, Department of Economic and Social Affairs, 2019). Yet, 44% of UN member states have yet to ensure systems to meet Goal 4 of the CRPD's Sustainable Goals (UN Flagship Report, 2018). Ironically, the US is one of only a handful of UN member states that had not yet ratified the CRPD.

The question arises, why is there such a lag between many countries' intentions and their actual implementation of CRPD principles? Alfredo Artiles, Elizabeth Kozleski, and Frederico Waitoller (2011) have described the global picture of inclusion in terms of "first generation" inclusion, which developed in "economically vibrant" societies such as Denmark, France, and the US, as compared with "second generation" efforts in the developing world. Yet, a striking irony is seen in two facts cited by John Richardson and Justin Powell (2011) in their comparative analysis of special education services globally. First, as increasing proportions of students have been identified as having special learning needs in many countries, segregated and inclusive schooling have increased simultaneously. Second, and most importantly, these authors note that the inclusive model has not yet been implemented in several developed nations.

As cited in the opening chapter of this book, Richardson and Powell's analysis of inclusive placements in 18 European countries in 2002 showed that seven countries evidenced full inclusion models, six had "multiple" systems, and five maintained a dual education system that served students with and without disabilities in separate settings. Of the latter five countries, updated reports by Eurydice (2019) indicated that the dual model continued to be maintained in Germany and the Netherlands, while both French and Flemish communities in Belgium had moved since 2015 toward partial inclusion of students with special needs. In Switzerland, a decentralized education system currently allows for a range of placements, including "full-time and part-time" integration, special classes, and special schools. Meanwhile, in the US, where inclusion is greatly lauded, the multiple track system provides for widely varying levels of inclusion/exclusion according to different localities and related to different disability categories. Moreover, as consistently revealed in annual reports of the Office for Special Education Programs (U.S. Department of Education, 2018), the issue of inappropriate placements is a continuing concern as students from low-status minority groups such as African Americans, Native Americans, and Latinos, experience disproportionately high rates of placement in disability categories based on clinical judgment (e.g. learning disability and emotional/behavioral disorder). Compared to their white peers, these students also experience placements in more restrictive (i.e. more separate) settings.

These globally disparate patterns indicate that commitment to inclusive education does not reflect simple features of "development". Rather, Richardson and Powell (2011) point to the difficulty of changing historical structures, and conclude that, in any given country, "economic, political, and historical differences that played a role in prior legislative events are considerable sources of resistance" (p. 228).

Globalization and the tensions between cultural continuity and change. The question of how the global "export" of second-generation inclusion applies to developing countries has stimulated a robust debate among international scholars. In considering how to evaluate the appropriateness of the inclusive principle in developing countries, Alfredo Artiles and his colleagues (2011) provided a very helpful perspective similar to that of Richardson and Powell (2011). Challenging "the long-standing assumption...that a laudable idea—inclusive education—can travel seamlessly across cultures and contexts" (p. 8), these scholars proposed two key considerations for the transfer of the philosophy to different geopolitical settings:

> First, [there is] a country's historical commitment to inclusive education and its attendant historical legacies about difference... Inclusive education models in countries with different historical commitments to this approach are affected differently by economic opportunities, systems of stratification, policy climates, levels of investment in social policies, educational expectations for the citizenry, cultural forces, social movements, and so forth... Second, we theorize that globalization and the tensions observed in a given nation between cultural continuity and change also shape how equity is addressed in inclusive education. (p. 7)

In other words, the appropriateness of inclusion depends on an understanding of the country's historical cultural philosophies and practices, and by its cultural responsiveness to change. Pressing this point further, Maya Kalyanpur (2015) applied this critique to her native India, a nation of 1.2 billion people with deeply ingrained social stratifications and vast diversity in languages, religions, and economic resources. She argued that, in a nation where access to basic needs such as sanitation, food, shelter, and electricity are yet unmet and education remains out of reach for many, the idea of inclusion is an inappropriate imposition. Kalyanpur described such "policy borrowing" as a form of colonialism:

> By placing governments in the position of defending their own implementation of the international agenda, a culture of apologetic inadequacy has been created rather than a sense of outrage that they are being held to impossible standards that the developed world itself could not have met during its own phase of development. (p. 66)

In an article entitled, "*International orthodoxy vs. national realities*", James Urwick and Julian Elliott (2010) offered an example of inclusion gone wrong. Like Kalyanpur's point above, these authors argued that the imposition of the principle amounts to a kind of neo-colonialism, as seen in their case study of the failure of the educational inclusion experiment in Lesotho. They concluded that the experiment attempted, unsuccessfully, to move the country "from a position of virtually no provision for disabilities straight to one of fully integrated provision" (p. 137).

Another focal point in the discussion is the fact that disability and poverty tend to be intertwined. Shaun Grech (2015) called for setting realistic economic priorities in countries with limited resources. Based on 11 years of qualitative research in Guatemala, his findings indicated that extremes of poverty and deprivation in that largely rural nation rendered issues of inclusion hardly relevant in the face of a struggle for basic survival. Thus, Grech argued that inclusion was a philosophy developed in resource-rich developed nations of the "global North" and exported uncritically to nations in the "global South".

How does the liminal situation of Trinidad and Tobago relate to these global patterns? When comparing Trinidad/Tobago to India, for example, one obvious commonality is a shared British colonial history that included the establishment of a democratic political structure and a Western academic education system with English as the medium of instruction. However, in Trinidad/Tobago, English is spoken by all, and an estimated 98% of all primary-aged children are in school. In India, by contrast, the wide diversity of languages, historical social stratification, and simply the vast size and population of the country make education, in Maya Kalyanpur's words, "an unattainable dream for millions of children" (2015, p. 64).

Inclusion in Trinidad/Tobago within the Caribbean context: A "piecemeal" process. Despite some historical similarities, Trinidad/Tobago is not India, Lesotho, or Guatemala. Nor is it the United States or Germany. A better comparison would be Jamaica and Barbados, two Caribbean nations of the same "age" and very similar colonial history. These countries' education systems are essentially the same, to the point that students sit the same high school graduation examinations, set by the Caribbean Examinations Council (CXC). Both countries also maintain a similar "dual" system of education regarding students with disabilities.

In her study of disability and inequality in Jamaica, Annicia Gayle-Geddes (2015) reported a literacy rate of 91%, a poverty rate of 17.6%, and an unemployment rate of 13.7%. Stating that Jamaica was "the first country globally to ratify the CRPD in 2007 and therefore remains at the forefront of disability provisions in the Caribbean…" (p. 2), Gayle-Geddes went on to offer a sharp critique of the country's progress on disabilities since that time. She explained that, until 2015, although the work of disability advocates had resulted in the National Policy for Persons with Disabilities in 2000 and in government benefits for specific disabilities, there had been no legislation to enforce these provisions. Specifying numerous benefits that were supposed to be available but were poorly distributed or hard to access, such as rehabilitation services, "concessionary bus fares and physically accessible public transportation", sign language interpretation, and others, Gayle-Geddes summarized the situation as follows:

> While the milestone benefits for PWDs [Persons with Disabilities] are commendable in Jamaica, access to benefits by the majority of PWDs proves unattainable…The National Policy for Persons with Disabilities remains unenforced, and …has not kept pace with expectations from the disabled citizenry. Absence of a programmatic framework for the development of PWDs and under-capacitation of the national coordinating agency charged with oversight of disability affairs undercuts the long-term livelihood prospects of PWDs. (p. 2)[1]

In a similar vein, Barbadian scholar Stacy Blackman (2017) outlined the 20-year stagnation of a hopeful inclusion policy developed by Barbadian government agencies in 1995. Citing issues such as negative teacher and peer group attitudes toward inclusion, and inadequate structures for assessment, teacher preparation, and support services, Blackman explained that the government's philosophy toward social justice in education has not been supported by a "fundamental commitment" to education reform.

---

[1] At the time of this writing, recent developments in Jamaica indicated that a legal mandate for the education of students with disabilities had been enacted. The form of implementation of this mandate, however, was yet to be determined (Gayle-Geddes, personal communication, February, 2019).

The intermittent attempts at policy change described by Blackman echo Gayle-Geddes' (2015) description of the education policy for persons with disabilities in Jamaica, which she describes as "piecemeal", and the provision of inclusive education as "a distant dream" (p. 22). This sounds very much like the situation in Trinidad/Tobago: A "piecemeal" process, proceeding in fits and starts, influenced in one moment by international pressure, in another by local political conveniences, and, in yet another, by economic uncertainties such as the recession of 2016.

Cultural Continuity and the Colonial Legacy in Caribbean Education Systems

In Trinidad/Tobago, we see a young nation with considerable economic resources, a strong democracy, a highly literate, largely urban population of approximately one and a half million, and a commitment to free public education from primary through tertiary levels. When viewed through this lens, it is hard to comprehend why students with disabilities—a tiny percentage of the population—should be excluded from publicly supported education services. Although the WHO-World Bank (2011) report on disability found that children with disabilities were always the last to be included in school, we wonder why that should continue to be the case in a numerically small and geographically accessible nation with a reported gross national product of 20 billion U.S. dollars.

To understand this continuing exclusion, it is crucial to understand the deeply embedded legacy of British colonial education. In the opening chapter, I quoted Trinidadian scholars Elna Carrington-Blaides' and Dennis Conrad (2017), who described this as "an elitist system that is deeply examination-oriented and focused on rewards for small percentages of the brightest citizens" (p. 35).

This examination orientation was explained in detail by Jerome de Lisle and his colleagues (De Lisle, Laptiste-Francis, McMillan-Solomon, & Bowrin-Williams, 2017), who described a stratified system enforced by high-stakes academic testing at multiple points in children's development. The resulting structure excludes in two ways, at the entry point into primary schools of differential quality, which correlates heavily with socio-economic or social capital, and then at specific points as children move through a supposedly meritocratic schooling process with a common curriculum. These scholars explained the structure clearly:

> The outcome is high levels of horizontal and vertical differentiation. A differentiated school system is the exact opposite of a seamless school system. Vertical differentiation means that some students are repeating grades or being excluded from certain tracks. Horizontal differentiation means that advantaged and disadvantaged students attend different schools…High levels of vertical and horizontal differentiation imply that the education system is not inclusive and does not accommodate all learners in high quality learning. (p. 92)
>   This emphasis on sorting may be fuelled by a pervasive philosophy of elitism inherited from colonial education…a belief-system that amounts to a philosophical mind-set with an elitist logic that influences both the design of the education and assessment systems. (p. 93)

These descriptions make it clear that the education system would require a dramatic overhaul to effectively include students with both mild and significant intellectual or communication disabilities, such as those who attend Immortelle and the other special schools. Significant modifications would have to be made to all aspects of schooling, starting at the macro level with the structures described above, and the requirement for one shared curriculum and assessment process. At the micro levels, huge changes would be required on issues such as class size, teacher preparation, the didactic instructional methods typically used in these schools, and the ethos of uniformity that still marks the social climate of schools in this society.

The challenge of change. By the foregoing analysis, we see in practice what Alfredo Artiles and his colleagues (2011) referred to as "globalization and the tensions…between cultural continuity and change" (p. 7). In Trinidad and Tobago, an increasingly urbanized and educated populace holds equality as an explicit goal, but struggles to pursue this goal within the constraints of an education system that supports a deeply entrenched academic and social elitism.

As noted above, Trinidad and Tobago is by no means unique in its resistance to the kind of systemic change that would be required for a truly unitary system. While developing nations hustle to create inclusive systems, economically strong, developed European nations such as Germany and Switzerland maintain dual education systems that serve disabled and non-disabled students in separate schools, and the US maintains tracks within schools, which may or may not include students with disabilities in general education classrooms. Reflecting on this pattern, Richardson and Powell (2011) concluded:

> The persistence of segregation, indeed its rising simultaneously with inclusion… indicates that although some international consensus on the importance of inclusive education has been reached at an abstract level, the deinstitutionalization of the dualism of special and general education is still just beginning…Inclusive education reform implies the restructuring of nearly every aspect of schooling—too much for most involved interest groups to bear, especially where the will of national and local decision makers and community support lags behind the ideals and principles articulated at the global level. (p. 282)

Allyson Hamel-Smith, the psychologist who participated in this study, placed the discussion of change in the context of developmental phases of a society. Allyson proposed viewing Trinidad and Tobago as being in a phase of development similar to that of the US before the civil rights movement of the 1960s, when it was still legal to exclude children with disabilities from public schools. Once more, a liminal space on the spectrum of "development".

This point, however, prompts a consideration of how this developing nation might learn from the mistakes of other more developed societies. For example, how successful have some of the special education trends in the US been? How well has "inclusion" worked? What have been the downsides of the categorical framing of school-based disabilities such as learning disability or emotional behavior disorders? How has this categorical approach failed to take account of students' identity intersections, primarily race and socio-economic status?

With these issues in mind, what would it take to provide an appropriate public education for the children currently served by Immortelle and the other "special schools" in Trinidad/Tobago? What should "inclusion" look like in this liminal space? One thing is clear: regardless of ideal models, Paul Sillitoe (1998) points out that a practical approach must be tailored to existing local structures and belief systems if reforms are to be sustainable.

It is worth recalling that the vision of inclusion was on the table, as demonstrated by the intended pilot program developed with the IADB

(2008) that was to be implemented and evaluated in 12 pilot schools. Whether the reason that this plan was abandoned was "too much politics", "too much bureaucracy", or not enough resources, it seems that a "seamless" model of inclusive services is not going to happen in the near future. Meanwhile, children with disabilities and their families struggle to find "an equal place" or, if they find one, they struggle to afford it. What is to be done? I believe that step one is legislation. Step two will be working out a model of implementation of the legal mandate that is feasible within the social and educational structures of the country. Step three will be the establishment by the government, with support from NGO's and private establishments, of an on-going, intensive public awareness program designed to promote and sustain increased understanding and inclusion of individuals with disabling conditions.

Government Helps, but…

There is a policy on persons with disabilities. A nice package. But there is no legal mandate, no law to drive the policy. So that's where it's falling down.
   —Sister Bertil, Lady Hochoy Home

The quotation above points to the largest gap in disability services in Trinidad and Tobago—the absence of a legal mandate. One of the most recurrent themes in this research project was, "government helps, but…"

The huge "BUT" at the end of this theme is what needs to be addressed. Exactly what constitutes this caveat? Sister Bertil pointed to legislation. Michael Reid implicitly agreed, but was not sure whether that law should be a "stand alone", or an amendment to existing laws. Across the study, all participants pointed to the fact that "subventions" to special schools, based only on a "policy", are not the answer because they represent add-ons, rather than integral features of educational services.

Maya Kalyanpur and her colleagues (2007), based on their work in Cambodia, noted that special education, particularly for individuals with intellectual disabilities, tends to be perceived as a situation of "high investment, low returns", which governments often see as not profitable. Kamal Lamichane (2015), however, in discussing education and employment for individuals with disabilities in developing countries, argued for public investment in human capital. Offering a broad definition of the concept of "investment", this author offered a view that shifts from the usual idea of investing capital in a business for profit, to investment in human development. In his words:

> The term "investment" is defined as the allocation of budgets and resources by states and societies into areas of human capital formation such as education, health, and employment, and for social capital such as accessible roads and transport and other infrastructures, to facilitate the participation of PWD [persons with disabilities] in economic, social and political spheres. (p. 9)

How could the government of Trinidad/Tobago truly begin to "invest" in developing the human capital currently untapped by a narrowly conceived education system? The participants in this study identified the caveats to the success of government's efforts and pointed to the following directions for investment as a way forward.

- *BUT* **Number 1—Legislation**. Government helps, but there is no requirement that children with disabilities must be provided with an education.

If an overhaul of the public system is not part of the nation's vision, why not at least ensure the existence and accessibility of a parallel system *fully* supported by public funds? Why not enact this requirement, even in the form of an amendment to the existing education law? The law would require that services be provided, while the nature and location of those services could be determined according to philosophical and budgetary considerations. Indeed, the draft policy statement of 2017 seemed to point in that direction.

The 2017 Draft Policy Statement: A plan for differential services according to disability. In 2017, the Ministry of Social Development and Family Services' National Policy on Persons with Disabilities provided a draft of a policy update that differed very little from the report of 2004. The draft of this policy was greeted with considerable critique by advocates and disability scholars, such as Dr. Jeanne Dunne (Newsday, November 14 & 21, 2016) and the Faculty of Law at the University of the West Indies in Trinidad (Mohammed-Davidson, 2016). The not-so-new but encouraging draft policy promised support for a wide range of needs, including transportation, public awareness, physical accessibility, information and communication, medical assessment and care, rehabilitation, and social protection programs for families in poverty. For education, the policy draft provided the following overall goal:

> It is recognized that there should be greater inclusivity of persons with disabilities into the mainstream education system. It is therefore important to facilitate access to education, from early childhood education to tertiary level, for persons with disabilities. An inclusive education system is therefore critical. There would be need for an approach to education that will meet the needs of all children with disabilities. The goal would be to implement progressive education programmes geared toward achieving an environment of completely barrier-free and accessible schools. (p. 17)

Toward this goal, the report identified several specific aims, which essentially reflected two key provisions:

> To provide the appropriate support services for children with disabilities that would facilitate their full inclusion in the education system [and] to establish appropriate educational facilities for persons with severe or multiple disabilities. (p. 17)

The language here distinguishes between "children with disabilities" and "persons with severe or multiple disabilities". One can only interpret this as indicating two types of services, mainstream inclusion for children with "mild" disabilities—perhaps those whom participants in this study referred to as the "invisible disabilities", and separate schools for those with significant disabilities. While inclusion activists around the world would no doubt object to this plan, it seems to be not out of synch with the preferences expressed by most participants in this study.

Are parallel services or "dual" systems necessarily bad? Certainly, all parents subscribed to the idea of an inclusive society in which their children would, as the anthem proposes, "find an equal place". Several pointed out that inclusion in the community and in the public education system should go hand in hand, since children going to school together would mean that they were growing up together, which would, in turn mitigate social stigma and isolation. Yet, they also agreed that this would take economic and personnel resources which, at present, have not been afforded to the education system. With no guarantee that the curriculum would be tailored to the individual needs of their children, or that their children would not be held to impossible standards and to the likelihood of increased stigmatization, most would prefer to keep their children where they were—even Renata, Daniel's mother, for whom this option was simply a heartbreaking "compromise".

At this point, I must acknowledge an important limitation to these findings: that these parents' views may be unique to a particular group whose children are enrolled in one private special school with which they are largely satisfied. Their views, therefore, may not be representative of parents whose children are in other situations. On the other hand, it is true that many of these parents did try "normal schools", and found them impossible for their children.

It was, therefore, telling, to hear the views of Glen Niles, the only voice in the entire study who was 100% behind the appropriateness of full inclusion in school and in the workplace. Glen argued passionately that the entire citizenry had bought into a culture of low expectations and acceptance of a negative status quo regarding disabilities. He felt that the failure to develop inclusion as a priority in all social systems simply represented a lack of will and vision on the part of the society and its leaders. Glen had no patience with views such as, "For now we have no alternative to special schools" or "We just don't have the resources".

While I can see no reason why an appropriate curriculum could not be offered in the same buildings as those who are "fully included", the question is whether the entire vision of schooling and curriculum *would* be modified to make such inclusive placement meaningful. If this were the case, I would say—certainly. If not, I agree with the parents who said that appropriate separate services would be better than inadequate or inappropriate "full inclusion". If they had to choose between a high-quality separate environment and a mediocre and unwelcoming mainstream, they saw no contest.

As many have argued, inclusion cannot be a one-size-fits-all approach. If we are to take seriously the statement of O'Rourke-Lang and Levy (2016) that inclusion should not be understood as "a place", then we understand that to be "inclusive" does not mean placing children with disabilities into regular classrooms solely for the sake of apparent "equity". Indeed, the argument has been made powerfully that to be equitable is not necessarily to provide the "same" treatments for all children. Rather, as Artiles and colleagues (2011) explained, equity means providing all children with what they need. This must also take into account the local realities of education. As argued by Charles Mouttet, a parent and Immortelle board member, the typical class sizes in Trinidad/Tobago primary schools would make "full inclusion" an impossibility: "Some of these kids you can't have more than four with a teacher and an assistant. How are these kids going to go into a class of 30?"

As confirmed by Richardson and Powell (2011), even in developed countries that tout the principle of inclusion, this seldom means "full inclusion" for all. In the US, where the Individuals with Disabilities Education Act of 1990 calls for "the least restrictive environment", it does not call for full inclusion. In fact, the "multiple track" model provides students with intellectual or multiple disabilities with a range of placements from full inclusion for a few, to separate and/or partially integrated classes within schools serving students with and without disabilities; to separate schools for students with particularly challenging issues such as severely disruptive behaviors or specialized medical needs.

The Trinidad/Tobago Equal Opportunities Act of 2000. If, as Michael Reid suggested, the government of Trinidad/Tobago were to consider it fit to amend existing laws rather than create stand-alone laws for individuals with disabilities, then why not go that route? In fact, the 2017 draft policy on disabilities addressed legislation, stating that new laws or amendments to existing laws, will be enacted "where necessary" (p. 15). Again, by comparison, in the US, the first legislation prohibiting discrimination based on disability was Section 504 of the Rehabilitation Act of 1973, which, as explained by Colin Ong-Dean (2009), "was nothing more than a paragraph appended to a bill funding vocational rehabilitation for people with disabilities" (p. 15).

In Trinidad and Tobago, existing law, the Education Act of 1966, requires the provision of public funding for education. It seems that the needed "paragraph" is already in the Equal Opportunities Act of 2000, which actually specifies disability as one of the "statuses" that must not be used as grounds for discrimination. Having defined "disabilities" very clearly, the Act further defines discrimination in education as "refusing or failing to accept that person's application for admission as a student" (Part IV, # 15a). I believe that, if the will was there, another paragraph in each or both of these laws is all it would take to specifically mandate education of students with disabilities. Of course, that means a paragraph with the funding to support it!

- *BUT* **Number 2—Funding**. The second BUT is that government helps by contributing to the costs of eligible private special schools, but children with disabilities continue to be the only ones for whom parents must search for a school and pay school fees.

As the theme, "Finding Immortelle" indicated, parents are not choosing to pay private school fees because they want to; they are enrolling their children in the only schools that will accept them. The government falls short of that basic provision found in all developed nations of the world. In fact, it falls short of its own vision of a free education primary through tertiary "for all". Here is one place where both feet need to be firmly on the developed side of the fence.

Michael Reid from the Ministry of Social Development and Family Services put it this way:

> *Michael.* I think that the private special schools have developed because of the need for services that are not found in the public schools. And I think there would always be that need. Yes, we want integration and inclusion but there are some children who need special attention, which, in a typical school that has a curriculum to fulfill, would not be feasible. And they are all private, so because they need specially trained people, the fees are sometimes very high. As a government we need to look at that. We have a policy of education for all from the nursery to tertiary but there is a group of people who have to pay for their children to go to school.

Despite Michael's support for public funding, two aspects of his statement are really striking: first, the notion that schools must have "a curriculum to fulfill", brings us back to the rigidly stratified structure of education in Trinidad and Tobago. The reality is that, to educate all children, a range of curriculum options are needed. The second point is that the government's commitment to free tertiary education, while commendable, indicates the high priority placed on advanced education for an intellectual elite. Conversely, it points to the low value on citizens who occupy the opposite end of the intellectual spectrum, whose parents must "pay for them to go to school". Moreover, the recession in Trinidad and Tobago in 2016 resulted in considerable cutbacks in some of the generous provisions of free tertiary education, providing a note of caution regarding creating sweeping visions based on a thriving but poorly balanced oil-based economy. As Shaun Grech (2015) noted:

> What value will rights and legislation have if the resources to implement and enforce them are absent or constantly shrinking in the persistent, neo-liberal cost-cutting exercise? (p. 264)

- *BUT* **Number 3—Bureaucracy.** The third BUT is that government helps, but "gets in its own way" because of the cumbersome bureaucratic structures for implementing educational and social policies regarding children with disabilities.

The stories told by parents revealed that numerous bureaucratic hoops were exacerbated by the negative attitudes of those charged with enforcing the policies. In the words of Dr. Esla Lynch: "Parents are forced to humble themselves, be humiliated, or exasperated in their attempts to get assistance". Esla's point was painfully illustrated in 2018 by parents protesting the government's three-year delay in opening the National Enrichment Center for the Disabled (the "Couva Centre"). During the protest, as parents chanted—"Open the Centre!"—one mother told a reporter, "We are begging! We not supposed to beg because this is our children's right. But we have come to the stage where we have to beg!" (Loop News, 2018). Indeed, the list of humiliations is long: families must return year after year to re-establish that a child with a congenital disability "still has" the disability. To become eligible for the "disability grant", families of children under 18 must weave their way through a maze of variable eligibility criteria that function in a truly unsystematic manner, subject to the whims of individuals whose "attitudes" often reveal contempt, or at least disdain, for parents and their children. Private schools and services that receive government subventions must find some way to get through long periods in which the promised subvention simply does not arrive. These schools have no recourse but to engage in frustrating and demoralizing strategies such as raising loans on which interest rates would cut further into their limited budgets; paying salaries late to staff who, in turn, have to pay their bills late; or in the worst cases, close school until the subvention finally arrived.

An easy fix. The fact that the situation with private school subventions could quite easily be improved was demonstrated in 2018, two years after the initial phase of my research, when Jacqui Leotaud told me that, as of that academic year, the government subventions had started to arrive on time. Her explanation for this dramatic and very important change amounted to two key events: most importantly, a pair of particularly efficient government employees had been assigned to implement the payments of the subventions and had taken charge of the entire process. Second, the Ministry of Education's physical facility had been renovated and all offices were now in one building, removing the cumbersome processes of moving paperwork through numerous offices located in different buildings.

Sadly, however, by the end of that year, this situation had been reversed. Phillis Griffith of New Beginnings reported it as below:

> *Phillis.* There was a period earlier this year when the payment process improved tremendously. There were two Ministry employees who took it on themselves to visit the schools and find out information and would trouble shoot any problems in the payment process. They were impressed with the schools—realizing how much we do. They started to organize the system and checks started to come on time. If there was a delay, we could call and ask what the problems were and get an answer. However, this was stopped when it was decided that what these two personnel were doing was not part of their portfolio.

This development demonstrates not only how simple some of the needed changes might be, but unfortunately, how the commitment to bureaucratic implementation of policy took precedence over efficiency. Clearly, these steps represented individual initiatives rather than sustainable systems change.

- *BUT* **Number 4—Attitudes**. The need to address "attitudes" must go hand in hand with a radical challenge to the stagnation incurred by ancient bureaucratic hoops that demoralize and dehumanize parents and children who are already supremely vulnerable.

All the BUTS above fall directly within the authority and responsibility of the government, but the pervasive presence of negative attitudes revealed a challenge which, according to Michael Reid of the Disability Affairs Unit, "cannot be legislated or forced". Michael pointed to this as an area for advocacy groups, but Teresina Seunarine, Director of the Autism Society, emphasized that advocacy groups need the support of government to do this consistently. She felt that, although attitudes cannot be mandated, it is possible to mandate a program that targets the improvement of the public's understanding and attitudes toward disabilities.

Participants in the study presented contrasting views of the issue of public attitudes to disability. The theme of "not nice" attitudes was supported not only by parents' reports of explicit public expressions of disdain or rejection of their children, but, worse, by accounts of callous treatment of parents by government workers tasked with implementing grants or services to which families were legally entitled. On the other hand, several people attributed these behaviors not to unkindness but to ignorance of disabilities. Speech therapist Penny Camps took this point further, arguing that despite a cultural characteristic of "caring", there was a tendency for people to "put on blinkers" that disguised the presence of disability, poverty, and crime until they "come up in your face". Penny felt that demonstrations of good intentions were evident in the public's welcoming response, for example, to a performing company that included persons with disabilities. Similarly, Sister Bertil, who had been involved in disabilities at the Lady Hochoy home for over 30 years, compared previous parental attitudes of shame and rejection to current parents' pride in their children's accomplishments and social activities. On Carnival day, for example, she said, "The parents are following the children's band. Long ago the children were dropped off and the parents would disappear. It's so different now!"

If we accept that both negative and positive attitudes toward disability do exist, it might be helpful to ask how the social processes and situations that convey these attitudes could be changed. I suggest we address this question by noting that all the "BUTS" above are interrelated and need to be treated as parts of a whole.

Attitudes and bureaucracy: An interactive cycle from the top down. Workers in government offices, or in any of a society's service systems, are influenced by the ethos of the structures in which they work. For instance, if it is common practice for subventions to be paid late, or for policies on benefits to be so vaguely explained that parents do not know whether they are eligible or not, employees who are providing these services gradually come to accept that this is how it is done, and therefore build up resistance to the sad faces or challenging voices of distraught members of the public. As cited earlier, speech therapist Penny Camps described this distancing as putting on "blinkers" that protect the average person from having to notice the pain of others.

Yet, several stories in the research suggest that, behind the "blinkers" of disinterest, lie beating hearts that can quite easily be touched through sympathy. When Crystal Jones reacted to the cold face of disdain by displaying her intense emotion for all to see, the workers in the government office responded with charitable offerings of help for her and her family. When Charles Mouttet walked into the government office with his multiply disabled son to apply for the disability grant, he received an immediate response of, "Oh, ok".

What would it take to move this response from sympathy to one of mutual responsibility? To convert this beating heart into a "system" with feelings? If the regulations were respectful and meaningful, would not those implementing them also behave respectfully? Could not the "caring" character of this society be built into the bureaucracy?

Attitudes and legislation: An interactive cycle from the bottom up. Another way of thinking about attitudinal change is to start with behavioral change and believe that, by behaving in a certain way, one can come to value that way of being. For example, Jacqui Leotaud's story about the rules she laid down for Racquel's siblings and relatives in their interactions with Raquel required everyone to behave in an inclusive and respectful manner toward her. They had to understand that if her siblings were invited to a family party, Raquel must be included, even if she did annoy everyone by sticking her hand in the birthday cake.

To stretch an analogy somewhat, I would say that the "behavioral" approach is what has occurred in the US, regarding civil rights. Through law suits and legislation, discrimination in schooling, housing, or employment has been at least partially eradicated by the imposition of the law. The civil rights movement did not have the full support of the nation's populace. Yet, racial integration laws were enacted and, although they took several decades to be fully implemented across all states, the assumption that separate schooling and separate public facilities based on race was inherently unequal gradually gained credence, if only because it was the law.

Establishing an understanding of "personhood". Finally, I turn to an intangible obstacle that might lie at the heart of negative attitudes towards persons with disabilities—the question of who is valuable as a human being. This question is not one that most participants in the study addressed openly. Yet, people who have family members with disabilities know that this question lies behind some of the rejection their loved ones experience. How can societies reach the "beating hearts" of average citizens whose lives have not yet been touched by disability, or who see those with disabilities as less than human in their value?

The principle of inclusion is based on the democratic premise of the rights of the individual. However, my interviews with participants did not suggest that this premise resonated particularly with the culture of Trinidad and Tobago. While it is beyond the scope of my research to speak with any authority on how this nation would fall currently on a spectrum of "collectivist" to "individualistic", my guess is that it lies within the "liminal" frame—moving between a traditional collectivism in which a focus on familial ties and community identity provided the backbone of the society, and a more Western model in which the individual has priority. It seemed to me that positive attitudes toward persons with disabilities were more reflective of what Michael Reid, Director of the Disability Affairs Unit, identified as a "human rights" approach. Indeed, the Ministry of Social Development and Family Services (2017) draft policy statement did identify this as the basis for its policy.

An example of the human rights principle in practice was presented in a qualitative study in India by Shrivedi Rao (2015), which detailed the daily strategies that Bengali mothers used to create an inclusive environment in the neighborhood by appealing to people's "moral conscience … evoking the sense of humanity that is implicit in all of us" (p. 241). In the present study, we saw the same approach in Crystal Jones' description of how she introduced her son, Tiba, who had cerebral palsy, to the neighborhood. In addition to her public battles on behalf of children with cerebral palsy, Crystal waged a gentle and persuasive war on negative attitudes to disability within her own neighborhood:

> *Crystal.* I would carry him outside and take him for a walk. Wherever I was going, my child was going. No shame! So the children knew him and I would teach them about him. So they would come to understand what was wrong with him. They would call him, "Talk, Tiba! Yeah!" They learned to interact with him. And I encouraged my children to bring their friends home, until my son became like a big celebrity. He started to be accepted by their friends. They felt no shame.

Crystal's cry of, "no shame" calls to mind philosophical arguments about what it is that constitutes human life and worth. As mentioned in the opening chapter, disability studies scholar Nirmala Erevelles (2011) summarized the key arguments around this question as centering on the assumption that humanity is characterized by reason and autonomy, but placed the debate in the context of the way the economic imperatives of capitalist societies frame disabilities. In an article entitled, "Lives worth Living", Ashley Taylor (2013), also a disability studies scholar, delivered a powerful challenge to this somewhat complicated philosophical discourse, pointing out that even to ask the question "What counts as a life worth living", is to support the premise that some human beings are less valuable than others. Thus, she explained, to attempt to decide who should be included in the definition of "human" is to "uphold rather than dismiss" the belief that there should be "qualifying conditions of personhood and humanity" (p. 8). Eva Kittay (2000), challenging the focus on autonomy as a key human characteristic, countered the belief that society should be seen as "an association of equals—independent equals engaged in reciprocal interactions" (p. 76). We do not, she argued, have to justify support to individuals who are dependent by trying to "equalize them", because dependency is an essential and valuable component of human existence. In an extended discussion of an "ethic of care", Kittay (2019) placed these questions in the historical framework of Western philosophy, which has sought to base moral principles on reason alone, and argued instead for a focus on "empathetic connection to, and understanding of the other" p. 175).

The parents in this study did not need to be informed on this philosophical discussion. Like Eva Kittay, Margaret and Rupert Jones, parents of Candace, who had multiple disabilities induced by meningitis at the age of seven months, interpreted their daughter's life as intrinsically valuable. For this family, that value was based in the Christian framework of a divine purpose, by which Candace's presence in the world represented a God-given opportunity for others to develop empathy and compassion. Lana de Gannes and Renata Texeira, whose children had Down Syndrome, offered similar interpretations based on God's will. Francis Escayg, father of Isaiah, a child who had multiple disabilities, believed that his own gifts as a filmmaker would bring meaning to Isaiah's life through a vigorous agenda of on-going education through the media. His film of his son, Isaiah, (Escayg, 2013, *Crossing the Gap*), presents a visceral understanding of this beautiful human being whose physical anomalies marked him as "different". Going straight to the heart of negative "attitudes", Francis' words were haunting:

> *Francis.* People need to understand that these are human beings. They have souls, they have spirits. They feel pain. They feel lonely. They feel afraid just like any one of us.

No More Buts: Building on Cultural Traits of Caring, Diversity, and Humanism

In closing, I focus on the theme "We need systems!" In my anecdote of arriving in the Toronto airport with Melanie, I believe that I was experiencing what participants in this study meant by "systems": policies, procedures, and practices so ingrained as to largely remove the need for personal appeals to get basic things done. Barring emergencies, one can assume that "things" will go as planned. The absence of such systems resulted in a continuance of inequity through an overreliance on personal networking and "contacts".

I believe that a commitment to develop "systems" should address the four "Buts" above, based on a four-pronged approach led by the government and supported by NGO's and charitable organizations:

- the enactment of legislation making special education services a required and integral component of the education system,
- the provision of public funding for both private and public special education services, with on-going support for appropriate teacher preparation,
- the development of a rational bureaucracy for implementation of that legislation, with on-going professional development for government employees engaged in implementation of the legislation,
- the creation of an on-going explicit public awareness agenda for valuing and respecting individuals with disabilities.

With a legal mandate, a reliable delivery system, and increasingly positive understanding of disabilities, I believe the transformation would begin. We should see personal and political agendas replaced by established goals and procedures by which payments would be made on time, plans for buildings and services would be detailed enough to ensure all potential logistics, and regulations would be followed in a rational and respectful manner. This would require both top-down and bottom-up processes—pressure from parents and community advocates and responsive decision-making from the government.

This book suggests that Trinidad and Tobago is poised for the development of systems that will include all its citizens. It suggests also that there are in place cultural traits of caring, valuing of diversity, and humanism that could be mobilized to shake off the shackles of lethargy encouraged by a slow-moving bureaucracy and a strong but overly rigid education system.

Since education is highly valued in this nation, and all parents expect and seek educational services for their children, I believe that full government responsibility for the education of children with disabilities should be the starting point for the change that is needed. The knowledge that every child is valued and respected enough to be afforded a place in school will begin the message of genuine inclusion throughout the society. The challenge is to modify educational provisions in ways that build on the nation's cultural strengths, existing institutions, and economic resources, while elevating public understandings of individuals with disabilities.

REFERENCES

Artiles, A. J., Kozleski, E. B., & Waitoller, F. R. (2011). *Inclusive education: Examining equity on five continents*. Boston: Harvard Education Press.

Blackman, S. (2017). From charity education toward inclusion: The development of special and inclusive education in Barbados. In S. Blackman & D. Conrad (Eds.), *Caribbean discourse in inclusive education: Historical and contemporary issues* (pp. 3–20). Charlotte, NC: Information Age Publishing.

Bourdieu, P. (1986). The forms of capital. In J. Richardson (Ed.), *Handbook of theory and research for the sociology of education*. New York: Greenwood.

Brown, K., & Jackson, D. D. (2013). The history and conceptual elements of critical race theory. In M. Lynn & A. D. Dixson (Eds.), *Handbook of critical race theory in education* (pp. 9–22). New York: Routledge.

Carrington-Blaides, E., & Conrad, D. (2017). Toward inclusive education in Trinidad and Tobago: Policy challenges and implications. In S. Blackman & D. Conrad (Eds.), *Caribbean discourse in inclusive education: Historical and contemporary issues* (pp. 33–52). Charlotte, NC: Information Age Publishing.

Central Intelligence Agency. (2018). *The world factbook*. Retrieved from https://www.cia.gov/library/publications/the-world-factbook/geos/t

Charmaz, K. (2014). *Constructing grounded theory: A practical guide through qualitative analysis* (2nd ed.). London: Sage.

Coleman, J. S. (1988). Social capital in the creation of human capital. *The American Journal of Sociology, 94,* 95–129.

Connor, D., Ferri, B., & Annamma, S. (2016). *DisCrit: Disability studies and critical race theory in education*. New York: Teachers College Press.

Crenshaw, K. (1996). Mapping the margins: Intersectionality, identity politics, and violence against women. In N. G. K. Crenshaw, G. Pellar, & K. Thomas (Eds.), *Critical race theory: The key writings that formed the movement* (pp. 357–383). New York: New Press.

De Lisle, J., Laptiste-Francis, N., McMillan-Solomon, S., & Bowring-Williams, C. (2017). Student assessment systems in the Caribbean as an obstacle to inclusive education: The case of Trinidad and Tobago. In S. Blackman & D. Conrad (Eds.), *Caribbean discourse in inclusive education: Historical and contemporary issues* (pp. 87–106). Charlotte, NC: Information Age Publishing.

Erevelles, N. (2011). *Disability and difference in global contexts: Enabling a transformative body politic*. New York: Palgrave Macmillan.

Escayg, F. (2013). *Crossing the Gap*. Cause an effect. Retrieved from https://www.facebook.com/cause.an.effecttt/videos/10151682077613669/

Eurydice. (2019). *Key data on education in Europe*. Brussels: European Commission. Retrieved February 24, 2019, from https://eacea.ec.europa.eu/national-policies/eurydice/home_en

Gayle-Geddes, A. (2015). *Disability and inequality: Socioeconomic imperatives and public policy in Jamaica*. New York: Palgrave Macmillan.

Goffman, E. (1963). *Stigma: Notes on the management of spoiled identity*. New York: Simon and Schuster.

Government of the Republic of Trinidad and Tobago, Ministry of Social Development and Family Services. (2017, June). *National Policy on Persons with Disabilities*. Port of Spain, Trinidad.

Grech, S. (2015). *Disability and poverty in the global South: Renegotiating development in Guatemala*. New York: Palgrave Macmillan.

Harry, B., & Klingner, J. K. (2014). *Why are so many minority students in special education: Understanding race and disability in schools*. New York: Teachers College Press.

Inter-American Development Bank. (2008). Trinidad/Tobago: Support for a Seamless Education System Project 3: TTL1005. Retrieved from https://www.iadb.org/en/projects.TT-L1005

Kalyanpur, M. (2015). Mind the gap: Special education policy and practice in India in the context of globalization. In S. Rao & M. Kalyanpur, *South Asia and Disability Studies: Redefining boundaries and extending horizons* (pp. 49–72). New York: Peter Lang.

Kalyanpur, M., Un, S., Kong, V., Kong, K., Lek, K., Bo, V., & Eng, M. (2007, April). *Evaluation of disability-responsiveness in FTI education policy and programs in Cambodia*. Milton Keynes, UK: World Vision.

Kittay, E. F. (2000). At home with my daughter. In L. P. Francis & A. Silvers (Eds.), *Americans with disabilities: Exploring implications of the law for individuals and institutions* (pp. 64–81). New York: Routledge.

Kittay, E. F. (2019). *Learning from my daughter: The value and care of disabled minds*. New York: Oxford University Press.

Lamichane, K. (2015). *Disability, education and employment in developing countries: From charity to investment*. Cambridge, UK: Cambridge University Press.

Loop News. (2018). *T&T Cerebral Palsy Society calls for new centre to be opened*. Retrieved from http://www.looptt.com/content/watch-cerebral-palsy-association-calls-new-centre-be-opened

Mohammed-Davidson, R. (2016, November 18). *Comments on National draft policy on persons with disabilities*. The Faculty of Law, University of the West Indies, St. Augustine.

Oliver, M. (2013). The social model of disability: Thirty years on. *Disability and Society, 28*(7), 1024–1026.

Oliver, M., & Barnes, C. (1998). *Social policy and disabled people: From exclusion to inclusion*. London: Longman.

Ong-Dean, C. (2009). *Distinguishing disability: Parents, privilege, and special education*. Chicago: University of Chicago Press.

O'Rourke-Lang, C., & Levy, R. V. (2016). The global context of disability. *Global Education Review, 3*(3), 1–3.

Rao, S. (2015). Just a member of the neighborhood: Bengali mothers' efforts to facilitate inclusion for their children with disabilities within local communities. In S. Rao & M. Kalyanpur (Eds.), *South Asia and Disability Studies: Redefining boundaries and extending horizons* (pp. 224–245). New York: Peter Lang.

Richardson, J. G., & Powell, J. W. (2011). *Comparing special education: Origins to contemporary paradoxes*. Stanford, CA: Stanford University Press.

Sillitoe, P. 1998. The development of indigenous knowledge. A new applied anthropology. *Current Anthropology, 39*(2), 223–235.

Taylor, A. (2013). Lives worth living: Theorizing moral status and expressions of human life. *Disability Studies Quarterly, 33*(4), 8.

The Borgen Project: Trinidad and Tobago poverty rate. (2017, October). Retrieved March 29, 2018, from https://borgenproject.org/trinidad-and-tobago-poverty-rate/

UNICEF Global Data Bases. (2015, October). Education: Adult literacy rate. data.unicef.org

United Nations. (2006). *Convention on the rights of persons with disabilities*. New York.

United Nations. (2018). *Human development reports*. Human Development Index. Retrieved February 25, 2019, from http://hdr.undp.org/en/content/human-development-index-hdi

United Nations Department of Economic and Social Affairs. (2018). *Flagship report on disability and development: Realization of the sustainable development goals by, for, and with persons with disabilities*.

United Nations Department of Economic and Social Affairs. (2019). Disability: Convention on the Rights of Persons with Disabilities. Retrieved March 14, 2019, from https://www.un.org/development/desa/disabilities/convention-on-the-rights-of-persons-with-disabilities.html

Urwick, J., & Elliott, J. (2010). International orthodoxy versus national realities: Inclusive schooling and the education of children with disabilities in Lesotho. *Comparative Education, 46*(2), 137–150.

U.S. Department of Education, Office of Special Education Programs. (2018). *40th Annual Report to Congress, Parts B and C*.

WHO—World Bank. (2011). *World report on disability*. Geneva: World Health Organization.

Appendix: A Word on Methodology

In conducting this qualitative study of the perspectives and experiences of 70 individuals deeply engaged in disability issues in Trinidad and Tobago, I followed traditional qualitative research procedures. I started with an overarching question and three supporting questions:

What explains the longevity of the Immortelle Children's Center as a well-reputed private school for children with disabilities in Trinidad and Tobago?

- What are the experiences and perspectives of parents, teachers, and community stakeholders regarding services for children with disabilities in Trinidad/Tobago?
- What has been the role of Immortelle in these experiences?
- How does the social context of Trinidad and Tobago contribute to the experiences described?
- What insights can be gained regarding the provision of services for children with disabilities in a developing/recently developed nation such as Trinidad and Tobago?

Blending ethnographic techniques of open-ended interviewing and participant observation with my own direct experience of the Immortelle Children's Centre, the book is a combination of ethnography and memoir. The strength of this approach is that it is tailored to the revelation of

© The Author(s) 2020
B. Harry, *Childhood Disability, Advocacy, and Inclusion in the Caribbean*, Palgrave Studies in Disability and International Development, https://doi.org/10.1007/978-3-030-23858-2

close-up and in-depth insights, while the challenge is to gain a balance between the data and the informed subjectivity that comes from my own lived experience. Because of my personal connection to the topic, I deliberately sought a range of contrasting perspectives that could tap into the complications and nuances of the data. Inevitably, because of my professional experience and positionality as a researcher in the field of special education, my framing of the study was greatly influenced by my knowledge of debates in the field, with particular regard to global discussions of inclusive education and interpretations of disability.

In order to provide some consistency to the open-ended interviewing process, I began by building my interviews around a framework derived from disability scholar Susan Peters (1993), who argued that, to understand disability issues in developing nations, it is necessary to explore three key dimensions: ideology, educational practices, and societal structures. To this, I added a fourth dimension—individual motivation—which reflected my personal and professional knowledge of the importance of individual agency and advocacy. I used these four dimensions as a flexible framework for the interviews with three groups of participants—parents, teachers, and community advocates. The style of the interviews was open-ended and ethnographic, following interviewees' leads, while probing for perspectives on all four dimensions.

All interviews were tape-recorded and transcribed verbatim. I then analyzed all the transcripts, using an inductive "grounded" process recommended by methodologists Barney Glaser and Anselm Strauss (1967) and Kathy Charmaz (2014), which seeks to develop theoretical or explanatory statements by looking closely at the most concrete levels of the data, and gradually comparing and reducing the information to develop more abstract levels of understanding. Since the sources of the data fell into three main groups—parents, teachers, and community participants—I first coded each set separately and then compared across the three sets to find common as well as distinguishing features of meaning.

At the first and most "grounded" level of analysis, I applied simple code names to chunks of data that share common or similar meanings. After initial revisions to those codes, I refined the list into 650 codes. Through a process of constant comparison, as described by the foregoing authors, I grouped these codes into 53 code families that reflected my perceptions of their commonalities. Comparing across these families, I then developed 14 main themes that showed cross-cutting inter-relationships and that captured my interpretation of the main issues and concerns in the entire data set. Moving to a level of greater abstraction and integration,

I constructed an amalgam of six central themes that represented the core of the findings. I named these themes as follows:

> *Nice or not nice? We are a caring people*
> *From "something not right here" to "she's wonderful"*
> *Contacts are essential: Individual agency and social capital work hand in hand*
> *Inclusion is an ideal, but...*
> *Government helps, but...*
> *We need systems!*

Following Kathy Charmaz (2014), I would describe this process as a constructivist approach. This means that, while using a systematic approach to coding and interpreting the data, I acknowledge that my interpretation is informed by my own sensitivity to the issues, resulting in constructions of themes that could have turned out differently had someone else done the analysis. Nonetheless, I feel confident in this interpretation because of the density of the information I gathered from interviews, observations, videos, and a range of supporting documents. As a final step, I conducted a "member-check" (Charmaz, 2014), with all interviewees whose words I intended to quote in the book. Through email, phone conversations, or in-person meetings, I presented each one with the exact quotes, invited them to adapt the statements if they wished, and give me written approval for use of the finalized version of the quote. In addition, I sought written consent of all participants to use their real names and the vast majority enthusiastically agreed. A common response to this invitation was, "I'm an advocate for children with disabilities; why wouldn't I want you to use my real name?" I used pseudonyms for the few who did not agree or whom I could not locate up to the time of completion of the book.

The final step in the analysis was the construction of a summary statement of my understanding of the big picture, with which I open the concluding chapter. I will not call this summary a "theory" as it is not sufficiently abstract to earn that title. I simply call it an explanatory statement, which I believe provides some insights into the processes by which a school such as the Immortelle may come into being and succeed in thriving over four decades, within the context of an unpredictable and constantly changing social, economic, and political climate. I conclude the book by weaving together the information from the study, informed by own sensitivity to the topics and to related literature, to present some realistic pointers to the way forward.

REFERENCES

Aldrich, C. A. (1947). Preventive medicine and Mongolism. *American Journal of Mental Deficiency, LII*(2), 127–129.

Artiles, A. J., Kozleski, E. B., & Waitoller, F. R. (2011). *Inclusive education: Examining equity on five continents.* Boston: Harvard Education Press.

Bernstein, J., Hamel-Smith, A., Leotaud, J., Lynch, E., & Palmer, L. (2013). Limin' n' learnin': Implementing collaborative service-learning programmes in Trinidad and Tobago. *Caribbean Journal of Psychology, 5*(1), 93–107.

Bettleheim, B. (1967). *The empty fortress: Infantile autism and the birth of the self.* New York: The Free Press.

Blackman, S. (2017). From charity education toward inclusion: The development of special and inclusive education in Barbados. In S. Blackman & D. Conrad (Eds.), *Caribbean discourse in inclusive education: Historical and contemporary issues* (pp. 3–20). Charlotte, NC: Information Age Publishing.

Bourdieu, P. (1986). The forms of capital. In J. Richardson (Ed.), *Handbook of theory and research for the sociology of education.* New York: Greenwood.

Brown, K., & Jackson, D. D. (2013). The history and conceptual elements of critical race theory. In M. Lynn & A. D. Dixson (Eds.), *Handbook of critical race theory in education* (pp. 9–22). New York: Routledge.

Carrington-Blaides, E., & Conrad, D. (2017). Toward inclusive education in Trinidad and Tobago: Policy challenges and implications. In S. Blackman & D. Conrad (Eds.), *Caribbean discourse in inclusive education: Historical and contemporary issues* (pp. 33–52). Charlotte, NC: Information Age Publishing.

Carver, J., & Carver, N. (1972). *The family of the retarded child.* Syracuse: Syracuse University Press.

© The Author(s) 2020
B. Harry, *Childhood Disability, Advocacy, and Inclusion in the Caribbean*, Palgrave Studies in Disability and International Development, https://doi.org/10.1007/978-3-030-23858-2

Central Intelligence Agency. (2018). *The world factbook.* Retrieved from https://www.cia.gov/library/publications/the-world-factbook/geos/t

Charmaz, K. (2014). *Constructing grounded theory: A practical guide through qualitative analysis* (2nd ed.). London: Sage.

Coleman, J. S. (1988). Social capital in the creation of human capital. *The American Journal of Sociology, 94*, 95–129.

Connor, D., Ferri, B., & Annamma, S. (2016). *DisCrit: Disability studies and critical race theory in education.* New York: Teachers College Press.

Conrad, D. A., Paul, N., Bruce, M., Charles, S., & Felix, K. (2010). Special schools in the search for social justice in Trinidad and Tobago: Perspectives from two marginalized contexts. *Caribbean Curriculum, 17*, 59–84.

Crenshaw, K. (1996). Mapping the margins: Intersectionality, identity politics, and violence against women. In N. G. K. Crenshaw, G. Pellar, & K. Thomas (Eds.), *Critical race theory: The key writings that formed the movement* (pp. 357–383). New York: New Press.

De Lisle, J., Laptiste-Francis, N., McMillan-Solomon, S., & Bowring-Williams, C. (2017). Student assessment systems in the Caribbean as an obstacle to inclusive education: The case of Trinidad and Tobago. In S. Blackman & D. Conrad (Eds.), *Caribbean discourse in inclusive education: Historical and contemporary issues* (pp. 87–106). Charlotte, NC: Information Age Publishing.

Eide, A. H., & Ingstad, B. (2011) *Disability and poverty: A global challenge.* Bristol, UK: Policy Press.

Erevelles, N. (2011). *Disability and difference in global contexts: Enabling a transformative body politic.* New York: Palgrave Macmillan.

Escayg, F. (2013). *Crossing the Gap.* Cause an effect. Retrieved from https://www.facebook.com/cause.an.effecttt/videos/10151682077613669/

Eurydice. (2019). *Key data on education in Europe.* Brussels: European Commission. Retrieved February 24, 2019, from https://eacea.ec.europa.eu/national-policies/eurydice/home_en

EYGM Ltd. (2015). Ernst and Young: Focus on T&T budget 2015. Executive summary, "The Paradox of Plenty" (p. 5). Retrieved from http://www.caribbeanelections.com/eDocs/budget/tt_budget/EY_tt_budget_analysis_2015.pdf

Fitt, A. (2015). *Aching to be.* Toronto, Canada: Ponies + Horses Books.

Gayle-Geddes, A. (2015). *Disability and inequality: Socioeconomic imperatives and public policy in Jamaica.* New York: Palgrave Macmillan.

Gayle-Geddes, A. (2016). A situational analysis of persons with disabilities in Jamaica and Trinidad and Tobago: Education and employment policy imperatives. In P. Block, D. Kasnitz, A. Nishida, & N. Pollard (Eds.), *Occupying disability: Critical approaches to community, justice, and decolonizing disability* (pp. 127–144). New York: Springer.

Glaser, B., & Strauss, A. (1967). *The discovery of grounded theory: Strategies for qualitative research.* New York: De Gruyeter.

Goffman, E. (1963). *Stigma: Notes on the management of spoiled identity.* New York: Simon and Schuster.

Government of the Republic of Trinidad and Tobago. (2015). *TT Connect.* Retrieved from https://www.ttconnect.gov.tt

Government of the Republic of Trinidad and Tobago, Equal Opportunity Commission. (2001). *Equal Opportunity Act of 2000.* Retrieved from http://www.equalopportunity.gov.tt/download-act

Government of the Republic of Trinidad and Tobago, Ministry of Education. (1967). *Education Act of 1967.* Port of Spain, Trinidad.

Government of the Republic of Trinidad and Tobago, Ministry of Education. (2001). *The Keenan Education Report of 1869.* Port of Spain, Trinidad.

Government of the Republic of Trinidad and Tobago, Ministry of Social Development. (2003, June). *Second periodic report under the Convention on the Rights of the Child.* Retrieved from https://www.ncjrs.gov/pdffiles1/Digitization/203642NCJRS.pdf

Government of the Republic of Trinidad and Tobago, Ministry of Social Development. (2006). *National Plan of Action for Children for 2006–2010.* Port of Spain, Trinidad.

Government of the Republic of Trinidad and Tobago, Ministry of the People and Social Development. (2005). *National Policy on Persons with Disabilities.* Port of Spain, Trinidad.

Grech, S. (2015). *Disability and poverty in the global South: Renegotiating development in Guatemala.* New York: Palgrave Macmillan.

Harry, B. (2010). *Melanie, bird with a broken wing: A mother's story.* Baltimore: Brookes.

Harry, B., & Klingner, J. K. (2014). *Why are so many minority students in special education: Understanding race and disability in schools.* New York: Teachers College Press.

Individuals with Disabilities Education Act, 20 U.S.C. 1400 (2004).

Inter-American Development Bank. (2008). Trinidad/Tobago: Support for a Seamless Education System Project 3: TTL1005. Retrieved from https://www.iadb.org/en/projects.TT-L1005

Kalyanpur, M. (2015). Mind the gap: Special education policy and practice in India in the context of globalization. In S. Rao & M. Kalyanpur, *South Asia and Disability Studies: Redefining boundaries and extending horizons* (pp. 49–72). New York: Peter Lang.

Keller, C. (1993). *Report of the National Task Force on Education, green paper.* Trinidad and Tobago, Ministry of Education, Port of Spain, Trinidad.

Kirk, S. A. (1984). Introspection and prophecy. In B. Blatt & R. J. Morris (Eds.), *Perspectives in special education: Personal orientations* (pp. 24–55). Glenview, IL: Scott Foresman.

Kittay, E. F. (2000). At home with my daughter. In L. P. Francis & A. Silvers (Eds.), *Americans with disabilities: Exploring implications of the law for individuals and institutions* (pp. 64–81). New York: Routledge.

Kittay, E. F. (2011). The ethics of care, dependence, and disability. *Ratio Juris. An International Journal of Jurisprudence and Philosophy of Law, 24*(1), 49–58.

Kittay, E. F. (2019). *Learning from my daughter: The value and care of disabled minds.* New York: Oxford University Press.

Kübler-Ross, E. (1969). *On death and dying.* Routledge.

Lamichane, K. (2015). *Disability, education and employment in developing countries: From charity to investment.* Cambridge, UK: Cambridge University Press.

Lareau, A. (2000). *Home advantage: Social class and parental intervention in elementary education* (2nd ed.). Lanham, MD: Rowman & Littlefield.

Linton, S. (2006). *My body politic: A memoir.* Ann Arbor: University of Michigan Press.

Loop News. (2018). *T&T Cerebral Palsy Society calls for new centre to be opened.* Retrieved from http://www.looptt.com/content/watch-cerebral-palsy-association-calls-new-centre-be-opened

Mairs, N. (1996). *Waist-high in the world: A life among the nondisabled.* Boston: Beacon Press.

Mairs, N. (2011). On being a cripple. *Researchomatic.* Retrieved June 2011, from http://www.researchomatic.com/Nancy-Mairs-On-Being-A-Cripple-75304.html

Mohammed-Davidson, R. (2016, November 18). *Comments on National draft policy on persons with disabilities.* The Faculty of Law, University of the West Indies, St. Augustine.

Morgan, P. (2014). *The terror and the time: Banal violence and trauma in Caribbean discourse.* Kingston, Jamaica: University of the West Indies press.

Oliver, M. (2013). The social model of disability: Thirty years on. *Disability and Society, 28*(7), 1024–1026.

Oliver, M., & Barnes, C. (1998). *Social policy and disabled people: From exclusion to inclusion.* London: Longman.

Ong-Dean, C. (2009). *Distinguishing disability: Parents, privilege, and special education.* Chicago: University of Chicago Press.

O'Rourke-Lang, C., & Levy, R. V. (2016). The global context of disability. *Global Education Review, 3*(3), 1–3.

Pennsylvania Association for Retarded Citizens v. Commonwealth of Pennsylvania, 334 F. Supp. 1257 (1971).

Peters, S. (1993). An ideological-cultural framework for the study of disability. In S. Peters (Ed.), *Education and disability in cross-cultural perspective* (pp. 19–38). New York: Garland Publishing.

Public Law 94–142: *Education for all Handicapped Children Act* of 1975.

Rao, S. (2015). Just a member of the neighborhood: Bengali mothers' efforts to facilitate inclusion for their children with disabilities within local communities. In S. Rao & M. Kalyanpur (Eds.), *South Asia and Disability Studies: Redefining boundaries and extending horizons* (pp. 224–245). New York: Peter Lang.

Richardson, J. G., & Powell, J. W. (2011). *Comparing special education: Origins to contemporary paradoxes*. Stanford, CA: Stanford University Press.

Rohlehr, G. (1990). *Calypso and society in pre-independence Trinidad*. Port of Spain, Trinidad: Gordon Rohlehr.

Sen, R., Goldbart, J, & Kaul, S. (2008). Growth of an NGO: The Indian Institute of Cerebral Palsy from 1974–2006. *Journal of Policy and Practice in Intellectual Disabilities, 5*(2), 105–111

Sillitoe, P. 1998. The development of indigenous knowledge. A new applied anthropology. *Current Anthropology, 39*(2), 223–235.

Singhal, N. (Ed.). (2013). *Disability, poverty & education*. Oxford, UK: Routledge.

Solnit, A. J., & Stark, M. H. (1961). Mourning and the birth of a defective child. *Psychoanalytic Study Child, 16*, 523–537.

Taylor, A. (2013). Lives worth living: Theorizing moral status and expressions of human life. *Disability Studies Quarterly, 33*(4).

The Borgen Project: Trinidad and Tobago poverty rate. (2017, October). Retrieved March 29, 2018, from https://borgenproject.org/trinidad-and-tobago-poverty-rate/

Titchkosky, T. (2008). Disability: A rose by any other name? "People-first" language in Canadian society. *Canadian Review of Sociology, 28*(2), 125–140.

Trinidad and Tobago Association for Retarded Children. (1984). *His special children*. Port of Spain, Trinidad: Horsford Printerie.

Turnbull, A., Turnbull, R., Erwin, E., Soodak, L., & Shogren, K. (2015). *Families, professionals, and exceptionality: Positive outcomes through partnerships and trust* (7th ed.). Boston: Pearson.

UNESCO. (1994, June). The Salamanca statement and framework for action on special needs education. Salamanca, Spain. Retrieved from http://unesdoc.unesco.org/images/0009/000984/098427eo.pdf

UNICEF Global Data Bases. (2015, October). Education: Adult literacy rate. data.unicef.org

United Nations. (2006). *Convention on the rights of persons with disabilities*. New York.

United Nations. (2018). *Human development reports*. Human Development Index. Retrieved February 25, 2019, from http://hdr.undp.org/en/content/human-development-index-hdi

United Nations Department of Economic and Social Affairs. (2018). *Flagship report on disability and development: Realization of the sustainable development goals by, for, and with persons with disabilities.*

United Nations Department of Economic and Social Affairs. (2019). Disability: Convention on the Rights of Persons with Disabilities. Retrieved March 14, 2019, from https://www.un.org/development/desa/disabilities/convention-on-the-rights-of-persons-with-disabilities.html

Urwick, J., & Elliott, J. (2010). International orthodoxy versus national realities: Inclusive schooling and the education of children with disabilities in Lesotho. *Comparative Education, 46*(2), 137–150.

U.S. Department of Education, Office of Special Education Programs. (2018). *40th Annual Report to Congress, Parts B and C.*

U.S. Department of State. (2014). Investment climate statement for Trinidad and Tobago. Retrieved from https://www.state.gov/documents/organization/227506.pdf

WHO—World Bank. (2011). *World report on disability.* Geneva: World Health Organization.

INDEX[1]

---

[1] Note: Page numbers followed by 'n' refer to notes.

© The Author(s) 2020
B. Harry, *Childhood Disability, Advocacy, and Inclusion in the Caribbean*, Palgrave Studies in Disability and International Development, https://doi.org/10.1007/978-3-030-23858-2

Trinidad and Tobago Ministry of
Education, 12, 13, 19, 33, 45,
148, 149, 192–194, 197, 203,
213, 214, 217, 218, 221, 222,
225, 260
Trinidad and Tobago Ministry of
Health, 18, 26, 190, 203,
205, 207
Trinidad and Tobago Ministry of
Social Development, 14, 17, 130,
131, 191, 226, 255, 259, 264

U
UNESCO, 9, 11, 12
UNICEF, 9, 237

United Nations (UN), 3, 6–10, 183,
185, 193, 217, 239, 246
University of the West Indies (UWI),
15, 60, 63, 185, 192, 198, 212,
213, 224, 225, 227, 243, 255
University of Trinidad and Tobago
(UTT), 15, 183, 192–194,
212, 213, 233

V
Volunteerism, 223–224

W
Wharton-Patrick School, 13, 216

Lightning Source UK Ltd.
Milton Keynes UK
UKHW020349091019
351227UK00002B/35/P